INTERNET
PROPHETS

INTERNET PROPHETS

Enlightened E-Business Strategies for Every Budget

Mary Diffley

CyberAge Books

Information Today, Inc.
Medford, New Jersey

Internet Prophets:
Enlightened E-Business Strategies for Every Budget

Library of Congress Cataloging-in-Publication Data

Diffley, Mary, 1959-
    Internet prophets : e-business strategies for every budget / Mary Diffley.
        p. cm.
    Includes index.
    ISBN: 0-910965-55-2
  1. Electronic commerce--Management. 2. Information technology--Management. I. Title.

HF5548.32.D534 2001
658.8'4--dc21

                                            2001047241

Printed and bound in the United States of America.

Publisher: Thomas H. Hogan, Sr.
Editor-in-Chief: John B. Bryans
Managing Editor: Deborah R. Poulson
Editor: Owen B. Davies
Copy Editor: Pat Hadley-Miller
Proofreader: Dorothy Pike
Production Manager: M. Heide Dengler
Book design: Jacqueline Walter and Kara Mia Jalkowski
Indexer: Robert Saigh

Cover design and Internet Prophet illustrations by Baker Vail Design

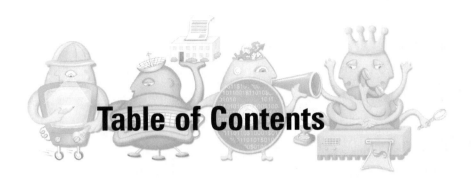

Table of Contents

Figures

Tables

Foreword

We don't live on *Little House on the Prairie* anymore and today's frontier isn't in the west, it's on the Net. We live in the Internet Age where change seems to take place at light speed. If you're in business today, it seems like you need a prophet just to make a profit and no matter what you think you need, you definitely need to be on the Net.

When someone once said, "Lead, follow, or get out of the way," he must have seen into the future and drawn a glimpse of the Internet. Because those people who are not leading or following will most certainly have to get out of the way and watch as their competitors tear on by.

The Internet simultaneously flattens the communication hierarchy while broadening people's access to ideas, information, products, and services. The Internet is to the world what the printing press was hundreds of years ago. It is to the world what radio and television were only decades ago. The Internet has opened doors and opportunities in a way beyond anything that has preceded it. In only a few short years an entire body of technology, vocabulary, culture, and marketplace has been born. Cyber entrepreneurs, customers, and a whole new economy have evolved at such a blinding speed that it is no wonder that many business people are at a loss about what to do and how to do it relating to the Internet and their business.

Understanding e-business fundamentals, creating an Internet business plan, developing and marketing a company's Web site, as well as understanding Internet regulation, are all new concepts to today's business professional. Those businesses that do not consider these issues today will most surely be a casualty of this new technology tomorrow. But more importantly, those businesses that do consider these issues today will be the success stories of tomorrow.

Internet Prophets is a comprehensive guide to e-business strategies. Mary Diffley has made the complex world of business on the Internet understandable. More importantly, she has provided a step-by-step blueprint for today's businessperson to follow, whether he or she is part of a large or small organization.

Your success on the Internet depends on many things, but mostly it depends on you and how you react now to this fast-changing medium full of opportunities and possibilities. You can be a casualty of the times or a business on the leading edge of the curve. Your company's survival will depend on your choice.

> Ivan R. Misner, Ph.D.
> Founder of Business Network
>   International (BNI)
> Co-author of *Masters of Networking*
> misner@bni.com
> www.MastersofNetworking.com

Preface

A year or two ago, most of us watched in amazement as dozens of Internet start-ups soared to the top of the stock market, even though most of the businesses they represented had never seen black ink. Many of the creative people who founded those companies became instant millionaires. Speculators grew rich almost overnight, just by putting their money into dot-coms whose business plans they did not begin to understand. What on Earth was that about? What, if anything, makes the Internet so valuable?

If you are not sure—if you even suspect that this magic "e-business" may be overrated—take comfort. Doubt and confusion are widespread. Whether you are a seasoned executive or brand new to the entrepreneurial arena, the traditional ways of doing business are probably natural to you, and the Internet often seems to violate all the old rules without offering much certainty of profit in return. No wonder so many businesspeople are baffled by the Internet!

Nonetheless, organizations of all sizes are still rushing madly to set up their shop online or to improve their exisiting e-business—this despite the abrupt failure of many dot-com companies in late 2000 and 2001. As you read this book, you will figure out why, for herein there are dozens of useful ideas for building your business in a fertile new world. A few hundred pages from now, you will understand how to make real profits from Internet technologies, reaching markets you could not hope to tap by any other means.

Why Bother?

Business professionals en masse are weighing the very issues that face you. The most stymied among them are still asking, "Why should I put my business on the Internet?" Others, earlier to e-commerce, wonder, "What happened to that e-miracle everyone promised? Why hasn't my Web site brought one cent of revenue?" Some, still a minority, mull the question almost everyone should be pondering by now: "I know my company needs its Web site—we have even gotten some business from it—but isn't there more we could do to increase our sales and compete more effectively in cyberspace?"

Answers to that first question are everywhere you look. Every business needs a Web presence simply because more and more consumers are relying on it for easy and convenient access to products, services, and information. In mid-2001, there were an estimated 391 million Internet users in the world, a number that will nearly double—to 774 million—in just the next two years. And in one recent study, 48 percent of Internet users already reported that the Web was the first place they looked for information when shopping for consumer goods. That represents an enormous, virtually untapped market for almost any product or service.

Further, the Internet is a gateway for global business. It levels the playing field. With businesses and individuals gaining Internet access in record numbers, basic tools like e-mail and Web sites enable even the smallest business to reach this growing worldwide market in an extremely cost-effective manner. Now is the time to master this technology. You will need it to survive the competition entering your marketplace from points across the world.

Also consider how long you plan to remain in business. If you are looking beyond the next few years, your future customers are still in high school. They are the "network generation," tech-savvy Internet users who have a profoundly different way of approaching the world than their parents. Thanks to the Internet, your future customers will think differently, work differently, learn differently, and communicate differently than any society in the history of the human race. Five or ten years from now, you will reach those customers in their native territory—the Internet—or you will be unlikely to reach them at all.

There is yet another reason to colonize this online world. Many companies have found that strategic collaborations with others are almost essential for success in the Information Age. Such collaborations promote efficiency and reduce expenses by allowing each partner to concentrate on its core specialties; they add value to your business and are critical to any e-business strategy. The sooner you start building these relationships, the sharper your edge will be. Net-shy businesses will be left out.

Finally—at least for our current purposes—the Internet can give your company greater control over the messages it delivers to consumers and collaborators. In the electronic future, it will take just 10 seconds for a business to earn a bad reputation—the time it takes a disappointed customer to fire off a scathing message that will be read by thousands or millions of Internet users. You need to be there, where you will have the chance to establish a positive reputation, and effectively position your business among its competitors.

What Lies Ahead?

What happened to the profits that e-business was supposed to bring, and how can you ring up more of them? That is the subject of this book. The Internet Prophets specialize in Internet profits!

Read this book and you will learn new methods for succeeding on the Internet. You will learn why Net-preneurs have measured success in different terms than traditional businesses. You will learn about a new asset presented on the balance sheet of growing, profitable Internet companies: customer loyalty. You will see why businesses are in a frenzy to attract and retain as many loyal customers as they can. And you will see how they are doing it.

A few chapters from now, you will understand that the value of these businesses is based not so much on immediate profit as on their ability to influence their customers. You will understand the importance of Web-site traffic: The more people visit your Web site, the more compelling your site becomes to prospective advertisers and other business owners with something to sell. You also will understand a host of critical new concepts that will help you dramatically improve your business performance on the Internet. Finally, the Internet Prophets themselves will have led you to several dozen resources and techniques that are specifically suited to your business, whatever its size and budget.

Read this book if you are:

- A business owner, professional, or corporate executive
- An advertising specialist

- A strategist at a marketing or PR firm
- Currently designing and developing Web sites
- An entrepreneur
- Interested in creating an e-business
- Determined to be successful in the new economy

Now less than 10 years old, the Web is still a new territory for all businesses. The Internet is vast and remains largely unexplored. Yet in this short time it has created a new economy. *Internet Prophets* is written for new pioneers ready to forge a business in this new environment. It's for business owners who want to know how to create a Web site for their company and to understand what benefits they can realistically expect from it. It's for those who have already established an e-business and need new strategies to enhance their online presence. It is a resource and strategies guide for those currently designing and developing Web sites. It's for traditional marketers and PR firms already in advertising, branding, and marketing, who should be offering their clients a full media package—one that includes the Internet. It's also for professionals with a client base or network of partners, whom they might better serve by using the Internet. In short, it is for everyone who does not wish to be left behind in an age of incredibly rapid change.

Internet Prophets is based on the real-time experience of working with hundreds of companies, small, medium, and large, that have effectively charted their course on the new frontier. These include the full range of industry—manufacturers, service organizations, and professional practices, sole proprietorships, nonprofits, small businesses, large corporations, and government agencies. Whatever your business, there is something here for you.

Throughout my Internet career, I have been an "Internet Prophet." I have consulted with businesses and organizations, designing innovative Internet applications to meet their objectives and fit their budgets. When I started my journey on the Internet, I looked for a book like this, but found none. I had no role models to follow. I had moved into uncharted territory, a frontier that seemed to continually reinvent itself. Internet business strategy was a guessing game. Trying to anticipate consumer and business patterns on the Web, to understand the evolving nature of the Internet and the demand for faster, smarter access to it was an entirely new challenge. Today, I look back and laugh. I often see features on Web sites and think, "Hey, I invented that."

This book will provide you with the knowledge you need to make your own way. It will inspire you to invent your own e-business strategies and build a more profitable enterprise. It will help you to chart your way through Internet territories that remain largely unmapped. Someday you, too, may be able to look back and see others following your lead.

Internet Prophets will help you gain an in-depth understanding of the new game of e-business. By the time you have finished reading, you should be able to assess the strengths and weaknesses in Internet business models. You will learn to create an online strategy that works for your company. You will be able to build, host, and manage a Web site, or—if you do not want to do it yourself— you will be well equipped to find a qualified individual or firm to do it for you.

Internet Prophets explains:

- The benefits of e-business and the new economy

- How to make your own rules in this new frontier

- How to make money on the Internet

- What's achievable within your budget (pick your personal Prophet)

- How to build, host, and manage a Web site: Do it yourself, hire in-house developers, outsource the project, or purchase the right products to get the job done efficiently and well

Since I first began touting these new technologies and selling Internet services, I have spoken to thousands of entrepreneurs and executives; you probably have a lot in common with many of them. I recognize that it takes time to grasp what the Internet is and what it can do for you. For this reason, I will also explain the background and history of the Internet and the evolution of the Information Age.

I understand that most people are put off by technical jargon and details, so wherever possible I will stick to everyday language and focus on concrete strategies and practical concerns, not on technology. But, let me tell you: The greatest satisfaction I have gotten in this business is not from building dynamic Web sites and watching the businesses succeed (as so many have), but that look in the eye of the technophobe who has hung in there and finally gotten it. When something finally clicks, a quiet, speculative smile appears. I can actually see the ideas start flying, and before you know it they are coming up with their own creative, innovative ways to use the Internet. It's a wonderful thing!

It usually makes sense to start at "A" and work to "Z," but for this book I will make an exception. We will begin with an overview of the changes in commerce and learn why the Information Age is so startlingly different from the Industrial Age. Next, we will talk about Internet business concepts, how to analyze your business and develop a Web site implementing Internet theories and concepts. We will bury the history, background information, and techno-babble in the appendices. But do not ignore that background material. Everything you do in e-business rests on that foundation. It is in your interest to master the basics, even when you already can use the practical techniques based on them.

This year *Webster's* inserted hundreds of new words into their dictionary, many of them related to computers and the Internet. If you do not understand and use them, you are already behind the times—and at a serious disadvantage in trying to compete against those who do. This book can help you become more Internet literate and effectively profit in this new world.

How Much Will It Cost?

In almost every case, the first question asked about Web site development is, "How much will it cost?" I hope this book impresses upon you the importance of creating a suitable budget for your endeavor. But some businesses must begin with a limited budget. Only when you have decided what you can afford can you choose and put into practice the strategies that could prove successful for your business. That is why I have put together my team of "Internet Prophets."

There are thousands of tested Internet strategies that can be implemented on Web sites. No doubt thousands more are still to be developed. The Internet Prophets help you sort through the best of them and identify the costs associated with each strategy. Each Prophet specializes in providing solutions for a particular budget level.

There are seven steps to follow in creating an e-business:

Step 1: Estimate your budget for Web-site development and support.

Step 2: Select an Internet Prophet for your business.

Step 3: Check out the fundamental Internet concepts presented in this book.

Step 4: Review your Prophet's "prophesies" for ideas for your business.

Step 5: Create a Web-based business plan.

Step 6: Create a Web-site project plan.

Step 7: Start making real profits from your Internet venture.

Internet Prophets provides a cost-of-production tour for building Web sites for businesses and organizations of all sizes. Within each chapter, the Prophets offer strategy suggestions with estimated costs of implementation for each. Before you read any further, get to know the Prophets, and select the one who specializes in your budget category. Then, read on. Get to understand the capabilities of the Internet, and listen most carefully to the prophecies of your Internet Prophet. Refer to the index of Prophet strategies to jump quickly to ideas and strategies for your firm. Your business will be up and running on the Internet in no time.

Good luck. I'll see you online!

About the Web Site

www.internetprophets.com

At www.internetprophets.com, Mary Diffley maintains an ever-expanding and frequently updated index of e-business products categorized by cost, as well as articles about emerging Internet business models and concepts, practical how-to guides, and product reviews.

internetprophets.com was designed with you, the reader of this book, in mind. As you develop your e-business strategy, you can use the Web site to create and manage your own database of available products and company contact information. You can rate the products you use or the customer service features of the companies you contact. We also invite you to write to us and tell us about your e-business experiences and success stories.

Enjoy your visit with Eenie, Meenie, Miney, and Moe, and send any feedback or questions to mary@internetprophets.com.

Disclaimer:

Neither publisher nor author make any claim as to the results that may be obtained through the use of internetprophets.com or of any of the Internet resources it references or links to. Neither publisher nor author will be held liable for any results, or lack thereof, obtained by the use of this page or any of its links; for any third-party charges; or for any hardware, software, or other problems that may occur as a result of using it. internetprophets.com is subject to change or discontinuation without notice at the discretion of the publisher and author. If you have difficulty finding any company or product referenced in this book, contact the author at mary@internetprophets.com for assistance or to locate a substitute.

Introducing
the Internet Prophets

Eenie   Meenie   Miney   Moe

Eeenie

Prophet Eenie

*The prophet of simple and basic
Web sites*

Prophecies

- Practical, quality ideas for small businesses
- Web strategies under $1,000
- Do-it-yourself guides

Eenie is the prophet of very small companies with limited funds for Internet development. Eenie prophesies to the business that wants to start with a simple online presence. Eenie companies will most likely develop a Web site to be used as a complementary marketing tool. Although Prophet Eenie suggests some transaction-based e-commerce solutions (selling products online), an Eenie follower will most likely need help with content development, presentation options, and how-to suggestions for creating a Web site. The companies that Eenie best relates to typically employ fewer than 10 people who are self-taught computer users with relatively little computer infrastructure, rely primarily on word-of-mouth advertising or self-promotion, and are just starting out on the Internet. Throughout the book, Prophet Eenie will present do-it-yourself ideas for getting started on the Internet.

Prophet Meenie

The prophet of enhanced, customized Web sites

Prophecies

- The "best bang for the buck"
- Web strategies up to $10,000
- Assessing Web-development firms
- Choosing cost-effective Web applications

Meenie is the prophet of small, but active and aggressive, companies. Companies with less than $5 million in sales—profitable, but without deep pockets. Companies that have an advertising budget, but usually concentrate on local or trade markets. These companies have no time for do-it-yourself, and they value outsourced knowledge. They typically hire freelancers and consultants to assist them with skills they lack, including Web strategies and development. They may look for entry-level personnel to manage their ongoing Web development after implementation. These companies recognize the importance of the Internet, but need a frugal approach; they can invest between $5,000 and $10,000 per year on their Internet strategies.

Prophet Meenie prophesies to the business that wants to create a strong and professional image and perhaps to sell some of its products online. Although Meenie suggests some creative applications, such as FAQs and simple database tools, a Meenie follower will most likely be in need of content development, graphical layout suggestions, and strategies for selling products or services on its Web site.

Prophet Miney

The prophet of transactional and interactive Web sites

Prophecies

- Strategies for outsourcing or hire-in
- Solutions up to $50,000
- Choosing interactive Web applications
- Active online marketing tactics

Miney guides companies that are ready to be serious about the Internet and have a fairly substantial starting budget for their endeavor. Miney prophesies to the businesses that want to create compelling Web content and features to attract new prospects and build loyalty among existing customers. They may also want to begin selling products or services online. Miney's followers understand the value of advertising and promotion, and they are prepared to implement a marketing campaign to drive traffic to their Web site. Miney will offer the best solutions for those companies with up to $50,000 set aside for e-business annually.

Prophet Moe

The prophet of full-blown e-business strategies

Prophecies

- Launch an aggressive campaign
- Solutions over $50,000
- Utilize elaborate and complex e-business technologies
- Choosing an Application Service Provider

Moe is prepared to offer the most sophisticated solutions to businesses with a solid Internet budget. These businesses will be willing to spend $50,000 or more annually on their e-business.

Prophet Moe prophesies to the business that wants to create a dot-com brand name. Moe followers are advanced, and they need to integrate some of their legacy computer applications with their online systems. They could be selling products, building online communities, or setting new trends. They will often strive to build networks of partners, leveraging the value of those relationships through the use of Internet technologies.

Moe's followers are interested in learning more about Application Service Providers (ASPs), which offer multiple application strategies and a full range of e-buisness integration solutions.

The prophets have a lot of ground to cover. They are determined to meet all your needs, to educate you, and to assist you in implementing strategies that really work. Which Internet Prophet is most suited to your business? Only you can decide that. Choose one, and follow your prophet throughout the book. However, do not ignore the others. Even followers of Miney and Moe will find that Prophets Eenie and Meenie offer ideas that are likely to be valuable for Internet businesses that can afford more ambitious strategies as well.

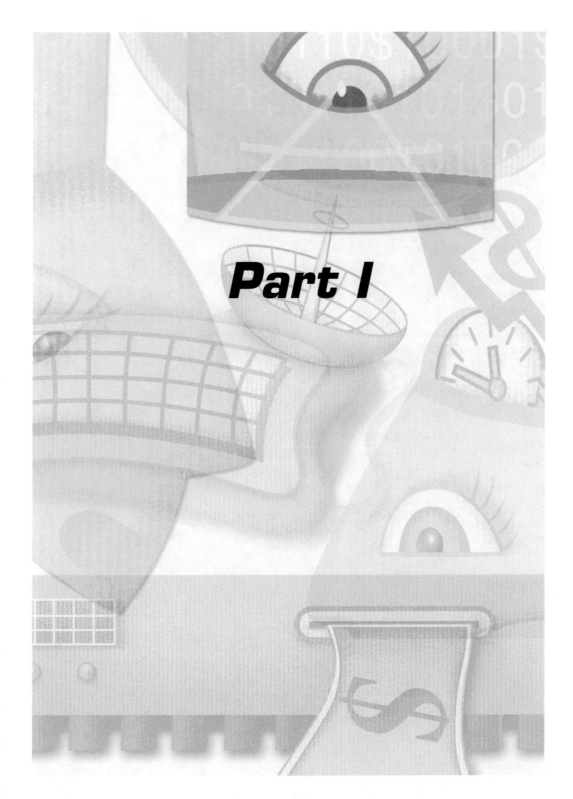

Part I

Part I
New Business Principles

Never in the history of the world has a technology been so widely accepted so quickly as the Internet. The adoption rates of other such devices—the printing press, the telegraph, radio, and television—pale in comparison. Once people heard of the World Wide Web, it took the Internet just four years to reach 50 million people; it had taken television 15 years to capture so large an audience.

The Internet is a tool of proven power and unimagined potential. Since the debut of the Web, Internet usage has soared at an unprecedented rate; it continues to grow exponentially. By 2000, barely six years after the general public became aware of the Internet, the Web had grown to more than 200 million users worldwide. By the year 2002, about 490 million people around the world will have Internet access, and almost 1 billion people will be online by 2005. Globally, both business and consumer segments are growing rapidly. In 1998, the number of e-mail messages transmitted over the Internet was double the number of letters delivered by the U.S. Postal Service. By 2001, in Europe alone, Internet users were sending each other more than 3 billion short text messages each month!

At the end of the '90s, the "New Economy" looked infallible. Yet in the first year of the millennium, over-extended Internet companies made daily headlines as they reported lower-than-projected income, huge layoffs, and often bankruptcy. Technology stocks traded on NASDAQ took a severe blow, and as a result many people began to feel skeptical about the future of e-business. Getting past the downturn may be difficult for some, but the truth is that e-business is here to stay.

In fact, we are just at the beginning of the revolution that the Internet and related technology will bring, as those technologies continue to evolve. The recent, highly publicized failure of scores of popular dot-com companies has taught us some important lessons, notably that quick-to-move but badly managed businesses are bound to take a hard fall. A shakeout was inevitable. Companies raced into the new frontier like pioneers at the dawn of the gold rush, but those unprepared to brave the elements were destined to fail. New e-businesses trying to capture enormous pieces of the Internet pie chewed through cash like there was no tomorrow. For many of them, there wasn't.

To ease your concerns for the future, it is important to understand that the Internet, the new medium of communications, will continue to create jobs and wealth. Internet companies will continue to attract capital, and they will help to sustain the overall economy.

For example, the quest for faster and smarter access is still moving at full speed. Telephone and cable companies continue to invest huge sums of money into fiber optics and other broadband technologies—and the wireless revolution has not even begun. The need for speed in this sector is a driving force: The newer, faster wireless infrastructure will require new applications, adaptations, hardware, and software. Every day, a startup with its sights on the future will scramble to fill whatever needs may arise.

Companies that use Internet technologies to cut costs and improve efficiency and productivity are reaping big rewards. Internetworking, information collection, and transaction immediacy can greatly improve the bottom line of any organization, across all industries and in government.

In the meantime, because of the so-called shakeout, the way we approach and value Internet business in the next few years is changing rapidly. Today's e-businesses need effective and efficient leaders, managing well-targeted and well-constructed ideas. For companies with a clear direction, focused on quality products and service to the customer, the opportunities for business continue to be boundless.

This book will be a helpful guide for those who are still skeptical of the Internet's business future, or are uncertain how best to take advantage of the opportunities available through the use of the Internet. Understanding the concepts that underlie a successful e-business is essential to charting a path through this still feral frontier.

I discovered the Internet in 1994, shortly after the release of the first Web browser, Mosaic. I gushed at the revelation of this phenomenon. I literally ran through the streets of my small community (go ahead, ask anyone—they'll tell you it's true), touting the power of this marvelous technology. I thought, "This is an incredible world, where all the information we could possibly need is at our fingertips." I didn't sleep much in those early years. I spent my time surfing the Internet for all sorts of valuable information that helped me grow my business.

I remember defending computing. "Computers will not create a cold emotionless world, leaving masses of people jobless," I told the skeptics. "They will create a society where people have more and better communication with each other, not less. Where there will be more satisfying jobs rather than joblessness, and where government will have more effective tools to listen to the people."

I prepared lengthy training sessions for business clients and colleagues and preached the power of the new frontier as if it were a religion. I started an Internet company that offered dial-up Internet access, Internet training, and Web development. But even though I prophesied every aching minute, I never imagined exactly how radical the Internet would become, how it would alter fundamental business processes, how it would revolutionize the way we live and work. How it would transform our relationships, our family life, and our leisure time.

A few years ago, on a beautiful, sunny afternoon, I decided to take a tour of New York City in a double-decker bus. I have lived close to New York all my life; I visit the city often and know my way around. Yet this tour was an opportunity to spend an afternoon and experience this familiar territory in a different way. I sat on the top deck of this open bus, and as we approached Times Square, I was filled with awe. There, about 30 feet above street level, it seemed that I was nearly eye-to-eye with billboard advertisements that may have been 50 feet high by 100 feet long—and every single one of them was promoting a dot-com.

At that moment, I began to recognize how large the Internet loomed over the world of business. I realized that the Internet as I knew it, that e-commerce as it exists today, is just the tip of the iceberg. We have yet to see anything like the full magnitude of the business transformation unleashed by the Internet. The evolution of the human condition, of our lifestyles, has barely begun. Opportunists, visionaries, and early adopters of Internet technologies have only scratched the surface of the possibilities inherent in this new medium.

At the risk of abusing the metaphor, the prospects for businesses today are comparable to those during the gold rush of the 1800s. If a business overlooks the power of the Internet, it is destined to fail. Those companies that embrace this power, that dive into Internet business with conviction and purpose, will reap the rewards. In order to be successful, today's business leaders need to grasp the fundamentals of this new business landscape. That is what Part I of *Internet Prophets* is all about.

Chapter 1

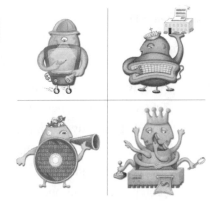

Industrial Age vs. Information Age

Ever since the 1960s, business pundits have been forecasting that computers would transform the way we do our jobs, operate our companies, and earn our livings. Decades later, the Internet is paying off on that promise. E-mail has multiplied the flow of information within and between organizations. E-commerce is revolutionizing the sale of goods and the delivery of services throughout the world. Yet we have barely begun to tap the limitless opportunities brought by this latest, most powerful expression of the computer revolution.

As you read the many practical e-business strategies that fill this book, you are likely to find your imagination bubbling with ideas for ways in which your organization can benefit from the rush to do business in the online world of the Internet. However, before we begin to consider those strategies, it may help to look at some of the reasons e-business has taken so long to get off the ground. This may put things into perspective and help you to see more clearly how e-commerce fits into your own organization's established ways of doing things. If you work for an old, established company, it also may tell you a little about what you are up against.

Few companies, organizations, or even government agencies today effectively use their computers, let alone the Internet. We hear the same excuses for this every day, in almost any organization. Computers are costly. (That was the excuse for Election 2000.) Computer "geeks," the employees needed to manage the machines, are hard to find. They are also hard to relate to, as they seem to speak a different language. In addition, it is very hard to evaluate the return on investment of adopting new technologies. All these obstacles, we hear, inhibit tradition-minded executives from adopting modern, computerized business methods.

In fact, this situation has persisted for a reason that has nothing to do with cost or the alien and mysterious nature of computers. For the first few decades of the computer revolution, few organizations had much incentive to use computers to their full potential, or even to think about how they might do so.

Most large corporations used computers routinely by the mid-1960s; by 1968, IBM had shipped 14,000 of its breakthrough Model 360 in just four years. Yet these mysterious machines, locked in climate-controlled rooms and operated by an off-putting technical priesthood, did very little that human beings had not been doing since the invention of bookkeeping. They assisted in the processing of data, and the data they processed was usually "yesterday's news"—last month's financial statements, billing reports, sales and expenses, and the like. When the day, week, or month was complete, the computers spat out records of the company's past transactions, perhaps with some rudimentary statistics attached.

This was known as "batch" processing, and it had little to do with the customer. It produced information for management of the company: It told managers in the Industrial Age how many units of a product to manufacture and distribute based on historical data and trends.

Companies in the Industrial Age did not really need much more than that. Their business was based primarily on the production of durable goods.

The Industrial Age

The Industrial Age was a time of mass production and mass marketing. An Industrial Age business accumulated great physical assets to build its strength. An automobile manufacturer owned not only the assembly plants, but rubber plants as well, and even shipping fleets to transport raw materials to and from the manufacturing locations. The key objective of Industrial Age corporations was to become mega-corporations, using their size and strength to isolate competition. For this reason, there were high barriers to market entry.

Industrial Age companies relied on economies of scale: They produced in high volume, thereby reducing their cost per unit, and flooded the market with their products. Production activities were fixed, and the goods were uniform; mass production did not allow for customization. Business improvement initiatives focused primarily on process efficiency and cost. There was little consideration for customer service. Processing customers' inquiries was not a priority; companies really had very little to do with their customers.

Hallmarks of Industrial Age Companies:

- Supply Economies of Scale
- High Barriers to Entry
- Mass Marketing
- Limited Customization
- Poor Customer Support

Supply Economies of Scale. In the Industrial Age, the more raw materials a company used, the more power it had to negotiate lower prices from its suppliers. In virtually every industry, this gave the largest manufacturer a powerful advantage over its smaller competitors. The larger the company, the less it had to charge to make a profit when it had to fight a newcomer to its markets, and the more money it could make when the smaller firm went under or was bought up and the market was again divided between a few giants.

High Barriers to Entry. It costs a lot to set up a factory, especially when making sophisticated products or churning out enough of them to serve a national or international market. It costs still more to set up branch offices, deal with legal restrictions in dozens or hundreds of different communities, and pay a host of other expenses. When companies grow large enough, they can take it all in stride. Startups in the Industrial Age faced yet another disadvantage.

Mass Marketing. Now add the cost of establishing and maintaining a national or multinational sales force and paying for ad campaigns in magazines, on the radio, and—most expensive of all—on television. Again, large companies can afford it, while small ones cannot.

Limited Customization. Henry Ford was eager to please his customers. They could, he famously said, have the Model T in any color they wanted, "so long as it is black." For a pre-computer manufacturer, tailoring products to the needs of individual customers is expensive; standardization costs far less. In the Industrial

Age, the ideal product was the Bic pen—a simple object churned out by the billion, each one as close as possible to being identical to every other. Thus, consumers faced an easy choice: They could accept whatever a manufacturer wanted to sell them, or they could hope to find another maker whose limited array of products included one that seemed more appealing. Customization was the realm of old-fashioned craftsmen, whose one-off creations could be afforded only by the wealthy.

Poor Customer Support. Mass production inevitably means mass consumption. And if one pen is identical to all the rest, then one customer is identical to the rest, for the manufacturer's purposes: One customer equals one unit of consumption, no more. Customer support becomes a kind of customization, a one-off expense to be avoided wherever possible.

This model of commerce was very satisfying for a while. By the 1980s, the output of consumer goods was higher than it had ever been, and consumers could choose from a wider variety of products than ever before. I remember when the shampoo counter in the supermarket had no more than five brands to choose from. Today, an entire supermarket aisle is filled with brands and subbrands of shampoos, conditioners, and hair products unimaginable in the '60s. As the variety became richer, consumer spending on what had once been considered luxury items rose rapidly. Corporate profits soared with them.

In those days, quality and customer support meant far less to producers than a good advertising campaign. Consumers were easily influenced by advertisements and promotions in all traditional media channels—television, print, and radio. Yet there came a turning point. Consumers in the last part of the 20th century became less and less enchanted by mere variety. Increasingly, mass production failed to satisfy them. Mainstream advertising ceased to excite buyers. Instead, consumers began to focus on the quality of the goods they bought and the service that marketers gave them. Poor product and bad service were no longer tolerated.

The Information Age

Enter the Information Age and the Internet, which many talk about as the force behind the transition from atoms to bits—the transition from the physical production of consumer goods to the digital production of information.

Suddenly, businesses and consumers had access to a ubiquitous network of information, rich in resources. Real-time communication offered unprecedented opportunities for conducting worldwide commerce. A different type of commerce emerged. This was electronic commerce—or e-commerce—and it was a totally new game, with new players and new rules.

Hallmarks of Information Age Companies:

- No Geographic Boundaries
- Smaller Barriers to Entry
- Improved Cost and Efficiency
- Customer Focused
- Innovations in Information
- New Organizational Models

No Geographic Boundaries. In the pre-Internet era, relationships with customers, employees, and suppliers were developed within shared geographic locations. A small retailer on Main Street primarily had access to the shoppers of Main Street. A large corporation could have access to shoppers in a much broader area, but only by developing a sales force and distribution network that effectively put a little piece of the company in each of those remote locations.

Today, because the Internet connects computers, and their owners, worldwide, geography no longer limits even a small company's access to customers. The Internet provides companies genuine access to a global village; there are no geographic boundaries. That little Main Street retailer now can sell its products to someone on the other side of the world. This is a dramatic change.

Consider it a frantic quest of—and for!—consumers worldwide. Consumers have finally been liberated and are able to search the globe for products and services that interest them. This is equally true for companies seeking to establish various business-to-business (B2B) relationships.

Thanks to the Internet, companies will increasingly be able to sustain important relationships at a distance, providing personalized service that meets the needs of unique customers, not just geographic market segments.

Smaller Barriers to Entry. Another important feature of the Internet is that in this new market the barriers to entry have shrunk. Unlike the Industrial Age, the cost of "setting up shop" today can be minimal. A company can create an Internet presence at very low cost. Prophet Eenie will show how a small company can produce a Web site that looks as professional as those of the big players who spend millions of dollars on their online shop, or can join an online mall in order to sell its products worldwide. The size of the company and its marketing budget no longer govern mass-market appeal. Promoting a business on the Web is relatively inexpensive compared to most forms of advertising. And, the business will be open 24 hours a day, seven days a week, including holidays.

Improved Cost and Efficiency. Improved cost and efficiency make this computer thing worthwhile. Computers are finally the productivity tools they were meant to be. This is to say that if computers are properly utilized, companies will see productivity improve greatly. If we can produce more in the same amount of time, with the same or less effort, costs of production go down. And computers are data-sorting tools. The better and quicker you can sort, store, and access critical data, the more efficient your business becomes. I am surprised at how many companies and organizations still use computers strictly for their word-processing tasks. Computers are not just glorified typewriters any longer, nor is the Internet just for sending goofy e-mails to your circle of friends.

I was recently looking for short-term apartment rentals in Tucson, Arizona. I was in New York, but had the greatest real-time tool imaginable—the Internet. I searched various places on the Internet and finally relied on a Web site at www.SpringStreet.com (part of the homestore.com network). Using SpringStreet.com, I was able to browse for apartment availability by location, size, monthly rental costs, and amenities. I was able to view photos and floor plans of the apartments. In some cases I was able to take a "virtual tour" of the properties. Although I am still in awe over the power of technology, today, Internet users tend to take this service for granted. It is painfully evident, however, that the owners of apartments not listed on this service or on the Internet were the losers.

I was able to customize SpringStreet.com by establishing a "My Stuff" section, where I kept a listing of the apartments that specifically interested me. I was able to instantly send e-mail to the apartment's leasing agent. The agents, using technology effectively and understanding the instantaneous nature of the Internet, were prompt and efficient in their replies. SpringStreet.com provided a link to maps and detailed directions, they allowed me to view neighborhoods and make note of shopping centers, parks, medical facilities, and other points of interest in the area. They provided moving and travel tips.

Computers, the Internet, data, sorting, customer interaction, good resourceful information—the experience was complete. What were the costs to the apartment lessors? Minimal! This Internet exposure cost far less than any other medium—direct mail, newspaper advertising, or catalogs. What was the exposure and potential for them to attract new lessees? Tremendous! Certainly, people in Tucson can use this tool when they seek relocation, but I was 2,600 miles away. This tool can be used by people on all ends of the planet. What was the efficiency for the users, both lessor and lessee? Unbeatable! How else would I have gathered this information as quickly and as efficiently? ... And the lessors and lessees who did not utilize computers and the Internet? Losers. Period.

Customer Focused. The information economy is allowing businesses to become more customer focused. Being efficient, effectively managing customer data, and meeting instant communication demands, a business can rebuild the consumer confidence that had been rapidly declining. In effect it is a revelation for businesses—it is actually possible to make your customers happy! Businesses must use technology as a tool to help customers tell them what they want. Proper implementation and use of technology allow the business to understand the needs of the customer and develop a relationship with each individual. In the Information Age, businesses cater to customer's needs on a one-to-one basis. My SpringStreet.com experience shows clearly how this online real-estate company set out to serve my individual needs.

In contrast to the Industrial Age, where the mega-corporations were in control, in the Information Age the real power is with the customer. Information Age customers participate in defining, creating, and consuming information/value. Sellers once held an advantage over buyers by virtue of their superior knowledge of product features, cost, and availability controls. Today, buyers have increasing access to this information. This knowledge has shifted from producers to users. Customers have the power of choice. When they surf the Web, their move to a new supplier is only a click away. They have the power of customization, because smart Internet businesses use technologies to personalize offerings.

Because of the Internet, people have begun to expect instant, 24/7 access to information and resources. The Internet allows effortless, fast, inexpensive communication at all hours of the day or night. (I was able to surf SpringStreet.com at two in the morning.) With all of this opportunity available to them, consumers expect and demand more. Customers want explicit product data, the best pricing, online order tracking, and lots of guarantees. They want rich, contextual information that is easy and quick to navigate or search. They also demand a large selection of goods and services to choose from. Even more, they want a personalized experience. They feel good about the personalized experience! If you are a business in the 21st century, you must give your customers this instant, individualized service in order to survive.

Innovations in Information. Businesses that have awakened to the power of the Internet are beginning to understand that it can and should be used as more than just a marketing and information tool. They recognize that the Internet is reshaping the culture of business and transforming the way organizations process information. They realize that their ability to collect, manipulate, and analyze information makes it possible for them to tailor their offerings to the needs of their customers. Those who take the most innovative and creative approach to this process are succeeding at lightening speeds.

These innovations are a continuing process. The ways in which organizations utilize information is constantly being discovered. New rules are made every day.

Competition in the New Economy will still be based on value, but in the e-economy "value" means more than product price. Knowledge is value, and the Internet is the ultimate knowledge medium. It is an open marketplace, where customers can tell you what they want and need. (I want an apartment in Tucson that accepts pets and is within five miles of a park.) Customers utilizing the Internet have the power of knowledge, which comes from access to near perfect information. This means that to attract and retain customers, sellers need to build two-way relationships that deliver real value.

Businesses that adopt the Web, focus on the offering of a value product, and accept the shift of power to the users of their value are the ones that will succeed. This shift of power, by the way, includes not only of customers, but employees and partners and anyone else even remotely relevant to the business process. Those who are most innovative will stand out in the crowd.

New Organizational Structures. Now, for all this to happen, companies must change the habits of decades. In the Industrial Age, businesses grew accustomed to operating as big fish in small ponds. Corporate leaders thought, "We are the market-makers, creating the market for our product, so just keep manufacturing." In this paradigm, process and efficiency improvements yielded much higher returns than innovation in the business model.

The rise of e-commerce has reversed the old priorities. Today's intense competition and free flow of information make it increasingly difficult for a single firm to force its vision upon others; collaboration becomes essential. Therefore new organizational structures are proliferating. Today's structures allow "turn-on-a-dime" execution of business strategies, greater transparency of the supply chain, and broad data sharing—among supply chain partners, customers, and even competitors.

Affiliate programs are a perfect example of business model innovation. Using the expansive power of the Internet, a company can quickly and easily form relationships with hundreds, thousands, maybe millions of partners that will eagerly and successfully advertise and sell their products. This is a simple process. Yet, if included in the company's business model, it can increase sales tremendously.

These partnerships are made possible by the networking of the world. Each partner with a presence on the World Wide Web is only a click away. Each partner's effort to sell the company's product is minimal, the expense is practically zero; partners merely add a link on their Web site to their partner company's product page. Yet they gain the opportunity to receive a steady stream of revenue, a percentage of the sales originating at their Web site. Nothing in the traditional brick-and-mortar business world could be so easy and effective.

SpringStreet.com is also an excellent example of the leveraging of partners and resources available to networked companies. Reaching out onto the Internet, SpringStreet partners with such sites and services as moving companies, cleaning services, electricians, lawn care professionals, and other home-oriented businesses. The most valuable partner for me (aside from apartment leasing agencies) was petswelcome.com, which provided me with a list of pet-friendly hotels on each stop of my journey across the country to my newly leased apartment in Tucson.

SpringStreet.com leverages these partnerships to offer personalized service that would be impossible for an integrated company stuck in the world of conventional, non-e-commerce. The site has rent and cost-of-living calculators that compare costs between different locations. It offers a free change-of-address service that not only notifies the U.S. Post Office of your move, but takes the extra step to alert catalogs and magazines, newspapers, credit card companies, colleges, clubs, and other mailing institutions. Every few days while preparing for my journey, I would get a countdown of the number of days until my trip. Each e-mail would contain tips about packing, safety, and all sorts of useful subjects. SpringStreet is a model for the effective use of the Internet and Internet tools.

There are many such opportunities to use the power of computers and the Internet. To survive in a world of such agile, efficient competitors, an Industrial Age company must integrate them into its overall automation systems.

Another good example is in sales and customer service, or what the industry refers to as electronic customer relationship management (eCRM). Today it is possible to track your customers' activity throughout your Web site, interact with them in real-time, and tailor your approach to their activities. Let's say the customer indicates that she is looking for a baby stroller. However, when the sales rep reviews her activity on the site, he sees that she has been clicking on infant strollers. This clarifies her objective and makes for more efficient sales and service. This is just one of many ways in which Net-savvy marketers can collect and manipulate critical information from customers, employees, and partners, and thus improve customer relationships.

Think also about the traditional advertising model. Say that you are a frequent flyer on one of the major airlines, and each time you have flown, you have taken your two children under the age of 12. In the traditional model, the airline is likely to target you with specialized advertising for family travel and vacations. Using the Internet, that same airline can "push" that advertisement to anyone searching their Web site for a fare that includes children. Whether the airline knows your history or not, it can recognize your immediate needs in real time and try to meet them with promotions and incentives.

These Internet techniques represent a fundamental change in the company's business model. In the digital economy, shorter product life cycles and new, agile competitors make such innovations critical. Capital, brands, and processes no longer give the company power in the marketplace. Instead, the company's ability to turn on a dime and change its business model to fit the needs of e-customers has become the key to survival.

In the chapters ahead, the Prophets will show us many different opportunities to make the Internet work for your agile, networked business, whatever its level of funding.

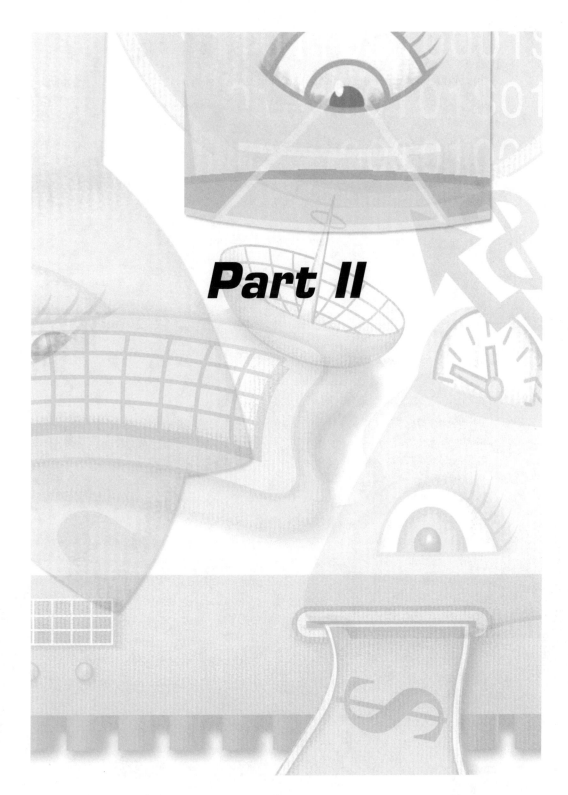

Part II

Part II

Part II
E-Business Fundamentals

So here we are. After several years of growth, aggressive companies that embraced electronic business were worth millions as the millennium opened. They are worth pennies today. NASDAQ has crashed, and Internet companies have downsized, gone bankrupt, or are heavily in the red. Some companies that ventured onto the Internet have lost hope, and some that once were ready to give the Internet a whirl now are extremely skeptical. Governments may feel that technology has failed them, and investors wonder what happened to the so-called "New Economy."

On the other hand, valuable lessons have been learned, and the most foresighted businesses are forging ahead with their e-business plans. Ambitions and expectations have leveled out a bit, and firms have begun to improve their Internet performance. Entrepreneurs each day are devising thousands of new strategies for making money on the Internet. New technologies are constantly being developed and improved upon. Wireless access to the Internet could soon be a mainstay for many business owners. New ways of servicing people have cropped up, and Internet usage is greater than ever before.

Despite the dot-bomb stock collapse, this also remains a time for optimism. Global competition has been unbound, and the Internet offers unprecedented opportunities for businesses and organizations of any size. Your company, too, can do well on the Web if it masters the rules of this new environment.

Part II of *Internet Prophets* introduces new business concepts brought on by the advent of the Internet. This section provides you with a solid understanding of the basic fundamentals, building blocks, and logic of Internet tools and applications. Regardless of what your business has done or will do with technology, it is important to review, embrace, act on, or reflect on the new theories brought into being in the new economy.

Chapter 2

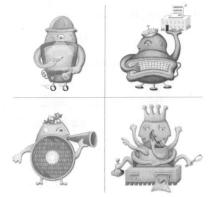

Online Shopping

The Internet allows users to look for and purchase almost any product from the convenience of their homes, 24 hours a day, seven days a week. Online shopping is less time-consuming than a trip to the mall, more convenient even than ordering by mail or telephone, and the worldwide selection of products cannot be matched. In an age when people are extremely busy and saving consumers time is critical, almost any company that offers its products on the Internet can build an important advantage over its brick-and-mortar competitors.

A newly released shopping study finds that 39 percent of those with access to the Internet say they go to a physical store or mall less often now that they can easily shop for a wide variety of products online. Nineteen percent of online shoppers say they do less traditional retail shopping. Twenty percent say they do less catalog shopping. And how about this: It is estimated that 50 percent of people with Internet access turn to the Web first for information about the products and services they need, and that Americans who use the Internet hold 60 percent or more of the buying power of the total U.S. population. These findings are significant to retailers.

The online arena is an intensely beneficial tool for consumers. The Internet makes it easy for shoppers to research a product, compare it with others, find the best price, order it online, and have it shipped to their door the next day.

That makes for shopping convenience that cannot be matched by traditional stores. Not long ago, I lived in a small town where there was a little market—something like the convenience stores we have today on every corner, but a bit more personal. The store had fresh meats and vegetables, canned and frozen goods, and household goods and toiletries. In a pinch I could get just about anything I needed from this store. In fact, I could run in and say, "Bruce, put this on my bill" as I held up a bottle of ketchup and ran back to my barbecue. "No problem," said Bruce, because he knew I would come back in a week to pay my monthly bill.

If Web sites are implemented properly, they allow every business to act like a small-town convenience store. Like Bruce in my local market, data management systems on Web sites enable each customer, anywhere in the world, to establish a personal profile when she first enters the site. From that point on, the customer can purchase what she wants in seconds. With a simple log-in and password, the system can remember who customers are, their credit card and shipping information, and anything else relevant to their purchase or experience.

The online arena offers tremendous advantages to the savvy business, as well. If you have products to sell, the Web will present them to an audience that you could not dream of reaching through traditional methods—it's that simple. And, once you have landed those worldly customers, Internet technology can help you keep them coming back

An online retailer can provide a whole host of convenience options to consumers. It can also solicit customers more cost effectively than any other means available today. The retailer can maintain databases of customers' personal information and keep an eye on ordering trends. An automatic trend analysis identifies suitable opportunities to solicit an individual customer with new product offers. For example, if a customer bought a Mother's Day gift last year, an online retailer's program could automatically send reminder e-mails to that customer every Mother's Day. The e-mail can be customized to say something like, "Dear Jackie: You sent a floral bouquet to Marilyn Conner last year. This year we would like to offer you a $10 discount on our wide selection of chocolates and other gift ideas. Visit our Web site at www.whattogetformothersday.com by May 5 to take advantage of this discount."

A retailer can send an e-mail that highlights the arrival of new products that are a good fit with the customer's interest, based on his shopping history. Let's say that a customer bought a fishing rod from your online store. An online retailer can send that customer e-mail offers for various types of fishing equipment. The e-mail could add value by including interesting articles about fishing and information about the best fishing spots in the customer's area. The online retailer might also establish a partnership with fishing resorts and boating companies, earning a commission on sales for each of his customers who uses the partner's facilities as a result of these messages.

One of the Internet's success stories is the online bookseller Amazon.com (www.amazon.com). On Amazon.com, a consumer can search for books by subject, author, or keyword. She can read reviews of books posted by ordinary book readers like you and me. I don't know about you, but I think these reviews are often more valuable than reviews published by professional book reviewers.

Amazon.com does a whole lot more to enhance the customer's buying experience. The company analyzes its customers' book requests and suggests other titles that may be of interest. When it presents a book on its site, Amazon.com

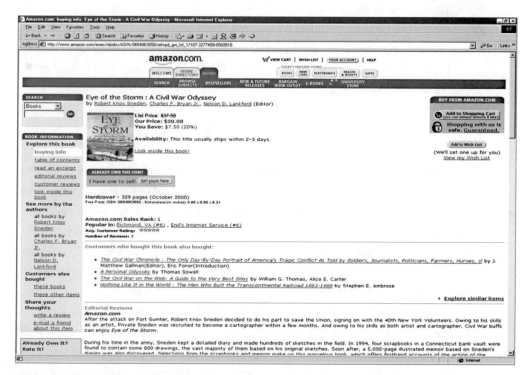

Figure 2.1. "Customers who bought this book also bought": When shoppers view one of the book selections on Amazon.com, they are provided with a list of similar books for sale.

tells the consumer something like, "Readers who purchased this book have also bought the following books," and displays a list of related reading. Amazon.com remembers who you are and maintains a detailed record of what you have purchased; when you return to the site, it greets you with information about titles that match your historical preferences. Amazon.com sends e-mail messages notifying you of the exact date of shipment of the book you just bought, so you know when to expect it. They send follow-up e-mails to announce new book offerings. Largely due to this high level of personalization in its customer service and marketing efforts, Amazon.com is among the most successful businesses operating on the Internet; the company has an extremely high percentage of repeat buyers and sells to a worldwide audience.

One of the most compelling features of the Internet and the behind-the-scenes applications employed by companies like Amazon.com is that the processes occur automatically—and they can be implemented at a fraction of the cost of acquiring and retaining a customer using traditional advertising, telemarketing, and print direct-mail campaigns.

Some e-tailers never even stock inventory. They set up shop on the Internet as a broker, passing orders on to suppliers and distributors and taking a percentage of sales.

One innovation that is of growing interest to many retailers is the online mall. The benefit of online malls is the aggregation in one "place" of a full range of products from a broad selection of manufacturers, distributors, and/or retailers. Every shop owner wants his store in a mall that is visited by millions of customers, and this is exactly what is taking place on the Web.

In the physical world, we visit shopping malls, not only to shop, but also to browse, to get out of the house, and to be entertained. Shopping online is not so different. There may be hundreds of other people visiting the same shopping mall at the same time and, while you may not see them (yet), you may be able to interact with them, if the site offers that functionality. For example, in many cybermalls online shoppers can post product reviews and merchant ratings to share their browsing and buying experiences with other patrons.

Companies with well-visited sites (such as search engines, portals, and Internet Service Provider [ISPs]) are rapidly adding shopping malls to their Web sites. This makes sense, because they already have a loyal group of users to whom they can provide an enhanced experience. Of course, malls can also provide an added revenue stream for the Web site.

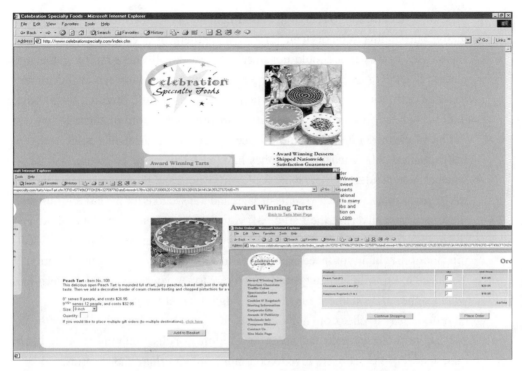

Figure 2.2. In this typical example, ordering merchandise online is very straightforward and easy.

Some online malls are striving to become the same sort of browsing and community gathering place as traditional malls in the physical world. An example is www.town24.com. Town24.com has an animated cartoon-style interface that allows visitors to select their destinations as if they were walking through a town. Each image, each building on each street, represents some type of product or service. For example, online insurance companies and other financial companies are organized in the "Financial District," while sports information, events, and products are found in the "Stadium." An animated airplane is the link to the "Travel" section of the site. In many such sites, there is a "Post Office" providing e-mail service.

Some electronic malls focus on the interests of targeted buying groups. For instance, www.surprise.com offers gift suggestions and ideas based on the gender of the recipient, your relationship with them, the type of occasion, and the recipient's preferences (such as: Are they an avid reader? Do they hate to cook? Do they have an unusual sense of humor?).

It is quite common to see large department stores represented in these cyber-malls, but smaller retailers can join most of them at a very reasonable cost. Businesses of all sizes should consider participating in these online gathering places. The key to success is choosing a mall that targets your typical customer. Before committing yourself to a particular mall, do a little research to find the mall best suited to your products, with a proven track record of success.

One of the most important things to take into account is the mall's traffic. Ask the mall's managers how many visitors they have each day, week, or month. Ask them whether they tabulate demographics on their visitors and the visitor's activity, and ask to see the data. Ask their volume of sales and transactions for the last few months.

Some malls advertise their site. Ask your candidate mall what kind of advertising or promotion they do to lead Web surfers to the mall. This is critical information, which you need in order to assess the viability of this "location." You need to know how many people are likely to see your product and determine whether the mall's audience is the right target market for you.

A good way to check out a mall is to contact other vendors who display there. Ask about their success, and about any failures or disappointments they have experienced. Internet users love to communicate and share their stories.

Once you have done your research on various malls and chosen the ones you like, there is no reason why you can't participate in more than one, provided the fees are affordable.

Your homework does not stop there, however. The success of any venture depends on the commitment given to it. You must promote your products in all venues possible. Even if the mall has an advertising program, it's important to recognize that your efforts to lure visitors to your specific products within the mall are going to be the real key to success.

For a fairly comprehensive list of Internet malls, go to www.malls.com.

Eenie Strategy

Join an Online Mall

If you have products to sell, you can easily and cost effectively join an online mall. In most malls,

all financial transactions are handled for you, and charges are minimal. Table 2.1 shows some popular malls, with comparisons of fees
and features.

Table 2.1. Eenie's mall strategies

Mall Address	Monthly Fees and Mall Commission	Other Features

Amazon.com
 zShops
	MONTHLY FEES
	 $39.99/mo for up to 5,000 items
	
	 MALL COMMISSION
	 Items priced to $25.00
	    commission = 5 percent
	
	 Items priced $25.01–$1,000
	    commission = $1.25 plus 2.5 percent of
	    any amount over $25
	
	 Items priced $1,000.01 and higher
	    commission = $25.63 plus 1.25 percent
	    of any amount over $1,000
		• Branded Web site using zShops URL
		
		 • Full billing history and payment status and statistics
		
		 • Additional fees for using Amazon Payments are $.25 per transaction, plus 2.5 percent of the transaction

AT&T Small Business Hosting Services **Attsbh.com**	*MONTHLY FEES* $75 for up to 100 items $100 for up to 250 items $115 for 500 items *MALL COMMISSION* None/Affiliated with Excitestores.com	• Branded Web site using your company domain name • Must have or apply through AT&T for merchant account • Quick access to orders, credit card transactions, and traffic reports
Yahoo.com **Yahoo!Store**	*MONTHLY FEES* $100/mo for up to 50 items $300/mo for up to 1,000 items *MALL COMMISSION* 2 percent of any amount over $5,000	• Branded Web site using Yahoo! URL or company domain name • Full reporting and statistics • Must have merchant account

Meenie Strategy

Build a "Shopping Cart" Web Site

You want to present yourself as an independent company, and plan to sell your products on your own branded Web site. You have two basic options within your budget:

Spend less on the shopping cart and more on design and content. Outsource the site's design and content development to creative Web designers. (Be sure to view their portfolio before giving them the assignment to make sure you approve of the quality of their work.) Then host your site with an Internet service provider that offers a simple template shopping cart solution. The template is a very simple, generic shopping cart that can be grafted into your Web site. Templates generally permit very little customization, but they are an inexpensive way to add this important function to your site.

The alternative is to spend more on a customized shopping cart, but less on design and content. Instead of hiring a Web designer, you outsource design, content, and application development to a firm that can create a custom shopping cart application. The benefits of this solution are more consistent branding and customized programming throughout your shopping site. The designers of a custom site typically work hand-in-hand with the application developers to create a seamless, well-branded site. An additional advantage to this approach is that the developers can create custom shopping cart tools based on your specific needs. This permits much greater flexibility than a template shopping cart. However, budget discipline is a must. It is easy to run the cost of extensive customization right out of the Meenie category.

See Table 2.2 for online resources to help with building either type of shopping cart site.

Table 2.2. Meenie's sample shopping cart strategies

Template Shopping Cart	Custom Shopping Cart
Spend less on shopping cart (template) and more on design and content.	Spend more on shopping cart customization, less on design and content.
Less customized shopping options	More customized shopping options
Outsource the design and content development of the site to creative Web designers (be sure to view their portfolio in advance to make sure you approve of the quality of their work). Host your site with an Internet Service Provider that offers a simple template "shopping cart" solution.	Outsource design, content, and application development to a firm that can customize your application. The benefit of this solution is more consistent branding throughout the site. The designers of a custom site typically work hand-in-hand with the application developers to create a seamless, well-branded site. An additional advantage to this approach is that the developers can create custom tools based on your needs whereas the template shopping carts have limited abilities. You handle fulfillment as you receive notification of each order.
ISPs with Template Shopping Cart Solutions	**Verio** at www.verio.com offers custom e-commerce solutions starting at $5,000 and feature online management of orders, inventory, and images as well as payment processing. Complex e-commerce apps include pricing for bulk discounts, gift registries, gift shipping, and related products.
EARTHLINK	
www.earthlink.com	
Initial setup: $175; Monthly: $54.95 With own merchant account	Starting at $9,000 Verio has content management applications that allow for easy publishing to the Web. Complex content management applications include image file management inside of articles, various levels of editorial approval, and can include direct links to items in our e-commerce store.
GATEWAY	
gateway-eservices.com	
Monthly: $19.95 for up to 10 items, up to 100 items is $69.95, and high volume stores are $119.95 per month	Verio has various add-on apps available to add extra functions economically. One example is their Mail Express application that collects customer e-mail addresses through a Web form and adds them to a list for bulk e-mailing, a simple way to notify your audience of new products or site news. Price: $5,000.
FRONTLINE COMMUNICATIONS CORP	
www.Frontline.net	
Initial setup $50.00; Monthly: $59.95 for up to 100 products, $89.95 for up to 500 items, $139.95 for up to 2,000 items	
Have your designers simply link from the content portion of the Web site to the shopping cart template. The shopping cart solution will provide you with details about each order and automatic online credit card processing. You would handle fulfillment as you receive notification of each order.	

Miney Strategy

Set Up an Efficient Order Fulfillment Routine

An outsourced fulfillment solution is available through a company called bizFulfillment.com (www.bizfulfillment.com).

They can assist you in establishing an efficient method to process and fulfill orders through your Web site. They will store and maintain your product inventories and pick, pack, label, and ship your product to your customers who order online. They even handle returned items and customer concerns. bizFulfillment.com also provides a full range of reports completely customized to your needs—so you can better plan and grow your business.

Why outsource? An entity like bizFulfilment.com has made the investments in fixed costs like warehouses and ordering systems, so you don't have to. You also save money through the economies of scale using a shared shipping contract and warehouse system.

Costs: Start-up and warehousing fees vary based on application customization and product intricacies. Fulfillment costs range from $4.75 to $9.50 per order.

Moe Strategy

Create Real-Time Customer Sales Assistance

You have the budget and ability to provide your customers and prospective customers with a customized, personalized, interactive, and entertaining shopping experience. In addition, you can utilize an application that allows your sales reps to close a sale while a prospective customer is on your Web site! A sophisticated solution by NewChannel, Inc. (www.newchannel.com) effectively analyzes Web visitors' movement on a Web site. It automatically ranks the customer's interest and creates a profile for them based on their behavior throughout the site. If the customer's behavior is indicative of a "hot lead," sales reps are alerted and can offer assistance to facilitate the transaction.

As an example, take a look at Consolidated Freightways Corporation (www.cfwy.com). This company is a large freight transportation carrier, providing transportation and logistics services to businesses throughout the world. Logistics purchasers visit this Web site seeking comparable service and pricing information. With NewChannel, Consolidated Freightway's online consultants are alerted when a prospect is most likely to need assistance and is ready to make a purchase. CF's online consultants can proactively extend an offer of assistance via a pop-up window on the computer screen. If the customer accepts the offer, a private dialog box appears, allowing the customer to chat and receive other information on a live, one-to-one basis with an experienced logistics expert.

Cost: NewChannel offers a fully hosted solution. Although pricing varies from customer to customer, there is a minimum annual fee of $350,000.

Chapter 3

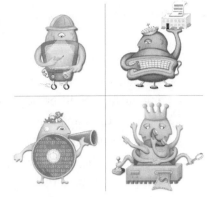

One-to-One Marketing

Every business-school graduate and marketing manager has learned the four Ps of marketing—product, price, place, and promotion. The principle of the four Ps is simple: Create the product, establish a price, place the product in a sales channel, and promote like crazy. Traditionally, businesses defined the features, benefits, and prices of their products and then mass-produced and mass-marketed them to consumers. Products were promoted aggressively through advertising, public relations, direct mail, and other in-your-face types of programs. Through the variety of media used, the business controlled the messages that consumers received and set the trends that drove their buying choices. Customers had very little say in the process.

Marketers always understood the potential value of developing relationships with customers, but until the Internet entered the mainstream there were no practical tools to accomplish it. Today, a ubiquitous, cheap, and interactive Net, combined with low-cost information-rich databases, allows producers to develop meaningful, direct relationships with prospects and customers. For the first time, companies can engage in a two-way, interactive dialogue with consumers on a mass scale.

This customer-focused approach has caused a profound rethinking of the marketing process. Say good-bye to the four Ps of mass production and mass marketing, and say hello to a concept referred to as "one-to-one marketing," serving "an audience of one." Put simply, one-to-one marketing is about developing relationships with individuals, one individual at a time. It is about businesses treating customers differently, finding out what they want, and narrowing the focus of services dramatically, so as to meet the needs of this individual audience.

In this new realm, it is the customers, not the companies, who create the messages that shape our perceptions of companies and their products. The Internet has given customers the tools to create public opinion online, as they communicate with one another. Marketers have the same tools as before, and they can push their messages through the Internet as well. Yet independent voices are heard just as clearly, and companies can no longer influence consumer perceptions as effectively as they did in the past. Now businesses are at the consumer's beck and call.

You might think this puts companies in a precarious situation. Instead, a newer, stronger, more effective and profitable kind of sales strategy has emerged from this change in the balance of power. Businesses can now focus on their core competencies. They have the opportunity to sell more of their products to fewer customers—if they can be flexible enough to customize their products and services to the needs of individual buyers. Success in the Information Age means not just getting more customers, but keeping existing customers and growing a strong relationship with them.

This new business model is extremely powerful. Think about it: It is much easier to sell (or up-sell—that is, market additional, often related products) to an existing customer, a customer you already know, and who knows you. Through their buying history, and the surveys and promotions they have participated in, you know the individual customer's preferences. And when you know enough about their values and needs, it is easier to satisfy customers and keep them happy—and loyal.

Transactions with these customers will be the most profitable transactions your business undertakes. These satisfied customers, who trust you and your products, are more likely to recommend you to others, thus increasing your qualified prospect base.

It gets even better. Through acquisition and development of a customer knowledge base, you become a smarter prospector. We all know that it is expensive to acquire customers. Without accurate consumer knowledge, many companies attract the wrong customers, and because the wrong customers do not stay loyal, this ends up costing the company much more in the long run than acquiring the right ones.

Using technology, you can improve your opportunities for directly acquiring the most profitable new customers. Through analysis of your best patrons' demography and preferences, you begin to recognize the attributes of a loyal and profitable customer. You do everything you can to attract and solicit a customer based on these profiles. So, getting to know your customers not only helps you maintain solid, profitable relationships with them, it also allows you to focus on attracting future loyalists. Do this, and you are way ahead of the game. The Internet enables companies to seize this knowledge opportunity.

A firm's most loyal customers may amount to as little as two percent of the total, or greater than 20 percent; it doesn't matter. The point is that to apply one-to-one marketing techniques effectively you must identify your most loyal customers and focus your offerings to them.

It is obviously easier in a small company to identify key customers. In fact, owners of small businesses (with less than $1,000,000 in revenue) can usually recite their key client list off the top of their heads. It may take a bit of information gathering for others. Larger companies must be nimble enough to integrate Customer Relationship Management (CRM) programs in order to provide better service to their customers. The goal, of course, is to generate more revenue through the ever-developing relationship with them.

The methodology should be approximately the same from company to company regardless of size. First, a business must clearly identify its customers and potential customers. Then it must group these customers, based on similar qualities and needs. Next, it must find a way to tailor its offerings to customers based on the individual's values and needs. Of course, this has to be done in friendly and personal ways.

Think about these questions:

- What do you know about your best and most loyal customers?
- Why would an existing customer want to buy more from you?
- What would they buy from you?
- How can you make it easier for them to buy additional products from you?

One-to-one marketing is a constant learning process. In an Internet worked environment, sellers and buyers can and should maintain an ongoing dialogue, so that each can learn about the other. The customers tell the business what they want. The business processes all the information received from each customer and tailors the products or services it offers to meet that individual's requirements. Consumers today actually participate in creating products; after they've told you what they want, they expect you to tailor your product or service to them.

Companies embracing the new philosophy are finding it truly effective. They discover that if they give customers the opportunity to communicate with them, consumers will do their part. Once the lines of communication are open and customers find that interacting with a business is beneficial, they continue to invest their time in this mutually profitable interaction. The more time a customer invests, the greater his stake in making the relationship work. At this point, it makes more sense for customers to stay loyal to the company than for them to groom a competitor. Businesses are discovering that serving a few regular customers extremely well can reduce expenses and generate more revenue than giving mediocre service to hundreds of occasional customers.

Many post-industrial companies consider management of this one-to-one customer relationship to be the most essential part of their business strategy. An Information Age company's assets are valuable in proportion to its ability to communicate with customers, suppliers, and other partners in order to engage in mutually beneficial transactions. Some consider the value of customer relationships more important than capital assets such as land, buildings, and even big bank accounts.

So, how does this one-to-one thing work? Well, although the basic methodology is the same for all companies, detailed strategies differ according to the firm's specific product or service. There are many applications on the market that specialize in meeting this one-to-one demand. There are many Application Service Providers (ASPs—technology consulting firms that offer a bundle of applications and strategies to their clients) focusing on electronic Customer Relationship Management (eCRM) strategies. There are both simple and complex methods that, when utilized properly, have proven benefits for the bottom line.

Let's see what it takes to create a one-to-one experience in the world of e-business.

Quick Response Is Critical

The Web never sleeps, and neither should your customer service department. Support staff may turn off the lights at the end of the day, but with e-mail, insomniacal customers have no mercy. Adding e-mail response and customer service forms to your Web site is the first step toward genuine customer interaction. But if you do not reply promptly, you will lose your opportunity. The quicker and more personalized the response, the more satisfied the customer will be. These days, people expect e-mail to alert you to their needs as instantly as a pager or beeper would. If you are serious about being an electronic business, you have to react in real time, or as close to real time as you can get.

This fast response time should extend to partners, employees, and colleagues. In the new economy, if you want to keep a happy employee, create a team environment, and collaborate effectively with your partners, treat them as you would a customer.

Registration Forms and Surveys

If you want to learn who your customers are, ask them. Find ways to entice site visitors to provide you with relevant information about them. Just collecting physical and e-mail addresses is not enough—you need to gather as much information as possible. Online registration forms, surveys, and even contests work really well for this.

On many successful sites, the customer is asked a series of questions, the answers to which help the business to serve them better, based on their personal interests. Think about this personalization technique. You can collect all kinds of information about the customer. You can expand your knowledge base to include more than just a profile of their use of your products or services. You can collect information about their families, pets, travel frequencies, and hobbies. You can even collect their birthday information and know their sun sign. Collect anything and *everything* that will help you personalize your efforts to reach them. All this information helps you to develop better relationships with customers.

Gentle Dialogue and Customer Recognition

A one-to-one relationship is built around the ability to create an ongoing dialogue with individual users. Successful e-businesses are implementing methods

ormation from their customers. These are sometimes
echniques. They collect information gradually, rather
ne-shot registration forms. Special promotions, rewards,
rage Web visitors to provide you with information about

d Individualization

Using ...... ffectively, a Web site can also recognize return visitors and build a knowledge base of interactions, preferences, and transactions that can later be used to offer personalized services. Individualization is the ability to modify information based on the user's needs. The Web site recognizes a user, often through a log-in or "cookie," a small file placed on the user's computer that "registers" the user with the server and often stores information about the customer. Based on the knowledge that has already been accumulated about that user, the Web site can individualize his experience in a variety of ways. This can be as simple as displaying the user's name and a welcoming message on the opening page: "Hello, Howard Gurock, welcome back!"

Privacy Policy

The issue of privacy cannot be over emphasized. Many new Internet users have read *1984* and have serious concerns about "Big Brother." The new marketing game is predicated on collecting volumes of personal data. If you set out to learn everything about your customers, then you have to be willing to safeguard that data. Your site should feature, prominently, a privacy policy that details how you collect information, how you use it, and how it is stored. These are vital steps for any interactive Web site.

Multiple Channels

Most importantly, integrate multiple interactive channels. Promote your URL everywhere, but don't drop the telephone, fax, and direct mail response campaigns. Use any and all communications techniques to gain customer information that can be used to strengthen and deepen your relationships.

Let's not fool ourselves, this new campaign is a lot of work. But the bei are great. Companies that focus on customers are typically 60 percent more itable than companies that ignore the value of relationship building.

In the end, a firm that builds personal relationships with its customers makes it convenient for a customer to be loyal. At a time when a company's margins are eroding and competitors are just a click away, the most effective thing a company can do to maintain a competitive advantage is nurture its customer relationships.

Eenie Strategy

Engage in a Viral Marketing Campaign

Increase your qualified prospect base by providing a means for your Web site visitors and satisfied customers to recommend you to their friends and colleagues. Use Let 'Em Know (www.letemknow.com) as a personal recommendation tool. Let 'Em Know features

- Easy setup—should take less than five minutes!

- Fully customizable—integrate it into your Web site however you want!

- Flexible—ask for (and optionally require!) one to five referrals at a time!

You must register your Web site with Let 'Em Know. Go to www.letemknow.com and fill out their signup form, and you'll be issued a Let 'Em Know Member ID number that allows you to use the service. Then, by adding just a few lines of HTML code to your Web page(s) Let 'Em Know will drive personally recommended, qualified traffic to your Web site twenty-four hours a day.

Cost: Free.

Meenie Strategy

Launch a Sweepstakes

You need to drive traffic to your site, to encourage repeat traffic, and to have visitors identify themselves. A sweepstakes is a great way to accomplish all of this.

A company called ePrize (www.eprize.net) can create a fully legal sweepstakes on your site within 24 hours. This means bonding and registration in appropriate states, full rules and regulations in compliance with sweepstakes laws, contest design, database programming, prize acquisition, etc.

ePrize will design the contest, prepare rules and regulations, collect and manage all user information, handle all legal work, manage the drawing and administration, verify all prizes, fulfill prizes with legal sign-off, and build an administration module that allows real-time data management.

The sweepstakes will include the ability to capture critical user data: name, e-mail, address, phone, age, sex, occupation, and an opt-in question of your choice. For example: "Do you want to receive our newsletter on such and such a topic?"

Prize options for this package include a week on a Hawaiian cruise for two, a Sea Doo GTI personal watercraft, paid mortgage for one year (up to $1,500 per month), or a three-year lease on a Porsche Boxster.

Cost: $950 per quarterly campaign.

Miney Strategy

Learn About One-to-One Marketing from the Experts

One of the leading consulting groups specializing in one-to-one Marketing is Peppers and Rogers Group (www.1to1.com), located in New York City. A senior team of Peppers and Rogers Group trainers will spend a day or more at a location of your choice, training a team of 10 to 20 executives. Prior to the course, Peppers and Rogers Group will review and customize program materials and curriculum.

Their 1to1 Learning Series courses include presentations, case studies, best practices, interactive exercises, and brainstorming sessions.

Cost: Varies, depending on amount of curriculum customization required, but averages between $10,000 and $40,000 for the group.

Moe Strategy

Build an E-Commerce Site, and Optimize Your Marketing Efforts While Targeting and Tracking Visitors

This strategy includes a wide variety of options, all designed to gather information about your customers so you can improve your service to them. These include the following:

- Offer samples, coupons, and rebates
- Hold contests
- Provide incentives
- Create loyalty programs

Most paper coupons are just mass-marketing ads with discounts. However, if used properly, coupons can be valid one-to-one tools, and an individualized coupon is an exceptional tool, at that.

You can manage and create your own branded promotional campaigns using BrightStreet's (www.brightstreet.com) patent-pending technology, which customizes offers using demographic, geographic, and profile information.

In addition to creating digital discounts and incentives, BrightStreet offers a network of affiliate sites that provide greater distribution for your promotions. This service can expand your marketing efforts on the Internet while supporting your existing bricks-and-mortar channels. Using the Web as a targeted incentive medium, you can drive consumers into traditional store outlets with securely printed, trackable coupons, rebates, and sales notifications.

Cost: $120,000 to start.

Chapter 4

Digital Delivery

For products that can be digitized, the Internet gives the added benefit of instant delivery of either samples or the real thing. A digital product can be shipped immediately over the Internet, anywhere in the world, with no distribution costs and virtually no processing costs. It is faster and less expensive to develop and distribute material online than to write, design, print, and mail traditional catalogs, brochures, and packaged products. Then there are audio and video. Online broadcasting, or "webcasting," is gaining popularity rapidly. Most of the traditional broadcasting companies have gotten into this new game. Even small players have no barrier to entry on this front, as producing and distributing digital files is cheap and easy.

I was able to replay Al Gore's concession speech on MSNBC almost immediately after he completed it. It is still available on the Web site—history teachers in classrooms across the world have continuous access to this and many other events that have been broadcast and held in digital libraries across the Internet.

I have a favorite radio station, WFUV (www.wfuv.org), which is broadcast out of Fordham University in New York. It is a smaller station, and I always had trouble with reception from my office building. WFUV recently took their radio station online. Now I can listen to it all day at work, with my computer instead of the radio, through the Internet. They have received hundreds of e-mails from people all over the world that are listening to WFUV. The

Internet has allowed this radio station to expand its listening audience to all points on the planet—another marvel of this networked age.

Internet radio is one of the Internet's "killer applications." A computer with a sound card and an Internet connection can give you access to an unbelievable variety of programming. Like everything else on the Internet, there are no geographic limitations. You can listen to a station from Hungary as easily as one from the nearby city. If you are interested in some obscure type of music that is not played on mainstream radio, you can probably find it on the Web. Or, like many of WFUV's overseas listeners, you do not have to be homesick for your hometown radio station any longer. And you will find more than just music. A huge variety of news, sports, talk shows, and other audio programming is available on the Web. Take a look at the listing of Internet radio stations currently online (www.internetradiolist.com), and you will find it all.

Internet radio is even better than traditional AM/FM programming. It does not need to be sequential; users can listen to an ongoing program, or to prerecorded pieces on demand. Also, the medium is not limited to sound alone. Online audio programs can be accompanied by pictures, text, and hyperlinks to related Web sites.

There are two ways to deliver audio and video over the Internet. The easiest way is simply to make the files available for download. Compressed formats such as MP3 for audio are the most popular, but any type of audio or video file can be delivered through a Web or FTP site. Once the user downloads the file, he can play it on his computer. The problem is that audio and video files are usually pretty large and take quite a while to download—especially on a slow Internet connection.

The most common technique for creating and transmitting digital media files is called "streaming." This technique processes data and distributes it across a network as a continuous stream. Streaming technologies allow Internet users with slow connections (56K and less) to download multimedia files fast and effortlessly. In order to receive streaming files, you must have a browser plug-in application that reads the files. With streaming, the plug-in can start displaying the data before the entire file has been transmitted.

A number of competing streaming technologies have emerged. For audio data on the Internet, the de facto standard is RealAudio. RealAudio was developed by RealNetworks and supports FM-stereo-quality sound. To hear a Web page that includes a RealAudio sound file, you need a RealAudio player (the plug-in). This plug-in is freely available from realaudio.com.

Most major ISPs offer streaming media as either a standard feature or an upgrade to their server packages. Streaming prerecorded content is pretty straightforward and could be done with an ordinary hosting account or virtual server account.

The digitization of media in the online world offers both consumers and businesses many options and advantages. No matter how you prepare the files, if you want to distribute original music or video online, it is a snap to do it.

The commercial benefits are endless. If one's favorite songs or videos are available online, they can be downloaded without waiting on those infamous store lines. The producer gains as well, because marketing through the Internet makes it possible to sell a single song at a time. This may sound odd, because we are accustomed to the old rules of mass production and distribution, and in that paradigm the company would make far less money by selling a single song than by selling an album. In the online world, producers can increase their profits through digital delivery of individual cuts.

Think about it this way. A typical music CD sells for around $16 to $20, right? There are probably 10 to 14 songs on an average CD. That means that each song is sold for, say, $2 per song. The producers of the CD have to press the CDs, mass produce them, package them in some sort of hard plastic to protect them in shipping, design and stick on some graphic imagery on the cover, shrink wrap the boxes, and distribute them. Distribution costs probably amount to nearly half of the cost of producing the product. You pay $2 per song, and the producers make $10 a CD or $1 per song.

Now look at the arithmetic when an online marketer sells me just my favorite song. If I paid $4 for my favorite song and could download it from the Internet, I could have all that I wanted, have it instantly, and basically save anything from $12 to $16 on the cost of an album. By selling a single song at $4 and eliminating virtually all distribution costs, the producers of the CD have just increased their profit on this song by more than 400 percent. As a consumer, I would probably buy this way regularly. I would spend less money, and yet profits for the producing company would grow exponentially. Forrester Research predicts that downloaded music will account for an estimated $1.1 billion in U.S. sales by 2003.

As for books, 45 percent of the cost of textbooks is in inventory and shipping. And you know, textbooks go out of print, sometimes rather quickly. Digital books never go out of print; they are always ready to be downloaded. With proper implementation of technology, you could download a chapter at a time.

And calling all authors! Have you ever wanted to write a book, but could not get a publisher's attention? Self-publishing is becoming more and more popular. It is feasible because of the power of the Internet. Companies have sprung up that not only deliver the book or chapters of the book digitally over the network, but will also print books on demand for readers who still want the physical atoms to hold.

You may have also heard about a new product called eBook. eBook is a hand-held device that connects to the Internet and downloads electronic books. eBook combines the atoms with bits—it is something for the reader to hold as they read their electronic book. The reading screen is about the size of a paperback book. It is high-resolution and backlit, so it is easy on the eyes. Users can build their own personal library on the eBook. The market for electronic books is growing at an incredible rate.

For a while there, some researchers wondered about the longevity of the printing press. If users can get all they need from the Internet, books, newspapers, and magazines may become extinct. And given that information on the Internet is free, how should *The New York Times* or *The Wall Street Journal* compete? Well, people still like tangible paper to hold. They like to read in bed and other relaxing places, and they really like the ability to leaf through pages of books and magazines. After all, what would Sunday mornings be without donut crumbs and newspaper parts scattered across the living room table? These are pleasures that no form of electronic publishing can yet replace.

Yet, digitizing and electronically delivering documents, music, video, audio, and other information is logical and practical. Have you considered other forms of real-time digital delivery? How about saving travel, meeting costs, and time by hosting online conferences? The Internet allows anyone and everyone to meet online from any location in the world. It does not matter how many people are involved in the conference. Bringing hundreds together often costs no more than a two-person meeting—and with today's Internet charges, at least in the United States, that is close to free.

One-to-One Web Presentations

The Internet brings dramatic new possibilities for small-scale communication as well. Companies now selling on the Web routinely field requests from prospects located in every imaginable corner of the Earth. In the traditional world, it often comes down to making a presentation to an individual or small group of decision makers. Large companies have traditionally positioned sales reps in all parts of the country or world, so they can get to the prospective customer and close the sale. Small companies, who cannot support such a large sales network and may find that traveling to a distant prospect is impractical or impossible, often lose out. But on the Internet, they have just as much "presence" in, say, South Africa, as the average multinational.

What the Internet offers business is its ability to extend marketing outreach and to save businesses money. With e-commerce, after you have reached a customer—across the country or across the world—you can save money by closing the sale without ever leaving your office. Using Web technology, you can give a presentation to one or many people, so long as they have a computer and connection to the Internet.

Web presentations offer several benefits over in-person presentations. Obviously you can save the cost of traveling, and you can schedule the interactive presentation on shorter notice than if the meeting required travel. Frequently, companies have groups of people working on a project from different locations. This can make it impossible to get the entire team together for a physical presentation and gather everyone's reaction simultaneously. With a Web presentation, you can make your pitch to people in different cities at the same time and get their immediate response.

The audio portion of a presentation can be carried over the Internet, or the presenter can use a standard telephone conference call. Most Web presentation companies provide software that transmits PowerPoint images to their server, where the images are broadcast to everyone in the audience for viewing in a Web browser. Some allow you to demonstrate running applications to the audience, a great tool when giving software or Web site demos. Many executives automatically assume that sales meetings with distant prospects will be their main use for Web presentations. However, other applications can be equally valuable. Web presentations are being used in-house for project briefings, updating the staff at remote locations, vendor briefings, and staff training.

Some vendors offer their Web conference solution only as a service, while others provide both services and software you can run in-house. Before bringing this type of application in-house, however, make sure your Internet connection has enough bandwidth to support the largest audience you plan to accommodate.

The versatility and low cost of Web presentation tools make it easier than ever to deliver your message with the impact of well-designed slides and live demonstrations. While nothing can replace the relationship-building value of meeting with people in person, Web presentations are a valuable tool to bridge the gap between a telephone call and a plane ride to a distant city.

When thinking about digital delivery of a product or service, consider all things that can be transferred into digital data: books, magazines, newsletters, research reports, video, audio, anything composed as knowledge and information both historically and in real time. Information databases can be manipulated to deliver specific digital content to a user at regular intervals. This is the concept behind personalization. Major databases such as LexisNexis have historically delivered targeted, fee-based content to lawyers practicing in specific industries. The Internet opens up the playing field, making fee-based digital information a reality to all industries.

Eenie Strategy

Publish Your Own Book

The written word is golden. Publish a book, and you prove your expertise on a particular subject. This gives you instant "expert" status, and perhaps even name recognition in your field. Books can also be used for more direct self-promotion and marketing purposes. Books are one of the most respected means of building your business. They also can be one of the most effective.

Publishing a book used to mean finding a publishing house, convincing an editor that you had both a marketable idea and the skill to write a book from it, and then investing anything from weeks to months of hard work in the writing. Then you would wait six months or more after delivering the manuscript before ever getting to hold an actual copy of your work.

The alternative is to try publishing the book yourself. Until recently, that usually involved paying a so-called "vanity publisher," a glorified printing house, to manufacture books that the author then attempted to market.

Internet services have arisen to help would-be self-publishers turn their ideas into books, both online and in print. Self-publishing venues include Iuniverse.com, Xlibris.com, and Ipublish.com. Their services include book formatting, usually with template formats, cover design, and marketing assistance. Help with marketing can include electronic distribution, chapter-by-chapter sales, listing announcements with online booksellers like Amazon.com, and sales partnerships with traditional booksellers like Barnes and Noble. These firms also provide print-on-demand services that make one hard copy at a time, when a customer orders it.

Cost: Fees to produce a book range from free to several thousand dollars and may include commissions to the online service.

Meenie Strategy

Conduct Live Meetings Online

Show your clients and partners that you are Internet savvy. WebEx (www.webex.com) has created a unique interactive environment for businesses to conduct live meetings through their Web sites. WebEx services fully integrate traditional voice and video communications with advanced real-time data-exchange capabilities. Participants in an online meeting can exchange integrated data, voice, and video; share presentations, documents, and applications; and co-browse the Web. WebEx also enables remote control of applications and desktops. The system utilizes integrated teleconferencing and/or Voice Over IP, and display real-time video.

Cost: $.45 per minute per user, or $100 per seat per month.

Miney Strategy

Deliver Electronic Presentations

Create a professional, fully interactive online presentation with assistance from Mshow (www.mshow.com). This company and its show directors provide help with pre-show content development, training and support, show management and monitoring, a live operator help desk, and audience data reporting after the show. Mshow also offers content archiving for on-demand playback of the presentation at any time.

Cost: Standard price is $.60 per minute per connection. Custom work is billed at $125 per hour. Archiving a presentation costs $500 for the first month, $100 per month thereafter, with unlimited use. The price for a custom registration page is $500. The fee for a post-show survey is $500. Volume discounts are available with annual contract.

Moe Strategy

Offer Rich-Media Content on Your Web Site

The digital delivery of rich-media information will have an enormous impact on the way businesses and individuals work, study, and play. Rich-media applications can bring the classroom to the Web, or make corporate training as close as an employee's desktop. Sites that can effectively offer this content at a high-enough quality will shape the future of the Internet.

A company called Brainshark (www.brainshark.com) allows the average person to self-author, deliver, and manage on-demand multimedia business communications. Users can create and access recorded multimedia presentations anywhere, anytime at their convenience.

To create and distribute rich-media content with Brainshark, basic knowledge of PowerPoint and the telephone is all that is required. To view content on Brainshark, users only need an Internet browser and a standard audio player.

The Brainshark application is currently available as a hosted service (ASP Model). Brainshark provides customers with a highly secure infrastructure on multiple levels, as well as additional security options to further enhance the privacy and integrity of data.

Cost: Based on the number of users and number of presentations stored, initial setup of the application, and the number of presentation views. Pricing starts at $24,000 for an annual subscription.

Chapter 5

Stickiness

Sticky sites, by definition, are places on the Internet where visitors stay for long periods. Stickiness is generally measured by the length of time a user stays on a Web site. AOL users average 60 minutes per session and 246 minutes per month. eBay, the online consumer-to-consumer auction, boasts an amazing 126.7 minutes per average visit. Such long visits are highly desirable. Stickiness is worth a lot of money to advertisers seeking access to consistent, identifiable Web site visitors.

Stickiness is proof of excellent content, clear navigation, and well-designed architecture. Stickiness often correlates heavily with dynamic, user-generated content such as chat facilities, message boards, and other tools where visitors participate in the site's creation. However, many innovative companies also create specialized applications that encourage users to return. These can be as simple as a mortgage calculator on a mortgage company's site, where users can calculate their payments after providing loan needs. The hope is that users will remember the site, return to it frequently, and tell others about its practical benefits and ease of use. Other companies create interactive entertainment to keep users coming back. Take a look at Web sites like www.benandjerrys.com, www.disney.com, and www.mcdonalds.com, and you will see a host of games, puzzles, and other entertaining activities that involve users for long periods of time.

All of the concepts covered in this book are intended to promote frequent customer interaction. All of the strategies presented by the Internet Prophets are designed in part to increase the stickiness of your site.

Eenie Strategy

Add Dynamically Updated Content to Your Site

Add news stories related to your industry to keep users coming back to your site. Using iSyndicate Express (www.isyndicate.com), you can add dynamically updated news articles aggregated from over 150 top news sources on the Web, stock tickers, and weather reports to your site. You choose relevant content from hundreds of content providers. You put a link to the content on your home page, and the content is dynamically updated as frequently as every 15 minutes.

iSyndicate also provides facilities to help you create your own online store and earn affiliate revenue. (See Chapter 22 for more information on affiliate marketing.)

Cost: Free with iSyndicate branding.

Meenie Strategy

Implement Online Project Management Tools

You want to encourage your most loyal customers to return to your Web site often. Offer them a project management tool that will enable them to track your progress on projects at hand.

Using the E-vis project management tool (www.e-vis.com), you can provide a valuable service to your best customers and keep them coming back to your Web site. E-vis is a comprehensive online project management and collaboration tool that is easy to set up and easy to use.

Cost: $89.00 per user per month.

Miney Strategy

Personalize Content on Your Site for Identified Users

A tool from YourCompass (www.yourcompass.com) gives Web site owners the power to form interactive relationships with individual users. Their application allows site owners to learn about the interests of each individual coming to their site, anticipate and meet their needs in real time, and recommend resources that reflect their preferences. It takes under 24 hours to set up.

Also consider joining their network, which they call True Network. True Network Affiliate Personalization enables online retailers with affiliate programs to offer customers personalized recommendations on each of their affiliate sites.

Here's how it works: When a user visits the site of an online retailer, and clicks on a specific product, the True Network software captures that information. Later, that same individual visits one of the retailer's affiliate sites. Because YourCompass technology recognizes that user as the same person from the retailer's site, the affiliate site displays a link to the product that caught the user's interest. With a little bit of luck, the user responds positively to an already favored product, clicks through, and buys it, thus generating a sale for the retailer and a commission for the affiliate.

Cost: $52.50 per 25,000 page views.

Moe Strategy

Create Customized Sticky Applications on Your Web Site

This strategy requires in-house Web developers who can manage and develop custom tools for your Web site. The details will vary according to your industry and target audience, so let us just look at a sample scenario.

Suppose that you are a utility company seeking branding identity in a broader marketplace. One effective approach would be to create online "learning tools" that teach young students about the discovery of electricity, how to avoid danger with electricity, what to do when they recognize the odor of gas, and so on. You might then offer your learning tools to schools for use in the classroom. These tools can be custom designed to meet the needs of your specific demographics and cover the services that you supply. The result: You attract a new audience through the incorporation of interactive tools on your Web site. Teachers, students, and parents return to your site frequently and use your site as a learning tool and resource for information about your full range of products.

Cost: Average salaries for programmers with high-end skills: $80,000 to $120,000 per year.

Chapter 6

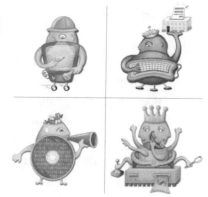

Online Communities

discovered my first online community in the early '90s after hearing of a very popular "community" called ECHO. ECHO was a Bulletin Board System (BBS) originating in lower Manhattan. While topics from the broader world occasionally were discussed, most of the exchanges on the board were centered on New York City. Within that focus, they ran the gamut from where to eat to the city's dog poop laws. This reflected the members of the community, who shared the common interest of living in or around New York City. Relationships that began on this BBS often moved into the real world, as ECHO members were invited to meet in a local restaurant once a month.

ECHO was typical of online communities then and now. The idea of these virtual communities was to allow people to come together to voice mutual concerns, discuss shared interests, and sometimes organize a grass roots response in the real world to issues raised online. Many people enjoyed philosophizing or merely ranting to others, and that is why they joined the Internet early on. Mostly though, the participants identified with the community. They congregated in spaces where they felt others shared common interests—places where they found other people whose ideas were challenging, interesting, or complementary to their own.

In the early days of the Internet, these e-mail lists, BBSs, and newsgroups existed only for communication and participation; there were no commercial motives. In fact, advertising was barred from the Internet for many years. The members of the community provided all content; it was the participants, rather than some outside sponsor, who gave these communities life. Many community members became so dedicated to their online worlds that they were vitally concerned about the well being of their community and each of its members. These online worlds were, and still are, a remarkable form of human connection.

However, as the Internet matured, the Web grew in popularity, and the number of communities continued to multiply, business inevitably recognized a potential market—thousands of them, in fact. After all, a large group actively discussing pet care constitutes an audience of people who have voluntarily identified themselves as being interested in pet care products and services. How better to target a market than to get involved in a gathering where you know there are hundreds, thousands, and in some cases millions of potential buyers of your product or service?

Many hundreds of these gatherings still take place online each day, and they offer unbelievable marketing opportunities. However, this potential customer base must be approached with care, for the cliquish, even xenophobic culture of the early Internet lives on. In many communities, strangers are viewed with suspicion until they establish themselves as belonging to the group.

Thus a new form of Internet community has appeared. In addition to enthusiast and interest-group communities, spontaneously organized by their participants, there are growing numbers of sponsored communities. In these, companies have established chat rooms, bulletin board systems, mailing lists, and other facilities and opened them to the public.

In a well-run sponsored community, participants find most of the benefits of a traditional online community, and some that are available only with organizational ties. They get the same chance to share information on subjects of common interest, exchange views, and build online friendships that often spill over into the real world. Online communities have entertainment value as well. Many people think of the Web as an alternative to television and other amusements, and an active community provides entertainment that a Net-savvy sponsor will help to foster.

Sponsors add something more. Once the company has established its knowledge and good will, members often discover that it can provide more authoritative information in its field than would otherwise be available. Without being heavy-handed about it, a good sponsored community also provides more sense of order than is found in many traditional communities, where a few disruptive members can damage the experience for others.

Sponsoring companies, in turn, can gain a variety of benefits. Build a useful and entertaining Web community for your potential customers, and they will reward you with loyalty beyond almost anything seen in real-world relationships. In a networked world, those customers will not be limited by geography or other constraints that previously kept you apart; in other words, online communities give companies and organizations access to potential customers they could never have reached by other means. They also allow companies to provide more finely targeted marketing and personalized service to their community's members. These are substantial benefits, whether you hope to sell directly to the community or will use your Web presence simply to improve customer service or market research.

While it can be difficult to measure just what an online community contributes to its sponsors' bottom line, it is clear that healthy online communities promote successful e-commerce. In a healthy online community, participants respond to surveys at much higher rates than in the real world. They also provide a steady flow of useful information between such formal research efforts.

There are more tangible rewards as well. When community members need an appropriate product or service, the sponsor is likely to be the first provider they think of. Online communities also are an excellent way to generate word of mouth support. Furthermore, if your site is well visited you will have a better chance of gaining additional revenues from advertising and joint ventures. This offers the chance for positive feedback. Added revenue and promotion of special joint ventures on your community Web site allow you to pass extra benefits on to your customers in the form of more content, services, and commercial offerings. This promotes still further growth, in an ascending spiral.

In setting out to build an online community, there are some important issues to consider. All communities, on the Web or off, live or die by a few basic principles.

First, their members must have a common purpose. People band together for some mutual interest, and the community must perform a necessary, or at least useful, function for them. It makes sense to build online communities where natural, real-world communities already exist. Sometimes, a real-world community functions better when it migrates online.

Communities also need rules to define who is a member and who is not, and what members can do that separates them from nonmembers. Without some clear definition of membership, there is no incentive to become a member and no ability to monitor access based on membership.

Of course, communities cannot exist without mechanisms for member interaction. All communities consist of participant interaction. The "logging" of this interaction typically forms the content of the site. The type of content that will be generated by the community must be clearly identified in advance; it is the most important feature of the site.

Communities also need the right communication tools for their purpose and members. Newsgroups, mailing lists, chat, and file sharing all are possible options. Knowing who the members are and what their objectives may be, and providing them with essential tools to meet their goals, is imperative. For example, a site for artists could thrive by enabling artists to upload images of their work for display and commentary. A teen site would be better served with chat and instant messaging tools. A site for business executives might offer the ability to compare spreadsheets.

Above all else, communities require trust. In the virtual world, nothing is so important as building trust between members, facilitators, and partners. Members must be able to trust each other. They also must be able to trust whoever runs the community not to abuse or exploit them. Trust is the most fragile asset of an online community. Any hint of a hard sell, or simply talking down to participants, will destroy it.

What else do you need to think about when building a community-oriented Web site? Consider the following questions:

- What is the demographic profile of your intended community?
- Who are you trying to reach?
- What is your objective once you reach them?
- What is your message?

Next, build a set of tools, services, products, links, and other activities that will help visitors to interact, and thereby keep your ideal audience coming back for more. Your capacity to provide important links to related sites, build relationships with other vendors, and attract the right kind of advertising to your site plays an important role.

This is not a one-shot project. In a community-oriented site, the process of building and maintaining relationships never ends. You need to continue expanding the site by adding new tools, new functionality, and new ways for customers to share their experiences and expertise. Stagnation is death for an online community, and failure for its sponsors.

The advent of the Web and the existence of online communities have introduced new ways of doing business. Communication has become far richer, and more rewarding, than in the prenetwork days. Businesses recognize the power of online communities as a way to engage and retain their customers.

As we have seen before, customers no longer passively receive whatever message a marketer delivers to them; they have become active participants in their relationships with those who would do business with them. They are at their most active, and accessible, in online communities.

Eenie Strategy

Add Community Tools to Your Web Site

Building an internet community is one of the most effective ways of opening the potential of your site. At Interprosolution.com you will find tools that allow you to

- Run your own Banner Exchange network
- Conduct Discussion Forums on your site
- Stay in touch with your customers by sending them newsletters
- Conduct interactive polls on your site
- Provide a Web searching service

You will not need to write a single line of code, install any product, or worry about database administration or system maintenance. All of the above services are remotely hosted by Interprosolution.

Cost: Free.

Meenie Strategy

Host Moderated Discussions on Your Web Site

You have at least two good options: eShare Communications's expressions community-building product (www.eshare.com) includes browser-based chat, moderator-led discussion, and database integration tools.

Alternatively, a company called ichat (www.ichat.com) provides a hosting service that allows you to moderate events or let your community chat away in a customizable environment. You can plug ichat ROOMS into a frame or pop-up on your existing Web site and save time installing the software, setting up the chat server, and monitoring performance, while retaining complete creative control over the chat site's look and feel.

Cost: eShare pricing starts at $995 for 50 concurrent users; the average cost is $2,000 to $5,000.

For iChat, initial set-up fees are $195. Thereafter, fees are based on the number of concurrent users. One hundred users cost approximately $195 per quarter. Five hundred users cost approximately $2,275 per quarter.

Miney Strategy

Host a Live Event on Your Web Site

Offer an ideal forum for real-time discussions in a safe, friendly, and civilized multimedia environment. Visitors can participate in a moderated live-chat event with speakers and hosts using Talk City's (www.talkcity.com) community applications.

Talk City's software lends itself to a wide variety of applications: celebrity events, product launches, training seminars, technical support, virtual press conferences, discussions with the CEO and company experts, stockholder meetings, distance learning courses, partner meetings, and employee communications. Functions as diverse as customer relations, product development, human resources management, and corporate communications all can benefit from this kind of event.

Web events, especially those with celebrity speakers, can generate a huge amount of traffic; they can also convert browsers into buyers. But live Web events must be done properly to be effective. They must provide a quality presentation that downloads quickly over the Internet. Talk City Marketing Group has produced hundreds of successful events. They have the appropriate skill, technical knowledge, and infrastructure to make it work.

Cost: $2,000 to $7,000 per event.

Moe Strategy

Give Visitors to Your Web Site the Ability to Build Their Own Interactive Web Site

If your company is an ISP, media company, or content portal, you will be aiming to generate new revenue streams, build customer loyalty, and build traffic to your site. A company called Moonfruit (www.moonfruit.com) is now partnering with some of the world's leading online businesses and provides simple integration of Moonfruit's Sitemaker 3.0 Web-site-building toolkit as a cobranded, hosted application that its partners offer to consumers for a subscription fee. Using Flash technology, Moonfruit's application provides end-users with simple-to-use tools for creating multimedia-rich Web sites.

Cost: Fees for setup and customization from $10,000; share of subscription fees are negotiable.

Chapter 7

Portals

The goal of a portal, or "destination site," is to be the starting point for as many Web users as possible—the page where all their Internet functions are organized, and the first thing they see when they go online. These visitors are its stock in trade, the "eyeballs" its managers will market to potential advertisers and comarketers in order to generate revenue.

Most Internet users require just one portal site, which they will designate as their starting page on the Web. Because of this, there is a limit to the number of portals that can succeed in the long run, and only the best of them can be expected to survive and thrive.

In order to compete with other destination sites, the successful portal must support all the most basic Internet services its users require. Portal services provide e-mail accounts, custom news and stories, member chat rooms, online calendar functions, stock tickers, personal portfolio managers, and much more. Recently, portals have started offering online tools and templates to help people create personal or business Web sites, which are hosted on the portal's server. Often, portal services are provided at no charge in an effort to secure user loyalty and to encourage regular visits. Stickiness is critical to the success of a portal.

Yahoo! (www.yahoo.com) was one of the first Web portals. Started in the early '90s by a group of students at Stanford University, Yahoo! (Yet Another Hierarchical Officious Oracle) was a hyperlinked directory of useful and interesting Web sites, organized by topic. Yahoo! quickly gained a reputation as an excellent starting point for Web surfers, and traffic to the site was unprecedented. This in turn brought in a level of advertising revenue that was unheard of for any Web site at the time, and Yahoo! became one of the first Web services to turn a profit.

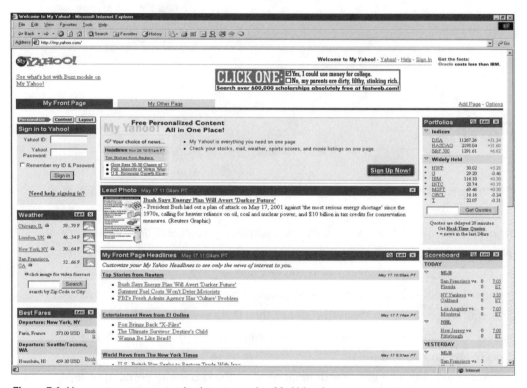

Figure 7.1. Users can create customized content using My Yahoo!.

While Yahoo! started out as a Web directory, today (as you see in Figure 7.1) the site offers services such as e-mail, shopping, auctions, and instant messaging. One of the most interesting services is "My Yahoo!," which allows users to set up their own home page so they can view personalized content whenever they visit the site. For example, users can configure their My Yahoo! to display sports scores, the local weather forecast, or the current price of the stocks in their portfolio. When it launched Local Yahoo!, this Web site became one of the first online information services to focus its research on local communities or regions.

Excite (www.excite.com), GO (www.go.com), and Netscape (www.net scape.com) are examples of portals that, like Yahoo!, offer a broad range of free, customizable services as they vie to become the be-all, end-all gateway for Internet users.

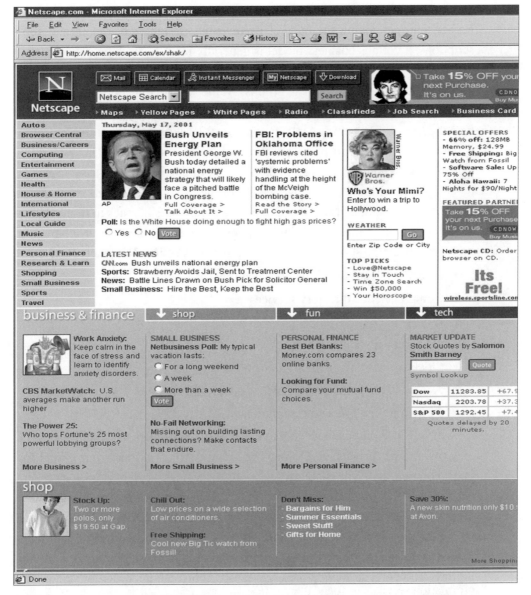

Figure 7.2. The front page of Netscape's Portal offers news and directory-style search features.

The vertical portal, or "vortal," is focused on a particular slice of the online marketplace, appealing to Web users who share a similar set of needs and interests. Some vortals are business to business (B2B), some are business to consumer (B2C), and still others are "enterprise information portals" (EIPs)—corporate portals focused on a specific company's news and information. (An intranet set up for the use of employees and partners is one example.) Rather than generating the bulk of its revenues through advertising and subscriptions, a vortal's business model is generally more focused on e-commerce.

Many manufacturers partner with vortals in order to aim their products at specific, hard-to-reach interest groups. Some industry leaders have jumped into the game and set up industry-specific vortals. Raytheon, for example, has launched www.EverythingAircraft.com—a B2B vortal that features not only Raytheon's own aircraft parts, but those of other manufacturers.

A relatively new type of vortal, the voice-portal, combines the easy access of the telephone with the knowledge wealth of the Internet. One such voice-portal is iNetNow (www.inetnow.com). iNetNow actually uses humans to research and answer questions while you are on the phone with them. In effect, iNetNow is a high-end concierge service. The most popular uses of iNetNow include:

- Directions from the road and travel reports
- Comprehensive directory services
- E-commerce
- Comparison shopping
- Stock reports and detailed financial news
- Access to personal contact and schedule information
- Restaurant reviews and reservations

iNetNow also claims to be able to check flight schedules, weather reports for any city, movie reviews, and more. The service will even read your e-mail for you! Through the "My iNetNow" section, the voice concierge can locate personalized content including an address book, calendar, and personal e-mail messages. (You also can set up a private folder, so that the "concierge" cannot read information you prefer to hold confidential.) iNetNow has partnered with merchants to offer an approved vendor program to users: Its vendor partners offer a 30-day, 100-percent money-back guarantee, plus online order tracking. For iNetNow customers, your concierge handles all the details.

Eenie Strategy

Create an Intranet for Your Company, Department, Sales Team, or Customers

An intranet is a private, secure space on the Web where your group can easily access and share documents, calendars, and event information. Create your intranet at www.Intranets.com, and use it to centralize important company information, let your users post documents, create group schedules, announce events, and more. All the interactive features are designed to help your group communicate and collaborate online. With just an Internet connection, everyone in your group has simple access to the same information, no matter where they are.

Unlike public Web sites, intranets can be password protected to give you control over who can access your information. This makes intranets perfect for sharing confidential information among the members of your corporate "family."

Some sites may be listed in the Intranet Directory, but ask that nonmembers with an interest in your information apply for access to your intranet. Once the proposed user's data has been reviewed, a password for her can be arranged. This kind of setup is perfect for screening potential customers who may need access to sensitive corporate information.

Other sites listed in the Intranet Directory allow users to enter as guests. This enables nonmembers to view certain areas of the intranet. This option is perfect for companies wishing to post public product information and yet restrict access to confidential data.

In addition, sites can be listed in the Directory and allow anyone to join. This is equivalent to an open-access Web site, but takes advantage of the Intranet Directory, where potential visitors can find your site.

Cost: $19.95 for four users; $5.95 each additional user.

Meenie Strategy

Turn Your Site into a Microportal

Using a site search engine from Mondosoft (www.mondosoft.com), you can seamlessly create a collection of searchable Web sites from your own site. MondoSearch expands the breadth of your Web site's content and enables your visitors to easily search a group of sites you choose. It is a convenient tool to bring together partners, associations, customers, and other topical sites for quick and easy searching. Your visitors can search your site only, or search all of the sites in the collection you select—a powerful customer management tool that helps facilitate Web partnerships and online distribution channels. Web sites of any purpose and focus can benefit from this service.

Cost: Prices range from about $300 per month for sites with fewer than 200 pages to about $5,000 per month for sites nearing 100,000 pages. For very large Web sites, prices are negotiable. The cost of a product license (CD) also depends upon the size of the Web site. The price begins at about $4,000.

Miney Strategy

Set Up a Portal for Your Company, and Allow Your Employees and Colleagues to Connect to Your Online Computing Environment from Anywhere in the World

With an outsourced solution from Offyx (www.offyx.com), you can significantly reduce costs and remove the burden of technology management within your organization.

Offyx provides your business with a state-of-the-art computing environment. All your computing resources (documents, databases, accounting programs, and so on) will reside on Offyx's systems; these systems become the digital existence of your business creating an online portal for all your employees, accessible from anywhere in the world. It does not matter how many employees you have or how many remote offices your business has; as long as your employees can connect to the Internet, they are ready to conduct business.

Offyx states that its average customers reduce their IT costs by 30 to 60 percent.

There can be other benefits as well. If you are a technology consultant, software vendor, and/or hardware and network integrator, Offyx's computing environment allows you to service your clients without ever leaving the office. You can focus on more strategic elements of your client's business, as Offyx effortlessly handles the repetitive, mundane tasks that previously would have required costly trips to client sites. And you can start a new revenue stream as Offyx pays commissions on new client acquisitions.

Cost: $100 to $140 per user per month.

Moe Strategy

Create an Information Portal

From broad-market to country-specific portals, the drive to create focused communities of Web knowledge has never been greater. Information portals need to manage massive amounts of data from multiple sources to provide fresh, timely content. Regional portals need to search in-depth local and Web-wide content. Whatever your needs, AltaVista (www.altavista.com) has the products and services that are right for your portal site. The following are just a few of things you can do with the latest AltaVista search technology:

- Retrieve information from multiple data sources: databases, Web servers, domino servers, and file servers.

- Create a large index or manage multiple indexes (either Web pages or internal documents, in xls, doc, pdf, and other formats).

- Build communities by delivering deep and rich topic- and region-specific content.

- Present search results using your own interface.

AltaVista supports over 30 languages, including Arabic, Chinese, Japanese, Korean, and Portuguese.

Cost: Pricing for AltaVista Search Engine 3.0 starts at $25,000.

Chapter 8

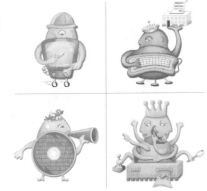

Auctions

So far, e-commerce can be classified into four acronyms: B2C, business to consumer; B2B, business to business; C2C, consumer to consumer; and B2B2C, business to business to consumer.

Within the past few years, B2C markets have led the way in e-commerce. Yet C2C markets have quickly become one of the most popular venues for small companies, as well as for individuals. If you are reading this book and have not yet heard of eBay (unlikely!) or visited www.eBay.com, then go to your computer now, get on the Internet, and take a good look at one of the most revolutionary and successful business models of the new age—C2C transactions through online auctions.

eBay has successfully established the Internet's most extensive C2C exchange, where users all over the world can post and purchase almost anything and everything you can imagine. (A few illegal or otherwise questionable products are banned; for example, one offer of a donor kidney for transplant patients was quickly removed from the site.) eBay has created otherwise unattainable revenue streams for individual consumers who are cleaning out their attics, basements, and garages and posting their unneeded treasures to the site—an online flea market or garage sale at its finest. A host of small retailers also use eBay to market products from computer software to power tools. With more than 2 million items for sale in more than 1,500 categories, eBay boasts one of the highest trafficked sites on the Web.

Prices for the goods are negotiated online in an efficient and automated manner. Sellers post their products to the site and list a starting bid price for each item. Buyers scan the site, typically by category, and make bids on items of interest. eBay's customers, whether they are the sellers or buyers, do most of the work, and they carry the burden of risk. The sellers carry the inventory, do their own marketing, and arrange for shipping of the product. It costs eBay next to nothing to add customers, and the company's fees are prepaid by credit card. And as it is all put together, there is a great deal of entertainment value in making the bids and watching the auctions. eBay has been making money, for itself as well as for its sellers, almost from the day it was conceived.

Predictably, eBay has been followed by hundreds, perhaps thousands, of imitators. Many portal sites, such as Yahoo!, now operate their own general-interest auctions. Some other auction operators, like www.onsale.com, simply bring auctions to traditional retail goods. Other auction sites specialize in certain fields, such as antique ceramics, collectible books, or used industrial equipment. There also is an active B2B auction market. If a given market is not yet served by an auction site, it probably soon will be.

Some of the features pioneered by eBay, and now available on many auction sites, include:

- Varying types of auctions such as Reserve Price Auction, Private Auction, Dutch Auction, and Restricted Access Auction
- Up-to-the-minute tracking of bids, which can be sent via e-mail as well as posted real time on the site
- "Feedback Profiles" of sellers, made up of comments (positive, negative, or neutral) from other traders. eBay refers to this as an "official electronic reputation"
- A community section where there are discussion groups and chat
- Specialty auctions like charity auction
- News
- A "My eBay" section of the site maintains a history of each customer's transactions. (See Figure 8.1.)

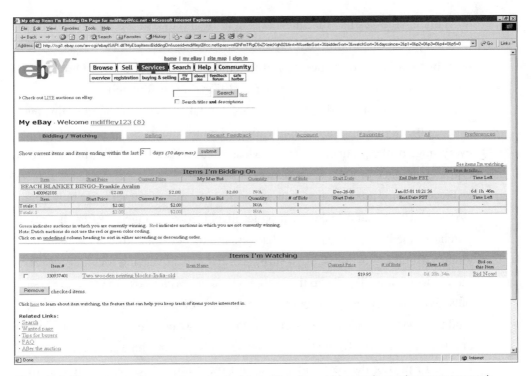

Figure 8.1. Shoppers on eBay can keep track of items they have bid on or items they want to watch.

eBay and its many competitors are the best demonstrations yet of how the Internet can benefit the smallest businesses. In the Industrial—that is, pre-Internet—Age, short of physically attending auctions, garage sales, flea markets, and specialty shows, the best venues for C2C marketing were classified advertisements in local or regional publications. If the prices were not fixed, one could "haggle" or "bid" for the best price when contacting the prospective seller. However, the process was burdensome and time consuming compared to the Internet alternative. The auction sites also show how dynamic pricing (a concept we will further explore in the next chapter) on the Internet can establish new intermediaries between disparate buyers and sellers, greatly extending seller reach and buyer access.

Many businesses use the Internet as a critical part of their strategy in order to reduce costs by more cost-effective marketing and processing of critical data, or to increase revenues by introducing a new sales channel. Online B2B auctions offer interesting prospects for still greater efficiencies.

Almost any business that has inventory can take advantage of an online auction or other dynamic pricing applications. Online auctions can help to leverage every stage of the product life cycle. Most effective is the use of online auctions to trade ancillary product components.

For example, imagine that you are a clothing manufacturer. You have retail stores with aisles and aisles of product displayed on hangers. After the buyer purchases the blouse or pants, the hangers are recycled and used to display new clothes. But there is inevitably a surplus of hangers at varying locations at varying points of time. Thanks to the Web, your business can now leverage these surplus assets by selling them or auctioning them off to the highest price bidder. And there will be bidders, even for a relatively low cost item like clothes hangers. It is a lot more efficient for a plant in Missouri or China to purchase more instead of paying the cost and waiting for the return of recycled hangers. Web auctions of these surplus hangers result in tremendous cost savings due to improved efficiencies in the business process.

Businesses must examine their overall product set and establish goals for this new dynamic pricing strategy. Then like any other business plan, they must implement it, observe the results, and adjust their strategy over time. Each implementation will vary by industry and market. Certain industries may see better results than others, when there are significant costs, market inefficiencies, or potential revenues that lend themselves to this kind of market. Consider an online auction if your company has products or services that become perishable when supplies run to excess, when inventory costs are high, when products become obsolete, or when costs are low but the volume of transactions is high and buyers repeatedly purchase the products.

Many businesses have already adopted Web auctions and dynamic pricing models as an important ingredient in their overall strategy. Those that move first, adjust, and optimize that experience over time, will realize the greatest success.

Eenie Strategy

Join an Online Auction, Link to an Auction Search, or Create a Simple Auction of Your Own

There are hundreds of online auction sites on the Internet. Some are general consumer-to-consumer (C2C) sites. Some are strictly for business-to-business (B2B) transactions. Some specialize in government procurement purposes (B2G.) Others deal in fine art and precious metals. The following are just a few of the sites that offer auction strategies to sell your products and services, and the market niches they serve:

www.eBay.com

www.haggle.com

www.cityauction.com

www.ubid.com

eBay is by far the most popular online auction service. On eBay as well as the other auctions, you will find many consumer-to-consumer offerings. But take special note to the businesses, just like yours, that use online auctions as a fully functional retail shop. Posting your products to one of these auctions makes them available to the worldwide users of the Internet. Vendors have been pleased to find that, in many cases, the users of online auctions have driven product prices to higher levels than they could have received in a traditional retail setting.

Cost: The above auctions have minimal or no listing fees.

Meenie Strategy

Automate the Management of Your Auction

If you are selling products on more than one auction site—and managing it manually—an automated management system will free up your time and allow you to sell more products. Andale (www.andale.com) offers powerful auction tools and services that will automate virtually any aspect of your selling cycle, freeing you to list more, sell more, and make more than you ever dreamed possible. Andale helps in creating ads, provides tools to list items and to re-list unsold merchandise automatically, tracks sales, automates e-mail, provides online check-out, supplies tools for shipping and payment, assists in creating picture galleries of your products, and provides feedback on the results of your sales.

Cost: Andale charges the following fees: $39.95 per month, 10mb image hosting, 275 items, plus a 2.3 percent fee per transaction.

Miney Strategy

Create Your Own (Multilingual) Auction Web Site

Implement a fully functional online auction that includes features important to businesses, such as private auctions by invitation only. Use www.beyondsolutions.com, whose system includes a translation interface, which makes it easy to switch between different languages. See demonstrations at:

http://auction23.beyondsolutions.com (Select Languages)

http://auction23.beyondsolutions.com/admin (Use admin for both Username and Password.)

Cost: $10,000.

Moe Strategy

Use the Power of the Internet's Worldwide Reach to Liquidate Product and/or Sell Off Used Capital Assets

DoveBid, Inc. (www.dovebid.com), one of the world's leading capital asset auctioneers and appraisers, has now gone online. Among other services, DoveBid holds Webcast auctions that bring their on-location, world-class services to distant markets by broadcasting auctions live over the Internet. Webcast auction participants can view asset descriptions and photographs online and bid in real time against both on-location and online bidders, increasing demand for the assets. DoveBid's Webcast auctions are facilitated by asset-experienced auctioneers. They also offer multilingual and multi-currency support. In addition, DoveBid supports asset sales with extensive marketing resources, technology, and tactics.

Cost: DoveBid's fees range on average from 10 percent to 15 percent of total gross proceeds of an auction.

Chapter 9

Dynamic Pricing Models

Almost anyone can understand the C2C and B2C auction models presented in the previous chapter. They just make sense, right? Put your product into the auction with the "lowest bid price;" this may be less than the going sales price—it probably should be, to encourage potential buyers—but at least you won't lose your shirt. Then, allow Internet users to bid the price up. Sold to the highest bidder!

However, new, much less intuitive pricing mechanisms are appearing on the Internet as well. In fact, some recent models do the opposite of a standard auction: The more users bid on a product, the lower the price falls. Now, this is an interesting concept.

And dynamic pricing models can be even more flexible than that. The Internet gives customers the power to set the rules. Customers may offer various prices for products, depending on conditions specified. For example, if the product is delivered today, they'll pay one price. If customers can buy quantity, they'll agree to another price. They may accept certain defects and pay yet another price. If someone else will pay A, then they'll pay B. Buyers and sellers exchange more information, and pricing becomes absolutely fluid.

In the Industrial Age, the mega-corporations acted as market makers and set broad rules. They governed the nature of the playing field, its boundaries, player eligibility, and the processes of competition. Not anymore. Talk about a shake-up! Facilitated by the Internet, negotiated transactions between buyers and sellers are challenging pricing habits in just about every industry. This is an unwelcome change for corporate executives accustomed to having pretty much their own way.

However, it turns out that properly deployed dynamic pricing has great advantages. As with other Internet technologies, if used in harmony with the company's traditional pricing mechanisms, dynamic pricing has the potential for dramatically strengthening the pricing portfolio of any business.

The pricing mechanisms that we are most familiar with are:

- Fixed Pricing—the old industrial megacorporation policy—very easy to administer and consumers have very little choice.

- Sale Pricing—of course, sales can stimulate demand and act as an incentive to purchase the product. Conducting sales has traditionally been the pricing weapon of choice among retailers. In fact, I know many retailers that set their prices too high, just to have an excuse for discounts—encouraging the sale, but making their target profit.

Now we have dynamic pricing. On the Internet, prices change not only from product to product, but also from customer to customer, and from one transaction to the next. Dynamic pricing delivers true mass personalization. Finding the appropriate mix of prices for a company's target market, and adjusting them over time, is imperative for the continued success of any business.

Online dynamic pricing applications can help businesses in a variety of ways. Because the Internet has global reach, there are no geographic boundaries; everyone can get in the game of competing for the best price. In the process, they create more efficient markets. Businesses on both sides of the B2B exchange can save time and money by eliminating paper trails, processing costs, and lengthy communications. They can increase revenues by selling excess inventory or reconditioned goods as well as one-of-a-kind products in high demand, reaching the most interested prospects in the most efficient way possible.

After products are retired, demand does not subside. Web auctions are ideal for the recycling of second-hand and refurbished products, thereby further strengthening customer relationships.

Dynamic pricing also offers a way to test prices when launching a new product: Let the community of users identify the price they are willing to pay for the product. Though this practice seems less secure than traditional pricing methods, it avoids the risk of predicting demand incorrectly and pricing items too high or low.

These pricing models have triggered dramatic changes in the B2B marketplace. Web sites are being constructed to facilitate transactions between buyers and sellers in vertical markets like steel, plastics, chemicals, apparel, etc. These vertical business communities are able to reach more trading partners more efficiently, but they also place greater competitive pressure on manufacturers and marketers.

Dynamic pricing not only helps businesses decrease costs and increase revenues, it has other benefits as well: Dynamic pricing applications can help companies deliver better Web experiences for prospective buyers. They provide more excitement, an increased sense of community, and a higher degree of personalization.

Better experiences are realized through:

- Entertainment—Placing bids and competing to win is engaging and stimulating. In addition to high repeat-purchase rates, dynamic pricing or auction sites are "sticky" even for the business consumer. Consumers stay at auction sites longer and come back more often than at traditional Web and fixed-priced sites. Sticky sites can generate more revenue, because they can offer potential advertisers more impressions and longer viewing times.

- More community—The combination of information with an event creates a community, and the interaction between participants creates goodwill and positive feelings toward the community.

- Increased personalization—Buyers and sellers can customize their own experiences by interacting as little or as much as they like. In addition, sellers gain valuable information about bidders during the auction, which can be used to target bidders and personalize their buying experience.

Eenie Strategy

Obtain Qualified Sales Leads

In order to deliver great experiences, businesses must learn about the purchasing habits of their customer bases. Web auctions and other dynamic facilitators provide a great tool for gathering this data. The customer information may include product interests, bidding methodologies, and price sensitivity. All this data can be used to improve the customer's e-commerce experiences by delivering more personalized content.

As the first and largest "reverse marketplace," www.imandi.com connects consumers to businesses across the street and across the country, who then compete for their business.

For retailers, imandi.com delivers qualified sales leads and the opportunity to benefit from the e-commerce explosion without having to manage a Web site or even use e-mail.

Cost: Free.

Meenie Strategy

Join an E-Marketplace

You can build extensive and detailed electronic catalogs of your products and classify them so that buyers can find them easily through electronic marketplaces. Using www.biz2biz.com you can participate in a vertical marketplace and manage your information in real time. Biz2Biz offers marketplaces for the following industries: aerospace, automotive, engineering, electronics, entertainment, plastics, and printing.

Biz2Biz solutions uses technology created by Commerce One (www.commerceone.com). For a directory of other marketplaces go to www.commerceone.com/customers/emarketplaces.html.

Cost: Membership in Biz2Biz is free to sellers who only answer RFQs, and only $49 per month with your full-featured electronic catalog.

Miney Strategy

Create Your Own Reverse Auction Web Site

A reverse auction allows buyers to post items they want to buy and sellers to compete for the best price at which the buyer will accept the items. This auction format is ideal for procurement.

AuctionBroker (www.auctionbroker.com) offers both traditional and blind reverse auctions with a variety of helpful features, including real-time credit card processing. The "Want List" is a "bulletin board" of items that buyers are looking for in the auction. "My Auction" allows the users of the site to create customized searches with specific criteria, as well as monitor items of interest. AuctionBroker can tailor your layout and will revise it to fit your needs for a period of six months.

Cost: $10,900.

Moe Strategy

Transforming Your Product Information into Powerful, Comprehensive E-Business Catalogs

Today, B2B sellers are confronted with the requirement to deliver more and better online product information to their customers through their traditional distributors and market channels. They are also faced with the new prospect of providing their online product catalogs to hundreds of eMarketplaces and customer eProcurement systems, all with different product content format requirements. Paper catalogs and even ordinary Web pages are not enough. Large suppliers have met this challenge head-on, transforming their product information into powerful, comprehensive e-commerce catalogs using SAQQARA ContentWorks (www. saqqara.com) and publishing their catalogs within a customer-centric B2B storefront with SAQQARA Commerce Suite solution. Small to medium-sized suppliers who cannot spend the time or money required to format catalog information can take advantage of the SAQQARA Cornerstone program, a hosted solution priced to scale with the number of catalog items that a supplier publishes. SAQQARA provides the infrastructure and applications necessary for suppliers to rapidly participate in the new B2B market and proactively manage its most valuable asset in today's Internet economy—product content information.

Cost: SAQQARA's application software license prices range upward from approximately $100K depending on the customer's specific catalog application requirements and configuration. For SAQQARA's Cornerstone application hosting service, small to mid-sized companies can get started at a lower monthly subscription price of about $3,000 per month for a catalog of up to 5,000 items, where SAQQARA handles all of the hardware and software issues.

Chapter 10

Customer Service

Without customers, would you be in business? Absolutely not! Customer service is about recognizing and valuing your customers and all of their needs and concerns. A healthy, effective customer service program tends to the needs of customers from the moment that they approach your business or Web site. It remains at their side when they buy your product or service, use it, and provide you with valuable feedback about it.

In short, how you treat each of your customers has a profound, immediate, and lasting impact on whether your business thrives or dives. Customer service cannot be merely a fallback measure for when things go wrong. Rather, it must continuously nurture the idiosyncrasies of each and every customer.

Customer service begins with client contact and fact finding. This fact finding is crucial to understanding the needs of your customers; it provides the knowledge you need to focus on your target audience, promote sales, and reduce the overall cost of customer acquisition. Once you really understand what customers need and want, a comprehensive customer service program can help you to improve your products and services and to build and retain customer loyalty.

If you have operated in a traditional distribution environment, largely cut off from your customers, the Internet will make it possible to identify, track, target, and stay close to them. You can interact directly with your customers through your

Web site, rather than communicating with them through distribution partners who are probably filtering or interpreting your customer's feedback.

Your online customers experience your Web site as if they were walking into your place of business. As in the traditional world, they decide to buy based on their impression of your products and services, your pricing, and how your total package compares to similar products. But they also decide based on the experience they have while at your Web site, just as they would in a real-world store.

Your products must be easily found, and the buying experience must be comfortable—and that's just the beginning.

What if customers are just looking for information? Break it down for them, and make it available so they can jump right to it.

What happens when you walk into a store and have to wait for a sales person to assist you? If no one is there, it is clear that that business does not value you as a customer. Personally, I walk right out. The same is true on a Web site. Make sure it is easy for customers to contact you. Online forms and e-mail addresses are absolutely critical, but sometimes it is even more reassuring to communicate with a business personally; be sure to include phone numbers, fax, and postal addresses as well.

All this sounds like a lot of trouble, but in reality it's just the e-business application of the old adage, "The customer is always right." In fact, like much of e-business, it is a lot more efficient than customer service in the real world. Once your Web site has been set up properly, it can serve many thousands of customers with little further attention. And the payoff can be enormous.

Nearly 35 percent of consumers surveyed said they would buy more if they could communicate in real time with the vendors. I recently received an e-mail solicitation that I glanced at half-heartedly. The sender wrote a very brief note, pleasant and to the point. Just as I was going to close the message, I caught the movement of an animated signature at the bottom of his e-mail. It simply said: "click below to call me now!" I clicked on the animated hyperlink and opened to a very easy-to-complete form that allowed me to communicate directly with the company (see Figure 10.1). All I had to do was send my telephone number to him, and he would call me right back. It was that simple—and very catchy.

Offering customers a variety of ways to contact you helps them to communicate effectively and appropriately. The faster, more convenient, and more complete your service is, the more likely casual browsers will turn into loyal

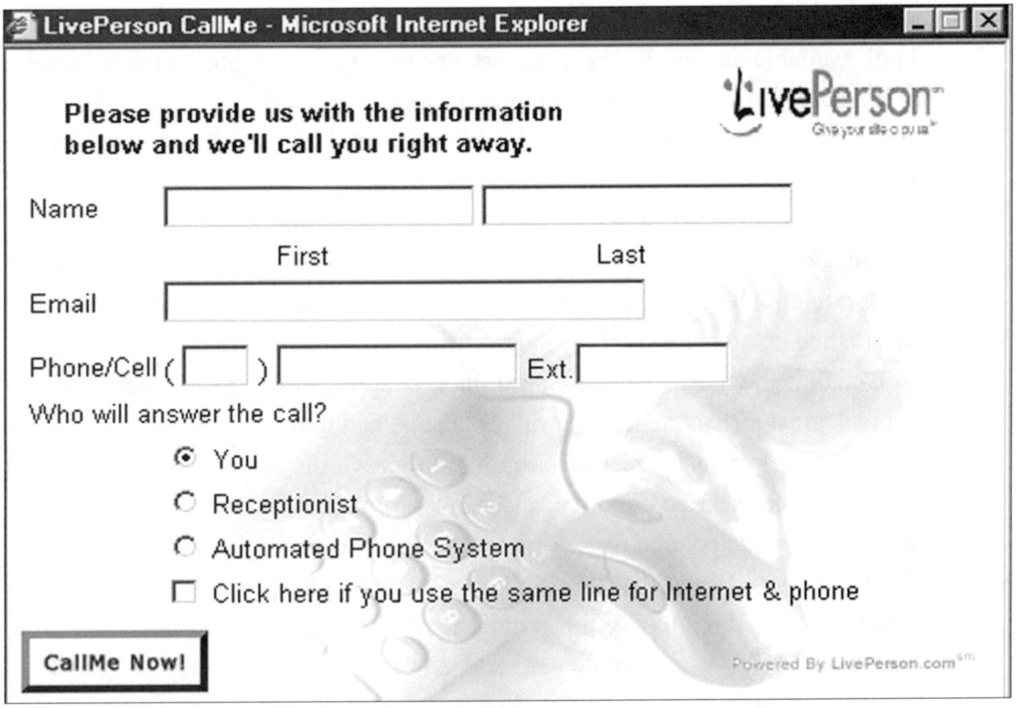

Figure 10.1. Web visitors who complete this form online receive a call from the company.

customers. Even more important, providing a means for easy communication gives customers the sense that their input is valued.

Say, for example, that you are a plumbing company. You repair and install bathrooms and kitchens. You prepare individual quotes upon physical inspection of the premises, and before doing so you must make appointments with your prospects. The easy way out is just to provide contact information for the prospects visiting your Web site. This misses endless opportunities.

With a little more effort, you can turn visitors into buyers. Customer service in this context means that you describe your services in detail, your pricing policies, and your inspection criteria. You can also post seasonal reminders of services a homeowner or company might need. You can offer tips about keeping heating costs in line by regularly maintaining heating systems. You can also display the products that you use, so that the customers don't have to wait to receive a brochure by mail.

Even this is not the end of your opportunities. Why make them contact you by another media just so you can fiddle through your appointment book? They might never call. To make your service still more complete, make your appointment book available on your Web site, so that a prospect can schedule a visit right there and then. All it takes is a simple online form.

Also, when planning for customer service, two issues are particularly worth considering: product returns and e-mail support.

Perhaps the truest test of customer service is how product returns are handled. If you can't deliver the product quickly, and then deal with mistakes gracefully, you shouldn't be offering it. It is said that it takes about four minutes for one unsatisfied customer to notify thousands of your future or prospective buyers.

E-mail is the most frequently used Internet application. The number of e-mail users is greater than the number of Web users, and many new users cite wanting e-mail as their primary reason for going online. Some businesses use e-mail as their customer service communications medium. They may have e-mail operators similar to telephone operators. Furthermore, e-mail responses can be automated or stored in a database and then mixed and matched. Phone support typically costs three to five times more than e-mail support. When establishing even the simplest e-mail customer service initiatives be sure to:

- Communicate positively—Answer inquiries promptly and with an upbeat message.
- Communicate quickly—Customers see response times as an indication of what it would be like to do business with your company. After all, the overall promise of the Internet is speed and convenience. In general, your goal should be to respond to your customer before he or she logs off.

Eenie Strategy

Enable Online Instant Messaging for Your Customers

Sometimes all the FAQs and information pages in the world don't help; your customers need a real, live human being to answer complex questions, make a decision, or just hold their hands. If you use Human Click (www.humanclick.com), visitors to your Web site can ask to chat with your support personnel. Human

Click provides the HTML code to embed a user button on your Web pages. When customers click this button, a chat window opens on the visitor's browser, and the site operator receives a "request to chat" alert. At that point, all it takes is pressing a key; you are ready to give your customer the most personalized, effective response possible.

Cost: Free, but the investment in trained personnel to handle customers can be substantial.

Meenie Strategy

Increase Productivity of Your Sales Force

To ensure top productivity for an entire sales organization, sales managers need:

- Oversight of the whole team's sales pipeline at a glance.

- Real-time forecasting and reporting that delivers consolidated information whenever it is needed, without interrupting salespeople to ask for updates.

- A complete calendar of all team members' daily activities to aid in management and coordination.

- Sales histories that capture the collective experience of the entire company so that it can be put to work for each salesperson.

Salesforce.com offers a sales productivity tool that each of your sales reps can access online. It provides all these functions, and more.

Cost: $65 per user per month.

Miney Strategy

Provide Full-Fledged Online Customer Support

Using LivePerson Exchange (www.liveperson. com), a high-quality CRM solution and ASP delivery model, you can offer your customers full-fledged online customer support through the use of a variety of tools such as Chat, FAQs, E-Mail, and Document Management.

Cost: The price range for the basic chat package begins with a $2,000 setup fee and $350 monthly fee per operator.

Moe Strategy

Provide Online Interactive, Multimedia Customer Service

Jeeves Solutions (www.askjeeves.com) provides companies with natural language navigation software coupled with customer intelligence systems to let a company's customers ask about the information, products, and services they're looking for, while simultaneously helping companies learn valuable information through the questions users ask.

Failing to provide users with fast and intuitive access to relevant online information leads to high phone and e-mail support costs and a possible loss in transactions. According to Forrester Research, the average cost to the company of a call to a contact center is more than $30 per call, and the average e-mail is over $10. But Ask Jeeves (www.askjeeves.com) has the answer to this costly problem—it allows users to easily service themselves (self-service). With Ask Jeeves search, navigation, and customer intelligence solutions, you can provide intuitive, self-service access to improve your customers' online experience while reducing costs.

Fees: Starts at $100K.

Chapter 11

Think Globally, Click Locally

Throughout most of this book, we focus our attention on using the Internet to reach the millions of potential users who are scattered across the globe. However, this is only part of the Internet's remarkable power. While this potent medium allows incredible geographic reach, it can be used as a local treasure as well. We can travel to the ends of the globe to find products, services, and people with common interests, but we are missing something really important if we forget our local, physical communities in the process. For business, government, service organizations, or almost any other Net user, the Internet can provide some of its greatest value at the local level.

In my heart, I click my ruby slippers together and chant, "there's no place like home." I crave a physical community that uses the power of the Internet to share information about everything that goes on—an online community where I can find out how to volunteer for local charities; get involved in local events; discover local art, theater, and music; or participate in a community board meeting because I have the schedules readily available to me.

In my practical consumer mind, I crave a community where I am able to check whether the video I want is in before I go to the neighborhood video rental, make reservations at a restaurant in town (or order a pizza for delivery), search through local store inventories to find out whether they carry products that I need, get the local traffic and weather report, and find out about the headline news in my area.

And I want to be connected to my government. I want to have public records available to me through my computer. Much as the U.S. government has made strides to put information online, the local governments should be clamoring to get into the game as well.

As for politicians, I want to know who is running for office at the local, state, and national levels. I want the opportunity to correspond with them and hear their views on issues of importance to me. I want to know (from their Web sites) why they think I should vote for them.

Well, figuring out how to bring all of this information together is no easy task. A truly open-networked environment could support such an endeavor, but it requires a level of partnership among all the community players—media and business, government, schools, nonprofit organizations, and, of course, the citizens. Developing a community portal that includes "everything you ever wanted to know about your community" requires a degree of convergence of these private and public sectors.

So far, it seems that the necessary parties never all get together; that's just the way it goes. Funding and operating a full-scope local community-based Web site is a messy task, which many of those who should participate construe as menacing. Besides that, the marketing efforts needed to produce a successful community Web site are enormous! Even though the target audience is in a small geographic area, building a brand that identifies the site as "the only," "the best," etc., so that people really utilize it is a monumental feat.

The need for localized content has clearly been recognized. Many of the major Web portals have set up community-interest areas within their sites in an attempt to meet the challenges. Examples include AltaVista Local (www.altavista.com), Netscape's Local Channel (www.netscape.com), NBCi's local pages (www.nbci.com), Yahoo!'s Get Local pages (www.yahoo.com), and the customizable My AOL (www.my.aol.com). Each of these sites offers city-specific news, information, and shopping services, as well as classified advertisements, event listings, restaurant listings, yellow pages, and more.

There also have been some hearty independent efforts to achieve the sense of local community. Most are smaller in scope and are more narrowly focused on the cultural aspects of a region than the all-inclusive community site of my

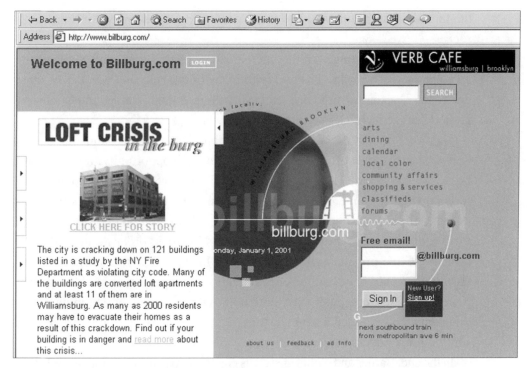

Figure 11.1. This Web site for Williamsburg, Brooklyn, is typical of the local-interest sites now serving many communities.

dreams. As an example, take a look at www.billburg.com, which was constructed by local enthusiasts for a small section of Brooklyn called Williamsburg.

Consider local Web communities from a different perspective. People really do value news, weather, and community service issues, but consumers also want convenience. Companies with a local presence must learn to leverage their brick and mortar in a way that provides added convenience for their customers—what the industry refers to as click and mortar.

One of the best lessons about brick/click operations emerges from the experience of Barnes and Noble, one of the largest book retailers in the physical world. While Amazon.com was establishing itself as the premier online book seller, Barnes and Noble waited nearly three years to get online. As Amazon.com built its online empire, Barnes and Noble bought real estate, built more physical stores, and set up coffee shops. By the time the company turned its attention to the Internet, it was both very late to the game and very aware of Amazon.com's success.

In hope of competing with the Internet-savvy giant, Barnes and Noble set up an e-commerce Web site (bn.com) with many of the bells and whistles of other dot-coms. The company did one really silly thing, though. Barnes and Noble forgot to leverage its brick-and-mortar investments.

There are hundreds of Barnes and Noble outlets all around the United States, and this asset offered the company a unique opportunity: It would have been easy to provide customers with a level of convenience that no competitor could match. Someone living in New York City, just a few blocks from one of the chain's book shops, should have been able to tap into that store's inventory, confirm that the book they wanted was in stock, order it, and then take a pleasant five-minute walk to pick it up. In this click-and-mortar nirvana, customers would have had the convenience of shopping for a book from their home or office computer, yet gotten it without delay or shipping costs. Amazon.com, without a single store in the real world, could never have offered book buyers such convenience.

In the end, Barnes and Noble missed its chance. Amazon.com remains the largest retailer of books in the online world—and has used that base to expand itself into a vast Internet department store—while at this time, bn.com shows little sign of making a profit. However, in its failure, Barnes and Noble showed the way for others.

Experts say that 70 percent of Internet surfers still prefer to shop in a physical store. This means that even a small retailer can leverage its bricks for online profit. There are Web services that focus specifically on this kind of retailing.

A site called www.Saleshound.com is a resource for people who want to find the best deals in stores in their communities. Saleshound.com says it offers a "comprehensive, current, and impartial" database of thousands of local sales and specials. Site users can search by product, category, store, brand, location, and/or ZIP Code to find information on pricing and special offers in their areas. Saleshound.com lists more than 250 product categories and 14,000 brands available in 110,000 stores across the country. The site will also help shoppers create customized lists to print and take with them when they shop. Shoppers can also get driving directions and street maps to the stores they find online.

Another attempt has been made by eBay, which recognized that the cost of shipping of its consumer's goods sometimes far exceeded the value of the goods themselves. eBay now has a "shop locally" section that features auctions in 20 metropolitan areas around the country. The advantages of this service include the customer's ability to browse items of local interest, to physically inspect the products, and to personally deliver them to the nearby customer.

As the Internet continues its global expansion, many companies are finding that local-interest sites are desirable because they offer consumers a unique level of convenience and efficiency. While the big players like Amazon.com have huge selections of goods and offer attractive discounted prices, local Internet businesses should be able to fulfill an order within hours. Local businesses that have capitalized on the need for this kind of convenience and rapid delivery are profiting from this new kind of e-commerce. In fact, the local model has been so successful that larger online merchants are working hard to build more efficient delivery systems through local channels. Speed of delivery is a major selling point for shoppers who are pressed for time, in a culture that is accustomed to instant gratification.

Eenie Strategy

Advertise in Local and Regional Portals and Directories

Use the following search engines to begin your hunt for appropriate advertising sites:

- www.wowworks.com
- www.the1000.com
- www.searchengines.com
- www.allsearchengines.com

Cost: Most listings are free.

Meenie Strategy

Set Up Shop in a Regional Mall

Create a storefront listing for your company in www.malls.com. They have city, state, and regional mall listings. Malls.com claims to receive approximately one million page requests per month and has averaged a 10 percent growth in visits every month for the last two years. It's easy to do (your store can be up and running within twenty-four to forty-eight hours).

Cost: Three months, $25/month; six months, $19.16/month; twelve months, $17.91/month. Six- and twelve-month listings get free Display Ads and Banners.

Miney Strategy

Advertise on Local TV and Sell Off the Web

A company called WebFill (www.webfill.com) gives local broadcasters an easy way to enter the e-commerce arena by creating, hosting, and maintaining turnkey retail "stores" that are seamlessly integrated into the Web sites of local television stations. They assist their local broadcast partners in bringing local advertisers' products online. After setting up a local retailer's virtual "counter space," they then handle every link in the fulfillment chain, from processing orders to packing and shipping. For local clients who feature perishable goods, such as gourmet food items, they offer a convenient drop-ship option. They also provide their broadcasters with key promotional tools, sending seasonal and generic on-air spots that can be easily tagged and customized by every television station.

Webfill also manages a national virtual store (shopthecountry.com Web mall) to showcase and sell products with cross-country visibility.

Cost: Local TV stations would need to make an average 12-36K investment. Fees for local vendors wishing to advertise begin at $10,000. Fees for high-end service including sponsorships could average $65,000.

Check out WebFill to see if your local network is participating.

Moe Strategy

Custom Develop Your Community Site

Every community has unique needs. What could be better than customizing your Web development plans to suit your specific needs? Develop your "blueprint," and go to a company like Blenderbox, Inc., (www.blenderbox.com) for additional ideas and to implement your site plan. This company's unique stock in trade is the combination of high-quality application development and extraordinary artistic expression.

Blenderbox works within a diversified portfolio of industries, but can also be credited for the development and management of the community Web site for Williamsburg, Brooklyn (www.billburg.com). Billburg.com allows people to create online art galleries, post classifieds, participate in forums, add listings, and add calendar events, among other important community tools. Other samples of Blenderbox's talent can be found at www.blenderbox.com.

Cost: Fees start at $25,000.

Chapter 12

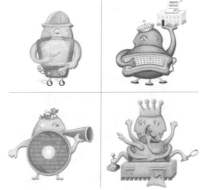

For the Cause:
Nonprofit Business on the Internet

According to the American Association of Fundraising Council, total charitable contributions in 1999 topped $190 billion! It's nice to know that people still care. Obviously, giving is big business.

What does this have to do with the Internet? Well...lots. Lots if you are a nonprofit or charitable organization, lots if you are the giver, and lots if you are a business.

For the rest of this chapter, I will assume that you operate a nonprofit organization. It does not matter what your nonprofit does. It might work to save the environment, encourage arts, seek to eliminate oppression, care for the less fortunate, or develop medical cures. Whatever the cause, nonprofits need money and support to pursue it. Well, the Internet brings you the same opportunities it gives to a profit-oriented business. It gives access to millions of people. It will allow you to get your message out to the masses, establish worthwhile collaborations, prospect for potential donors and volunteers, collect donations, and rally for supporters. The Internet is invaluable to you.

Just like businesses, nonprofit and charitable organizations come in all shapes and sizes. Which e-strategy is best for you depends on your scope and budget. If you are a local organization, your scope is regional. If you are national or international, the scope is much greater. Either way, there are strategies that, if used effectively and with the appropriate amount of commitment, can help you make great strides toward your goals. For example, most nonprofits rely on telemarketing and direct mail to solicit support. E-mail marketing can be far more cost effective.

According to a study entitled "Socially Engaged Internet Users: Prospects for Online Philanthropy and Activism," conducted by The Mellman Group for Craver, Mathews, Smith, and Company Interactive, the universe of potential online activists and donors is much larger than the pool of people that nonprofits now reach through direct mail. The study claims that while the traditional, direct-mail donor universe is approximately 12 million individuals, the number of Americans with Internet access who report giving time or money to social causes represents 25 percent of the adult population. That is approximately 50 million people!

The study narrows down this figure to consider only those who say they are willing to take an online action, such as send an e-mail to an elected official using a charity or public interest group Web site. That leaves fully 16 percent of the adult population, or about 32 million people, all with the potential to become online activists. No less than 8 percent, or about 16 million adults, are willing to make a donation to a charity or public interest group over the Internet.

The study also points out that the potential universe of online donors and activists is a younger, more ideologically diverse group than the traditional direct-mail donor universe. A survey conducted by the Mellman Group in 1995 of progressive direct-mail donors found that nearly two-thirds (64 percent) were age 60 or older. The average age among these donors was 66. By contrast, 85 percent of socially engaged Internet users are under the age of 60, and the average age of this group of potential online donors/activists is just 42.

There is a political difference as well. In addition, the 1998 Hart survey of progressive direct-mail donors found that 60 percent identify themselves as Democrats, while only 19 percent call themselves Republicans or Independents. In contrast, online activists are almost evenly divided between Democrats (39 percent) and Republicans (41 percent), and between liberal (43 percent) and conservative (44 percent).

Despite their involvement in social causes, few of these Internet users have utilized the Web's potential for contributions, activism, or communications. Two-thirds of socially engaged Internet users remain unaware of opportunities to take action on social issues. The online donor universe is huge, vibrant but barely tapped.

Under the circumstances, developing a Web presence for your charitable organization is absolutely the least you can do. This vast new stream of potential exposure and revenue is just waiting for you!

All of the concepts in this book work in the nonprofit world as well as they do in the business world. Many nonprofits have already set up Web sites and some, like Goodwill (www.goodwill.org), have put their stores online as well. Nonprofits on the Internet set up shopping sites and one-to-one marketing programs; there are charity portals, auctions, and affiliate marketing programs. Online charities also understand the value of online communities.

America Online's AOL Foundation runs Helping.org, a new philanthropy portal that is designed to provide an easy and cost-effective way for Americans to donate money or time to a wide range of charitable organizations. Calling it the most comprehensive philanthropy portal on the Internet, the AOL Foundation said that the nonprofit site connects users to over 620,000 charities and 20,000 volunteer activities.

Sites such as WebCharity.com and iGive.com also have a big branding presence across the Internet. WebCharity gives Internet users the chance to donate new and used items to be auctioned, with the proceeds going to their favorite nonprofit cause. A user on iGive.com can purchase products from one of the mall members, and up to 15 percent of the cost of the product will be donated to the buyer's favorite charity. Igive claims that it raised $815,910.78 in 2000.

Other giving malls include 4charity.com, CharityMall.com, MyCause.com, Non-Profit Shopping Mall (www.npsmall.com), and ShopForChange.com.

Schools have their own set of giving malls, including SchoolCash.com and Schoolpop.com.

If your favorite charity isn't online, make your voice heard. And make sure your charity can accept donations online. I've found nearly two dozen companies that help to Web-enable various facets of the giving process. For starters, try GivingCapital.com and CharityWeb.com.

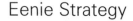

Eenie Strategy

Get Involved Wherever You Can!

Look around the Net and you will find hundreds of places where your organization can set up shop for free. For example, you can list your events—especially protests or rallies—on www.protest.net. (Of course, it makes sense then to tell your constituency to stay attuned to protest.net for upcoming events.) You can look for volunteers on www.servenet.org or www.helping.org. Or you can join a giving mall and increase contributions to your cause. Some examples are www.Mycause.com, www.Charitymall.com, and www.Igive.com.

Cost: Free.

Meenie Strategy

Host Online Charitable Auctions

Hold an Internet auction? Why not? Auctions have been a money-raising staple for charities for decades; watch your local public television station during the funding season for a good example. Auctions are one good way to turn donated items into cash.

Fundraising auctions can work even better on the Internet than in the offline world. Using the Internet, even a local nonprofit organization can solicit donations from a worldwide community. Auctions also provide welcome free advertising for your business supporters and sponsors.

A company called AuctionAnything.com will display your charitable listings throughout their network of community sites. More eyes on your offerings mean higher bidding and more money for your charity. Plus, you will have the branding opportunity to get your message out to millions of people who would want to help in your goal.

Cost: Packages start as low as $249 to set up and $79 per month with no commissions or other fees. In addition, charitable organizations receive a 50 percent discount.

Miney Strategy

Create an Online Community Dedicated to the Needs of Your Organization

Set up discussion boards, Web pages, private e-mail, newsgroups, e-mail lists, real-time chat, calendar, and many other features using a hosted product from Web Crossing (www.webcrossing.com). Your administrators can customize virtually any of your site's features and functions. Web Crossing's Professional Server Hosting Package will enable you to get your advocacy community fired up.

Cost: $245 setup plus $495 per month.

Moe Strategy

Get Serious About Garnering Grassroots Support

Grassroots Enterprise, Inc. (www. grassroots.com) provides technology solutions for impacting public policy and cultivating strong grassroots relationships. The company's flagship software, Grassroots Multiplier, integrates the technologies that organizations need to grow, manage, and mobilize members. Grassroots Multiplier offers a step-by-step interface for personalizing communications to members, creating online tools for taking action, managing member data, and generating detailed reports to analyze the effectiveness of advocacy campaigns.

Using Grassroots Multiplier, organizations can

- Easily centralize and manage a scalable member database

- Quickly launch HTML and rich media e-mail to supporters

- Increase response rates with highly personalized calls to action and online content, based on members' interests, demographics, and past actions

- Publish branded Web pages that replicate the look and feel of existing Web sites

- Enable members to target decision makers accurately using ZIP Code-to-district matching

- Guide future strategy and communications based on knowledge gained from real-time tracking of member actions

- Demonstrate campaign successes through vivid, graphical results reports

- Provide media with searchable database of news releases

- Eliminate the need for costly software and hardware installations, maintenance, and upgrades—Grassroots Enterprise securely hosts all data for organizations

By using Grassroots Multiplier to strengthen relationships with members, organizations can hope to increase loyalty, campaign participation, and retention rates that they need for winning public policy battles.

Cost: Fees determined by organization size and need.

Chapter 13

E-Government

Imagine being able to apply for a building permit from the convenience of your home. Imagine being able to sign up for local recreation programs, to pay traffic violations (c'mon everybody gets them), to dispute traffic violations (c'mon everyone tries to), or to look up land records as you plan to buy, sell, or build property—and do it all without racing through traffic on your lunch break. In some communities, it is already possible.

Just as the Internet has changed the way businesses provide products and services to consumers, the Internet is changing the way the federal, state, and local governments serve their constituents. The delivery of interactive, transactional-based government services on the Internet is referred to as e-government.

Government is huge. Just at the federal level there are countless thousands of agencies and subagencies set up to pursue countless disparate activities. Then there are state, city, local governments, all busy with their own concerns. Though there is a master (federal) plan, each level of government implements its own priorities. Each has a unique strategy for generating revenue, and each has its own budget for expending funds. Some have already incorporated the techniques of e-government into their plans and practices. Most have not.

Some agencies within the federal government have rolled out decent initiatives toward e-government. For example, the Department of Patents and Trademarks (www.uspto.gov) has its own database online, and users can search for registered patents or trademarks. This Web site has a detailed overview of the rules and regulations that govern patents and trademarks, and even keeps a fairly up-to-date listing of patent and trademark attorneys, who are not always easy to find. The IRS put its entire tax form library online several years ago and most recently has begun to allow the electronic filing of income taxes. Many agencies, however, are content simply to list their departmental phone numbers. Many others are not yet online at all.

This is true of the states as well. Many have launched Web sites that attempt to meet their constituents' basic information needs. States have posted visitor information, such as points of interest and recreational facilities, and information about the state's policies. Some have even made it possible for residents to register automobiles online and for businesses to apply over the Internet for incorporation, business licenses, and environmental permits.

Some city governments have been really trying to get out there for their constituents. Visit www.NYC.gov and see that New York City's Web site offers updated city news and allows users to pay selected taxes and parking tickets online. (Parking violators can even plead their case online.) The site also has links to sites where users can view several types of property-related statements, including property tax history, SCRIE reports, water bills, and real estate tax bills. One of the simplest features promotes this site above many other city Web pages: It has an index that users can consult to locate all of New York City's online services. Too many other sites provide only general information and leave you guessing what else might be available online.

Local administrations are the last place we'd find aggressive partisans of e-government. At this level, many are content with a basic Web presence, such as a site that merely lists departmental phone numbers but has nice pictures of the local leaders and municipal buildings. Many still have no Web presence at all.

Aside from constituent information, doing business with the government is big business. Many years ago, the U.S. government established a procedure for doing business that would reduce all the paper-processing costs governments were incurring. This was the basis for the Paperwork Elimination Act, which requires agencies to accept forms electronically by October 2003. The government started this initiative before the launch of the World Wide Web and sought to enable transactions through a system called EC-EDI (Electronic Commerce/Electronic Data Interchange). Transactions were processed

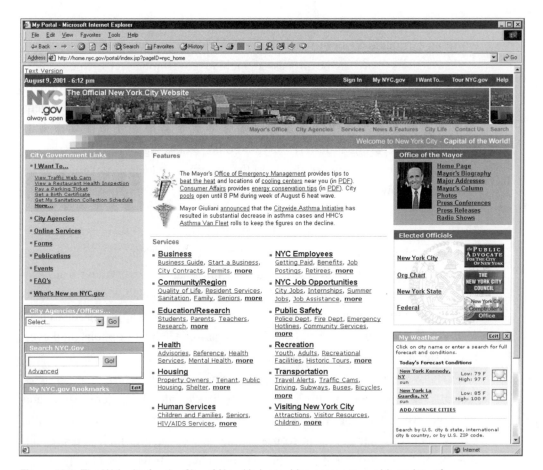

Figure 13.1. The Web site for the City of New York provides access to a wide variety of city information and services.

through a third-party vendor, and both buyer (government) and seller (business) had to use the same transaction system.

Recently, the Treasury Department launched another e-commerce initiative designed to streamline the process of doing business with the government and to assist agencies in meeting their goals under the Government Paperwork Elimination Act. The effort, called Pay.gov (www.pay.gov), is a secure payment and collection portal. When Pay.gov launched, citizens, businesses, and federal agencies were given the option of processing a wide variety of transactions via the Internet, most of which are currently handled through Automated Clearing House (ACH) collection systems or in person, over the counter. Ultimately, Pay.gov could process 80 million transactions each year, worth an estimated $125 billion.

Transactions that can be processed include government fees, fines, sales, leases, donations, loans, and certain taxes. Pay.gov claims it will save tax dollars by providing a central infrastructure for processing e-payments. The government says the new initiative will also reduce the Treasury's collections costs and eliminate paper processing at the Treasury and other federal agencies.

The new Internet site will also help the government keep better track of its money and allow the Treasury to provide more timely and extensive accounting information to other agencies.

The U.S. government also has launched its own portal Web site at www.first.gov, which provides a single point of entry to more than 20,000 Web sites. FirstGov allows users to browse a wealth of information—everything from carrying out research at the Library of Congress to tracking a NASA mission. It also enables users to conduct important business online—such as applying for student loans, tracking Social Security benefits, comparing Medicare options, and even administering government grants and contracts.

FirstGov claims to be a "one-stop shopping" site for government services. Actually, it is an index to the various Web sites created by federal, state, and local governments. The FirstGov site provides only information and links. Consumers who actually want to use online services to file their taxes, check their Social Security benefits, or buy stamps have to leave FirstGov for other government sites that vary greatly in quality and design.

Even within that limitation, however, FirstGov represents a big advance in e-government. Visitors to the site can browse through a selection of topics and find information about the most common government services; the listing includes topics such as Agriculture and Food, Arts and Culture, and Learning and Jobs. Or they can use FirstGov's search function to scan the government's entire library of 27 million online pages in less than a second!

All this is just the primitive beginning of e-government. One recent report forecasts that once government is fully online, a radical restructuring will take place. This reorganization will be driven by constituents and lawmakers who, seeing the entire structure of their government laid out on the Web, will begin to wonder why so many departments offer overlapping services.

The predictions also say that government agencies in the United States eventually will roll out almost 14,000 services online. Most will come from the country's 35,000 cities and towns. The report said that deployment of these sophisticated online offerings will be "slow," because governments will have to figure out ways to link legacy systems to new pay and authorization services. Yet it forecasts that virtually all of those 14,000 services will be available on the Web by 2006.

An increasingly demanding and wired public is looking for speed and convenience from its government. Even though constituents are concerned about privacy, and are not much interested in paying convenience fees, users see the value of online government. They want those services now. It appears that they will not have long to wait.

Eenie Strategy

Turn Your Paper Forms into Electronic Forms

Under two pieces of legislation—the Government Paperwork Reduction Act and the Government Paperwork Elimination Act—agencies are required (by 2003) to move many of their traditional printed forms to digital formats and make them available for their constituency on the Web.

Using Omniform by scansoft (www.scansoft.com), you can scan your forms and instantly turn them into a digital form that can be edited and filled out on your computer. OmniForm recognizes form fields so you can fill the form out on your PC.

Cost: $149.99 for software package.

Meenie Strategy

If You Are a Municipality, Make Your Code Available on Your Web Site

Local citizens will be able to find the information they need, and companies researching site locations in your area will be able to find the zoning and land use legislation they need, without calling your offices. Your government actually improves its customer service by providing easy, 24/7 access to information, even as it saves money, because staff spends less time fulfilling requests on the telephone and in person.

General Code (www.generalcode.com) is a company that specializes in digitizing municipal ordinances into a numbered and stylized document that is easy to read and easy to access. It can also put your Code on the Web. If you already have their electronic product (PC/CodeBook), the job can be completed quickly and very inexpensively.

Cost: PC/CodeBook starts at $1,750. Additional hourly fees are charged for scanning or data entry, as needed. The fee for E-Code, putting Code on the Web, is $200.

Miney Strategy

Implement Content Management Software for Teachers to Publish Curriculums on the Internet

RedDot Solutions Corporation (www.reddotsolutions.com) has developed an innovative, browser-based WYSIWYG editorial interface for content contribution across the enterprise. Users can develop Web content without knowing anything about HTML and route it through a workflow engine for multilevel approvals before the content is published to the live site. The RedDot interface is so simple and intuitive that no training is required, guaranteeing rapid acceptance among users and facilitating a fast return on investment. Implementations of any size are simple and straightforward.

Cost: Starts at $30,000.

Moe Strategy

Set Up Procurement Automation in Your Agency

Using ecweb.net, an electronic commerce center for public sector agencies and their suppliers, Federal, state, and local agencies can post requests for quotes, requests for proposals, solicitations, make awards, issue delivery orders, and more. Suppliers for these agencies review opportunities, place bids, and receive awards online.

Cost: EC Web charges government agencies $51,000 for an annual subscription to ecweb.net, a fee that includes an unlimited number of transactions. Use of the system is free to vendors, unless they want customized delivery of agency postings.

Part III

Part III
Creating an Internet Business Plan

In previous chapters, the Internet Prophets have offered a variety of ideas for you to think about. By now, you should have a good understanding of basic e-business objectives. If you are serious about taking your business onto the Internet, you probably have been considering which possible models would work for you: Selling through an online mall? Auctioning your products? Developing an online community? Some combination of these techniques?

In fact, if you are like many entrepreneurs, your head is swimming already with attractive, money-making ideas for your site. You could provide great graphics! You could wow 'em with streaming audio and video, hold online conferences, and do demonstrations! You could create a community and haul in millions of users a week!

At this early stage of developing an Internet business, it can be hard not to hear a voice, rich with promise, telling you, "If you build it, they will come." It's not that easy, and believing that it is can be the biggest mistake that companies make when developing their Web site.

Push all those ideas to the back of your mind while working on the next step in creating a new Web site or improving your existing one. Before sitting down to plan your Web site, there is a lot of preparation to be done. This stage of developing a Web-based enterprise has very little to do with the Internet, but everything to do with business.

In Part III of this book, we will examine what it takes to plan the commercial side of an Internet business so that it rests on a sound footing. You need to develop clear objectives for your Internet business and figure out where your

Internet strategies fit within your overall business plan. This may well mean examining your existing business, analyzing how it operates, and figuring out which parts of it can be made more efficient and profitable by going online. It will certainly require figuring out a realistic budget for developing and operating your Web site. There are other issues to consider as well.

As we saw in Part II, the digital frontier is about a healthy combination of information, relationships, and entertainment. Every feature of an effective Web site is designed to attract potential customers and build lifelong relationships with them. It is about recognizing who your customers are and strengthening your ties with them. A Web site must be active, dynamic, and fulfilling for all who use it. Do it right, and people will come back again and again.

But all that is in the future. Mishandle the business preparations for your Internet enterprise, and the best Web site design in the world cannot save you. Our goal in the next three chapters will be to guide you successfully over these hurdles.

Chapter 14

Planning for Web-Site Development

By now, it should be clear that there is nothing terribly difficult about start-ing a business on the Internet. Anyone with a little experience in creating a Web page, using the site-creation tools in a browser package, or even Microsoft Word, and utilities freely available online, can have a modest e-commerce Web site up and running in an afternoon, complete with facilities for accepting pay-ment by credit card. This does not mean that it is a good idea.

E-commerce is not some miraculous new money machine; it is just one more form of business. Making a go of it requires every bit as much planning as any traditional business, whether opening a real-world store, manufacturing widgets and marketing them wholesale, or setting up a mail-order retail operation.

The first step is setting realistic goals. If you are adding an Internet pres-ence to an existing business, what business are you in? How have other par-ticipants in your industry approached the Internet? How successful have they been? If you are just getting into business, how much competition are you tak-ing on? Why are you heading for the Internet, rather than using a traditional brick-and-mortar business model? (Limited start-up costs may not be a good enough reason, unless you can get by on limited profits or cope with hefty investments in expansion later on.) In either case, new start-up or existing busi-ness, are your profit targets in line with what similar businesses have achieved on the Internet? If not, what makes you think you can do better? In short, what are you really looking for from e-business? And can you really expect to get it? We will ask many more such questions in the next chapter, when we examine the development of business strategies in depth.

When developing an Internet strategy, it is important to look beyond the Internet as a mere marketing or sales tool. Take the time to review carefully everything your company does, and figure out where the Internet can be used to make those transactions run more smoothly and efficiently. The power of the Internet can offer practical solutions for attracting new customers, increasing revenues, reducing costs, and efficiently processing information.

That is just the beginning of your preparations. Next, you need a comprehensive business plan and budget for the Web site itself. This will give you a budget and timetable, as well as your target for return on investment, to help focus your activities. The Web-site business plan will help steer you in the right direction. It should be incorporated into the company's overall business plan to make sure that the objectives of the entire business are effectively met.

A thorough and complete Web-site business plan will identify the key personnel to be assigned to the project. You will need designated staff to manage the site once it's launched, to keep the content fresh, to analyze the successes and weaknesses of the endeavor, to answer inquiries, and to provide superior customer service. You may need to build an entirely new department or integrate Web functions into many departments within your company. You may want to consider building strategic relationships with related partners. The plan will also include milestones and timelines to make sure your goals are being achieved, as well as a budget for planning, development, hosting, and marketing.

Simply budgeting for Web-site development can be complicated. Determining the necessary resources will depend on whether the Web site is a part of the existing business or a new endeavor. It depends on how big the site is going to be and how much maintenance is projected for it. It depends on whether the site is going to be strictly informational or a point of sale. If it is informational, how often and extensively will it need to be updated? If the site aims to sell your products, how much of a commitment will it take to manage inventory, post new products to the site, or announce product specials? What about product fulfillment? How will it be handled? What about customer service? Merely deciding how much you need to spend on computers and software hardly even begins the process.

Companies fall into some common errors during the planning and development process:

- Ignoring the prior business model or sales channels; the existing marketing, fulfillment, inventory, and accounting procedures; or your established customers
- Building a site with bells, whistles, and so-called "cutting edge" design or complex navigation that actually obscures the message
- Creating Web pages heavy on graphics and media files, so that the pages download slowly and try your customers' patience
- Making it hard to find products, product information, or service and contact information on the Web site
- Not considering security and privacy issues or giving enough weight to consumers' concerns about them
- Failing to build a back end that is easily managed and powerful enough for the current and planned needs
- Building a site that is harder for customers to use than ordering or communicating by telephone or fax

Avoiding these and other potential problems is what planning is about. At best, impulsiveness, impatience, and lack of planning can waste your fledgling efforts. They may cost you potential business from a user who will never return to your site, even after you have gotten your act together.

Now let us consider some of the specific issues to be faced in the formulation of a business plan for your Web site.

Planning Budget

Planning takes time and resources. You need to allocate a budget and timeline for the planning phase of Web development.

First, though, what does it take to plan a Web site? For a start, you will need to do some general research and an internal business assessment. What you learn from these activities will help you to build a specific business model, based on your company's characteristics and ability to serve an Internet audience.

Having figured out what you want the site to do, it is necessary to consider what is practical within your budget. How do you plan to finance this venture?

Will you use existing cash flow and carve a part of your traditional marketing budget for Web-site development? Have you considered a bank loan or even venture capital to support your idea?

Consider personnel issues as well. You may want to create the next Amazon.com, but your plan is doomed if you lack the knowledgeable staff required to bring it off. You will need someone, perhaps an entire team, who can dedicate time to planning and developing the site. Think about where your resources will come from. Do any of your employees have "down time?" Do you need to hire additional employees? Are you willing to oversee the project yourself? Whoever you involve in this plan should have adequate knowledge of the Internet and more than adequate knowledge of your business.

The people assigned to develop the Web site should have a variety of skills. You cannot just hand the project over to your IT department, because technicians rarely understand marketing, design, or critical business processes. On the other hand you cannot give it to someone in marketing, because they probably lack the technical skills or business process skills.

That leaves relatively few alternatives, all of which require a substantial commitment. You can pioneer the whole thing yourself. Budget permitting, you might hire consultants to learn about the company and its organizational processes and then develop a Web strategy to suit your needs and capabilities.

Another approach used by many larger companies and organizations is to create a team with members from many different departments to develop a Web strategy. These people should have some knowledge of the Internet or be forward thinkers. Some should be technical people, the folks who are responsible for the current computer infrastructure within your company. However, representatives from marketing, customer support, billing, and warehousing all should be present for the planning sessions.

How much time you need for planning depends on the quality of people you have and how much of their schedule they can dedicate to the project. That time is not free. You must calculate the opportunity cost of involving your people on this project. ("Opportunity cost" is the lost profit associated with pulling your staff away from their normal business service.)

Research

It is important to do a little bit of research on the Internet to help you in developing your ideas for an e-business venture. Research Internet demographics and statistics, industry trends, and information on Internet marketing. One of the best sources for Internet statistics is www.cyberatlas.com. A series of Web sites launched by Economy.com also may have some helpful information:

- The Dismal Scientist (www.dismal.com) provides analysis of economic indicators and daily economic commentary.

- Research@Economy.com (www.economy.com/research) offers research reports on industries and on the U.S. and world economies.

- FreeLunch.com (www.economy.com/freelunch) provides free access to over 1 million sets of economic, financial, and demographic time series data.

Through your research, identify target markets and customer behavior patterns. To serve your customers best, you have to know how and why they do business with you. Obviously, you will build your Web site based on those needs. You will want to find out about your customer's age group, income, education level, gender, level of computer literacy, and more. As you learn more about your target market, it will become easier to attract new customers and encourage others to do business with you.

You will also have to make some decisions about selling to the international arena; after all, everywhere in the world, your Web site will be just a click away. Research and an internal business assessment will help you define your international potential. One key decision: Should you translate your site into other languages in order to maximize international exposure?

You must also research your competition. Use Internet search engines to find competitors. Remember, in an online setting your competition might be located far outside your customary geographic market—across the country or across the world. Review their online strategies to see what they are doing, and compare it to their traditional business model, and yours.

Eenie Strategy

Get Practical, Quality Advice from Experts

Visit Inc.com (www.inc.com), and use its online tools and reports to evaluate your e-business potential. Inc.com claims to deliver "best of breed" information, products, services, and online tools—aggregated from a variety of sources—for almost every business or management task. Inc.com, a product of Inc. Magazine, is widely considered a reputable source of information for the small to medium-size business market.

Inc.com provides its users with a detailed overview of how to establish an e-business. Its reports include how to attract visitors to your Web site, how to create customers, process orders, and maintain your site. In addition you will find information about how to develop a professional and comprehensive business plan to assist in clarifying your objectives and managing your progress. Inc.com also offers Web site evaluation worksheets, search engine submissions, and a variety of detailed research and analysis.

Cost: Most articles and reports are free; other services are priced affordably.

Meenie Strategy

Use the Resources of One of the Web's Most Popular "Research Marketplaces" to Create an E-Business Plan

AllNetResearch (www.allnetresearch.com) is one of the most complete marketplaces for Internet research on the Web. Reports cover e-commerce, computing and Internet services,

Internet marketing, demographics, telecommunications and wireless, Internet finance, and international issues.

This firm offers credible and useful reports, newsletters, directories, and databases from more than 80 publishers in the Internet industry. Their subject areas include computing/Internet services, demographics, e-commerce, geographics, Internet finance, Internet marketing, and telecommunications. Somewhere in this collection, you are likely to find information that can aid in making critical business decisions.

Cost: Prices start around $50 per report.

Miney Strategy

Access Industry-Focused Research
When Planning Your E-Business

Forrester, at www.forrester.com, is a leading independent research firm that analyzes the future of technology change and its impact on businesses, consumers, and society. Companies use their research as a continuing source of insight and strategy to guide their business technology decisions. Forrester provides objective research, strategic business, technology, and market assessment tools for this purpose.

Forrester provides a wide array of advisory services, by phone, e-mail, or fax, or in person. They provide customized assistance for applying data, research, and analysis to their customer's e-business strategies.

Forrester holds a number of executive events, forums, and workshops worldwide. These events cover a wide range of topics, such as marketing, healthcare, and executive forums that are current and pressing.

Cost: Forrester's minimum annual subscription fee is $10,000; the average client pays $25,000 per year.

Moe Strategy

Hire a Qualified Consultant to Help with Your Plan

Interlucent Internet Solutions, Inc. (www. interlucent.com), is an e-business solutions provider whose goal is to help you evaluate the latest technological trends and to identify those that will best enhance your company's competitive position. When the time comes to work out your e-commerce business plan, Interlucent's team will assist you in determining your goals and options, and in identifying innovative opportunities for achieving them.

Costs: Free initial consultation. Consulting fees start at $50,000.

Chapter 15

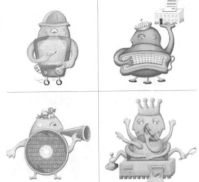

Business Assessment

Business assessment is the most critical step in planning a Web site. Take an objective look at your business. Who are your customers? What products or services do you provide? Figure out the current strengths and weaknesses of your business. Review the competition and what they have implemented on the Web. Then ask the following questions. Some are generic and may require a lengthy response, others are cut and dried.

- What is the business objective?
- What is the mission statement of the business? (The answer may not be the same as the one above.)
- As clearly as possible, define the business's product or service.
- Is the product informational/intangible or tangible real goods?
- How are orders placed?
- Does the business accept credit cards?
- Who are the target customers or clients?
- What do you know about the business's customers?
- Are the clients local, regional, or international?
- How do these customers now find this business?
- What type of marketing does the business currently engage in?
- How successful are those marketing efforts?

- Does this business have a sales team?
- What is the sales strategy?
- What types of sales collateral are used in the sales process?
- What is the main obstacle to closing a sale?
- Why do customers contact this business after a sale is made?
- Does this business do repeat business with existing customers?
- What type of customer service is provided for this business's products?
- What kind of ongoing dialogue does this business have with its customers?
- What are the most time-consuming tasks performed in this company?
- What type of work do the employees of this business detest the most?
- What type of work do they love the most?
- How would a Web site fit in with the company's overall strategy?
- Would a Web site be an extension of the existing business or a totally new business endeavor, using a new business model?

Ask yourself, "What processes are currently in place in this business that can be streamlined through the use of the Internet?" This is the fun part—let yourself dream a bit. The sky is the limit. For the time being, forget about Eenie, Meenie, Miney, and Moe, production costs, and other complicated issues that could derail your free thinking. The Internet is a totally new arena. It's a new game and there are no guidelines!

I have worked with many business owners and professionals whose main concern is what everyone else is doing. I say, "This is a revolution! You make up your own rules! We're all waiting for a sleeper idea to emerge, to be the next Amazon.com."

In previous chapters, we have seen a slew of new emerging business models. Review them. Have your team review them. See how they might apply to your business. Then think some more, and make your own model. That's how you will get ahead! The more innovative the Internet offerings, the greater the likelihood that the site will attract attention, the greater the likelihood of success. Innovative thinking comes from this pie-in-the-sky process. You would be amazed at what ingenious ideas might surface.

Now, after reviewing the results of your business assessment and the Internet business concepts presented in this book, consider the following:

- What is the essential value proposition that we can offer our customers?

- What are the most effective, value-added contributions that we can make that will reinforce our leadership position in this industry?

- How do I design my Web site as a customer service network, where all participants—not only customers but sales reps, customer service reps, and other customer relationship departments—have the knowledge and the motivation to focus on our customers?

- How do we work with vendors and suppliers to develop partnerships to improve efficiency and quality?

Now ask yourself, what kind of performance can we expect from the Web site? Do we want it to turn a profit? Is that the primary goal? (By now, you understand why profit is not always the ultimate goal right out of the starting gate.) Is the primary goal for additional branding of your company? Is the goal to gather more information about your customers and prospective customers? Or is it to conduct marketing tests? If our site is properly developed, launched, maintained, and marketed, what kind of traffic can we expect?

A more in-depth analysis is often beneficial in assessing the most effective transition to Internet technologies, depending on the specific business. Here are some examples:

- When assessing transactions at a local organization, the Arts Council of Rockland (ACOR, www.artscouncilofrockland.org), it became painfully clear that a great deal of time was spent in processing a monthly calendar of events. ACOR publishes a regular newsletter and maintains a Web site where this calendar is one of the main features. Hundreds of local arts organizations submit information to ACOR about upcoming events. The process of updating the calendar takes several hours per month. That was a problem, because it represented personnel time that ACOR could ill afford.

  Here's our Internet solution: Invite the local organizations to submit their own listings through an easy-to-use online database. When submissions are received, an e-mail goes to ACOR, to get approval for the submission. Once items have been accepted, they are automatically posted to the Web site. ACOR then can retrieve the data from the online Web site and post it in the printed newsletter. This streamlined, Web-based process saves the organization eight to ten hours each month.

- A local municipality receives hundreds of calls per month regarding necessary road repair. Unfortunately, many callers phone in to complain about roads that are not under the town's jurisdiction. To ease this needless workload, the municipality posted a complete database on its Web site of all the roads in their territory. Users now go to the Web site, look up the road by name, and are directed to the proper state, county, or town agency in seconds. Time saved: approximately 30 hours per month.

- A research company in the medical industry relies on feedback from lab technicians and scientists about discoveries in the use of their products. Using the Internet, this company solicits feedback from a worldwide audience to build its knowledge base. The company allows technicians to post comments about their products to their Web site, and a representative responds to requests and posts each addition to the FAQ on this Web site. The FAQ is searchable by topic or keyword. It represents a tremendous resource to the medical industry.

Identifying Objectives

Once you have completed your business assessment, you are better able to focus on practical implementation of your Web site. Consider the following basic objectives for developing a Web site:

- To develop a marketing presence on the Web.
- To provide enhanced customer service.
- To reduce overhead expenses.
- To increase revenue through sale of products and information.
- To build a dot-com brand.

Most businesses can justify one or many of the above goals for their Internet strategy. In fact, you can look at many Web sites and find all of the above strategies in them. Dell Computer, found at www.dell.com, is a good example. Obviously, Dell has a strong marketing presence online, and it is backed by a traditional advertising campaign. Dell sells millions of dollars worth of computers through its online efforts. The company provides extended customer service through value-added information on their site. Not only will Dell sell you the computer, but the Web site even has tutorials to teach you how to use it. The site also drastically reduces Dell's overhead expenses as the Internet automatically transmits orders directly to the fulfillment center, with virtually no human intervention. Dell has implemented dot-com branding and offers a variety of tools and options that keep customers coming back.

"Well of course, Dell is a huge company with lots of marketing muscle," you say? "With millions of dollars to back such a campaign?" Sure. Yet even the small folk can implement and benefit from similar strategies, at a fraction of the cost. Remember, the Internet levels the playing field, so that small companies can be perceived as big players and be just as competitive.

Let's take this apart objective by objective.

Developing a Marketing Presence

Every business that plans to stay in business should have at least a minimal marketing presence on the Internet. It's that simple. Think of the influence a Web site can have. Imagine, people can use the Internet to gather valuable information about companies when determining whether to do business with them. Why would they choose a company that withholds this information when so many competitors offer it freely?

Business cards are a must for the business professional—but, ah, they were so limiting until the advent of the World Wide Web. Think of the power of having a Web site for the sole purpose of printing it on your business card! Picture this: You're at one of those cheesy networking meetings. Everyone is shaking hands, spilling out the successes of their respective products or services; at these meetings, everyone is a business prospect, or everyone knows a prospect. A Web address on those 2"x1" cards justifies this experience, because back in the office, while still digesting the chicken that was served at lunch, your prospects have a *real* look at you.

Prospects can take the time to read the information posted to your Web site in an effort to understand what you can offer. They get a feel for the professionalism of your company. I have spoken to people so disappointed by Web sites that it was the deal breaker. On the other hand, a professionally designed Web site can be a deal maker. "I was able to tell from the company's Web site that they had a commitment to quality," said one of my clients, who was concerned that his company's Web site be designed in the most professional manner possible. I recently interviewed an employee who told me that she wanted to work for me because I had a cool Web site. A Web presence is a statement about your business and your professionalism. Done properly it can substantially improve your business success.

Enhanced Customer Service

There is no question that it is difficult for businesses to compete in today's highly competitive business market. Customer service is the key element that makes one company more successful than another. Regardless of how good a product or service is, if it is not backed by a real commitment to customer service, the bad word travels fast. The Internet provides countless opportunities for businesses of any size to improve their customer service programs. In fact, the most successful sites think of the customer first.

To start with, the best Web sites make it easy for customers and prospects to find the information they need, and products are just as easy to buy. Customer service features can range from prompt response to e-mailed questions to tracking purchases and shipment information. After analyzing the traditional processes of an existing business, opportunities for customer service should present themselves clearly.

One client, a debt-management/debt-restructuring firm, came to me for help in differentiating itself from its competition on the Web. I asked the managers about their business process. They told me that they interviewed each customer by phone, reviewing with them their particular debt concerns. The service this company offers is to negotiate with the customer's creditors to stop the accruing of interest, consolidate debts, and manage the customer's payoff in low monthly increments. Telemarketing sales reps use a form to document each creditor and the amount of debt on each account. They simply add up the balance and use a formula to project the monthly payoff.

This was an obvious opportunity. The Web lends itself very well to such a simple application! Now, users can come to the Web site and complete their own form, click the "calculate" button, and instantly get an estimate of their monthly payment.

Why use the Internet instead of telephone customer support? The Internet is "open" 24/7/52—24 hours a day, 7 days a week, 52 weeks a year—without the cost of extra customer-support personnel. Better, it offers potential clients privacy. People get into debt for all sorts of reasons, some of them—such as job loss during an economic downturn or sudden, unexpected medical bills—not their fault. Yet debt is frowned upon in our affluent society, and many debtors are shamed by their circumstances. On the Web, these prospective customers can remain anonymous as they feel their way to recovery, calculation by calculation.

Users perceive the Web site as "interactive"; it gives them instant gratification, something everyone in this fast-paced world appreciates. The likelihood of purchase is very high, because the Web site is able to respond so quickly to the customer's needs.

Reduce Overhead Expenses

The debt management firm above did not just improve its customer service, it cut its overhead expenses. The company receives hundreds of calls by "shoppers," or not-so-serious prospects. Having a Web site will allow the company to weed out many of these shoppers, since most of their questions are being answered online. It also saves time to have the customer "submit" data for online verification. This automated process powerfully streamlines the heavy demand on telephone customer service.

This is true in any type of customer support. Providing customer support is a customer service application, yet imagine how much time in labor (which translates to dollars) is saved with online message boards, FAQs, and the like.

Now think about all the paper that businesses traditionally use. Thanks to the Internet, newsletters, promotional materials, and any and all types of communication can now be paperless and distributed at a mere fraction of the cost.

Increase Revenue Through Sale of Products and Information

With all the hype and media attention that surround holiday-season sales on the Internet, one would think that selling products online is the sole purpose for having a Web site. As we have seen, that is not true. Yet there is no question that consumers love the ease of buying online.

A Web site dedicated to sales could be as simple as a listing of products, plus a telephone number to call and place an order. The most effective and successful Web sites, however, allow consumers to order products instantly online for immediate delivery. If you have not yet purchased your first product online, I suggest you get to it. Online shopping is a new experience. Later we will talk about the quality of that experience and how it varies among Web sites. Before long, you will understand how to develop a profitable Web site.

Business-to-business transactions are soaring in use and popularity. A successful B2B Web site can minimize routine sales calls and increase revenues by making ordering quicker and easier using online forms.

Building a Dot-Com Brand

The Web has spawned a host of new business ventures, while luring household names on board. A few years ago, Yahoo! was nothing more than an exclamation, and trading stocks without a broker was impossible. Now, Yahoo! is one of the most visited sites on the Web, and dozens of online brokerage houses such as E*Trade compete against real-world, full-service stockbrokers. Even United Airlines has found a comfortable place on the Web. What makes these sites role models is the fact that they have built a loyal customer base through one-to-one concepts.

To create a brand presence, you must differentiate your Web site, your product, and your service. You must also create an identity that your customers can and will remember. Admittedly, a corporation with a large budget has the advantage when creating slick ads and buying media space. But with ingenuity you can create effective branding for your e-business endeavor without deep pockets. The bottom line is that you must be creative, consistent, and aggressive. Branding is building recognition through name awareness, visuals, and the ability to deliver exceptional value, so that potential customers can tell your business from the competition.

Branding is not about getting targeted prospects to choose one company over another. It's about making sure that the prospects see the branded company as the only solution. It's the story of Kleenex and the wall covering brand, Sanitas. Kleenex is a brand name for a specific company's facial tissue product, as Sanitas is the name brand for a specific company's fabric-backed wall covering product. These traditional branding campaigns were launched by the respective companies decades ago, and to this day consumers ask for Kleenex when shopping for facial tissue products and Sanitas when buying wall covering. Wall covering consumers seldom even know that there is any other fabric-backed wall covering than Sanitas—in fact, they don't even know the qualities of the wall covering they are buying—they only know it's Sanitas that they want. Meanwhile there are dozens of manufacturers of facial tissue and fabric-backed wall covering who have been far less successful in branding the same quality products.

Brands project credibility and trust. A well-branded product or Web site creates emotion in the user. It has a personality and projects that personality effectively. It motivates the consumer to engage with the site. Over time, it creates strong user loyalty. Brands even have an attitude or point of view. Having some people disagree with you is not so bad. You can't be all things to all people, and trying to do so leaves you undifferentiated.

How do you create a dot-com brand? First you make sure your goals and objectives are very clear. Develop a brief mission statement—and be careful, the Web changes minute by minute, so it must be concise, yet scalable.

Next, select a domain name that people will remember easily. When people think of your Web site, the domain name should pop into their heads. Choosing and registering a good domain name is probably the simplest thing you can do to brand your site and make it easy to find.

At that point, it is time to create the brand. Create the look and feel that will best appeal to your target audience. Make sure the graphics are recognizable and distinguish your company from your competition. Make sure the Web site gives its prospective customers a quality experience. The site must be easy to navigate and must have intuitive and informational design. Every aspect of the site, from functionality to logo placement, communicates your brand.

When you are ready to go, you will need to raise the awareness of the brand by relentlessly marketing and promoting your Web site as being the most innovative, as having the best products and services, and as treating customers as its sole reason for being.

After all that, the work still is not over: You have to maintain the integrity of service by seeing to it that your business practices are up to par with your customer expectations, that your systems and products deliver what your customers want and expect, and that your customer service is solid. Brand maintenance is a job that never ends.

Create a Mission Statement

Once the objectives of the Web site have been identified, a mission statement should be written that clearly and accurately defines the Web site plan. Make sure to include those objectives into a concise, ready-to-go-to-work statement.

My favorite mission statement is that of the Motley Fool at www.fool.com: "To educate, amuse, enrich." They don't get much more clear and concise than that. The Motley Fool was conceived in mid-1993 as an educational resource for people interested in personal finance and investing. It debuted on America Online and moved to its own full-fledged e-business a few years later. Its Web site is chock full of investment theory. There are numerous discussion boards, where subscribers interact with one another and discuss investment strategies. Motley Fool sends several electronic newsletters to subscribers daily. It sells books, research papers, and ad space. All of its products and communications are forever strident in its mission: "To educate, amuse, and enrich." All of the information produced by the Motley Fool is presented in a lighthearted, amusing fashion, and it is extremely informative. By vigorously adhering to a clear mission statement, it has built one of the best-known brands in this highly competitive e-market.

To create a mission statement for your endeavor, begin by asking yourself the following questions:

- What service or product does your company offer?
- Who is the target market?
- What are three to five words that describe the company's image?
- What type of service can you deliver?
- What are your "specialties?"
- Do you want to become a leader in your field, or do you want to service a focused constituency?
- What are three to five goals that you want to achieve with this Web site?

Understanding the Commitment

Do not let me, or anyone, fool you. Any company that develops even the simplest site must make a substantial commitment if it hopes to succeed. It may seem that Web sites run themselves, and you may have heard that once a Web

Figure 15.1. The mission statement for The Motley Fool: Educate, Amuse, Enrich.

site is created, you can sit back and count the inflow of revenue. If life were that easy, we'd all be rich.

It is true that a Web site that works effectively for a company will reduce transaction costs, generate increased revenues, and help to automate some of the traditional customer service features of a business. However, it takes a great amount of effort and commitment to implement, maintain, and market this new endeavor.

That commitment does not end when the Web site goes online, it must continue for as long as the site is active. For example, if a Web site's customer service fails due to lack of commitment—and that is the most common cause of failure—you're plain old sunk! You will never get a customer who suffered from your inattention back to your site.

I have seen it hundreds of times: Companies and other organizations invest money in a Web site and then neglect the incoming e-mail inquiries. I've seen important, critical, and timely data go stale.

A local government agency set up a Web site in 1996. It was a pretty good, basic development effort. Prophet Eenie would have approved. However, the site became the laughingstock of the community when its managers failed to update the data. Three years later, they were still promoting their 1996 calendar of events! No doubt the site's developers started out enthusiastically enough. However, they did not understand the continuing commitment that would be required to make a success of the project. They quickly lost focus, and the Web site fell by the wayside.

Managers who claim to be too busy to maintain their Web site are the same ones who complain that their Web site gets no traffic. Well, you can revisit that government site to laugh if you want, but why else would a user return? There is no value in stale information, nor in any Web site whose managers obviously lack the commitment to run it well.

Information maintenance and customer service are just two of the continuing demands that a well-run Web site will make on your organization's resources. We will run into many more as we continue exploring your options in building and maintaining a good Web site.

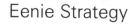

Eenie Strategy

Complete an E-Business Readiness Diagnostic Questionnaire

Determine your e-business readiness by visiting http://strategis.ic.gc.ca/cgi-bin/sc_indps/ebiz/diagnostic/ebiz2.pl. Answering the questions in this diagnostic will give you an opportunity to test your e-business readiness and identify action priorities. It has been designed to help you learn about what is possible for your firm in the digital economy and to assess your own e-business potential. Even if you are already experienced in Web-based operations, you may learn some tips from the questions that will help improve your profitability.

This tool helps you increase your competitiveness and profitability. The assessment will only be useful if it is based on your best evaluation of how your firm is doing at the moment ... not how you would like it to be performing.

Cost: Free.

Meenie Strategy

Implement Audio Training Initiatives to Help Your Employees Grasp E-Business Concepts

Several companies offer audio training products. One well known participant in this field, Gartner Group (www.gartner.com), offers a service called "Talking Technology." It offers a course on CD entitled "Technology Literacy for Business Professionals." This course approaches IT issues from the point of view of the lay business professional. It is nontechnical without being simplistic, unintimidating without talking down to nonspecialists. Talking Business illuminates how business goals and competitive advantage can be achieved through strategic implementation of IT.

Having taken the audio course, management personnel should be comfortable with technology. They will have learned IT concepts in terms that nonengineers can easily grasp, so that they understand the uses of information technology and can "talk the talk" with tech specialists.

Cost: A subscription to Technology Literacy for Business Professionals is $500 per year.

Miney Strategy

Conduct In-House Training to Create Employee Awareness of E-Business Requirements

Improve your business and technology strategic planning methodology, increase your teams' skill and productivity, and discover cutting-edge management techniques with in-house training from Cutter Consortium's (www.cutter.com) expert senior consultants. Ranging from negotiating techniques, to just-in-time training using a live project, to leadership development, their extensive list of in-house workshops can be customized to meet your enterprise's needs.

Cost: Fees begin at $3,500 for in-house workshops and depend on workshop content and length.

Moe Strategy

Hire a Top-Notch Consulting Team to Get You on the Road to E-Business Success

The Sutherland Group (www.suth.com) is a global electronic customer-relations management (eCRM) company, recognized as a leader in the innovative use of technology for reaching, retaining, and taking care of a client's customers most effectively. Sutherland says its mission is to help clients increase their productivity and customer satisfaction by linking all facets of the front-office and back-office interactions and making them accessible over the Internet.

The company's proposition is unique, because it offers three methods of deploying multichannel customer-care solutions:

- On-premise: Sutherland will design, configure, and deploy Web-based CRM solutions at the client's site, integrating call centers, Web sites, e-mail, wireless communications, and back-office systems.

- Hosted CRM infrastructure: This company can also give clients access to Suthernet, the company's secure CRM business and communications infrastructure.

- Process management: Sutherland also can manage the end-to-end customer-interaction operation on the client's behalf. This includes the management of human resources deployed to handle specific business functions for a contracted period and ensuring specific business results.

Cost: On-premise efforts typically start at $100,000, either as a fixed fee or priced by time and materials. Use of Sutherland's hosted CRM infrastructure requires a one-time fee of $10,000 to $200,000 for consulting, customization, and setup, plus monthly service fees ranging between $100 and $1,000, depending on the number of users, CRM package, service-level agreements, additional functionality, and length of contract. Contracts for process management range anywhere from $500,000 to $5 million.

Chapter 16

Defining Success

As you plan, you must be able to rationalize your expectations. At the beginning, the Internet looked and felt like a bonanza, with companies growing at rates never seen in the traditional economy. But as we learned in the first year of the new century, more businesses fail than succeed, even in the magic world of the Internet. Set realistic goals for your business. Understand that you probably will not see the results of your efforts for at least six months after full launch of your site. We have enough history now to know that a successful venture usually ramps up for three to five years before it becomes profitable. Defining long-term success is part of the planning process.

In fact, the first step may be figuring out just how success is best measured, given the objectives of your Web site. It will be calculated differently for each business, and for each of the business models you may choose.

If you hope simply to increase revenue by selling products and information, it is relatively easy to measure success. Obvious criteria include:

- Number of customers and repeat customers

- Number of sales

- Revenue generated

What if you want to develop a marketing presence? It sounds like almost the same goal as before, but your definition of success quickly becomes more complicated. Now it can be important to consider such factors as:

- Number of visitors to the site
- Number of registrations
- Feedback and comments
- Increased company recognition
- Increased credibility with your target audience

The goal of improving customer service or reducing overhead might be measured by still other criteria:

- Number of visitors to the site
- Quicker resolution of problems
- Reduction of incidents requiring staff response
- Average time spent on the site
- Number of registrants on the site or for newsletters, support alerts, etc.
- Decreased marketing and distribution costs

Success in building a dot-com brand may be the most difficult to measure of all. Though a few dot-coms, such as eBay, have been profitable almost from the first day, some of the strongest brands in e-commerce—think of Amazon.com—are still spilling red ink by the gallon after years in operation. For this goal, suitable measures of success might include:

- Number of visitors to the site
- A strong media presence (everyone's talking about you)
- Quality of the data gathered by visitors
- Credibility with your target audience

Many tools are available to help you analyze the results of your Web site. Much of the necessary information is collected as log files maintained by the Web server and recording all the activity that takes place on your Web site. It may be supplemented by data compiled in user registration databases resident on your site, recorded by databases handling site transactions, and bought as reports from third-party services that compile and verify data for the site.

If you have your own server, you can purchase or develop a custom statistics analysis application, depending on your need. The best known Web statistics application on the market today is Webtrends (www.webtrends.com). However, many other applications are available. Some are free, while others cost several hundred dollars or up to several hundred thousand dollars.

Webtrends has a number of products, but the company's basic log analyzer can be purchased for as little as $150.

If your Web site is being hosted by an ISP, make sure it is compiling log files for your site. For a small additional fee, most ISPs offer a tool for analyzing these log files. Log files are the first step in collecting user information. They can record the following types of data:

- How many "hits" have been recorded. Hits refer to the number of files requested by a user. In the early days of the Web, the number of hits was an important indicator of traffic. As we have grown more sophisticated however, we have come to recognize that measuring a site by the number of hits recorded can be deceiving. Later on we will learn how a Web page is composed of several types of files. Your home page could contain five graphic images along with a few welcoming paragraphs. When a user "calls" your home page by typing in the URL, www.yourhomepage.com, the log file will not record one hit to this page, but six. It counts the five images and the HTML or text page. Thus, counting hits is a poor measurement of traffic. Even if we understand what is going on, this kind of "hit inflation" is deceiving.

- How many "impressions" have been recorded. This gets a little better. The number of impressions is the number of times a single page is requested. Basically this data records only the HTML pages that are accessed, rather than HTML and all other file types.

- How many "unique users" have visited your Web site or a page within your site. Now, this becomes even more interesting. The "unique user" is identified by a computer user's address. The computer user's address is assigned by the service provider through which the user connected to the Internet. You see, when a user's computer links to the Internet, that computer is assigned an IP (Internet protocol) address. (See Appendix B for an overview of IP addressing.) So, log files can track user sessions by IP address only. Analysis tools that count "unique users" merely record the first time that the new IP address arrived at your Web site.

  Now, while unique user data is better than hits and more informative than impressions, it still lacks precision. Most service providers today use a system known as dynamic addressing. A computer's IP address is not fixed; instead, a new address is assigned each time the computer connects to the Internet. This means that today I was 209.94.121.7, and tomorrow I might be 209.94.121.22. Thus, I will be recorded as a unique user each day, even though I am not. Again, we have a kind of statistic inflation.

Recording unique users has one other limitation: Unless your visitors actually sign in and tell you who they are, you don't know them as individuals. You do not know their names, their e-mail addresses, and certainly not their physical addresses. While the number of unique users gives you an idea of how many people are visiting your site, and whether the number is growing or shrinking, it does little in helping to establish a relationship with your customers.

- What time users access the site. Analysis of this data will show activity levels at different times of the day. Perhaps your site is most heavily visited after 6:00 p.m. You might deduce that the majority of users are visiting your site after work. Maybe users visit your site more on a weekend. This information can help with future marketing efforts and bandwidth concerns.

- What state or country the users come from. Although we cannot know personal information about the people who visited the site unless the user offers it, studying IP addressing can at least indicate their state or country of origin. Every Internet Service Provider is provided with a block of IP addresses, which they then distribute to subscribers as they dial in. If an ISP in Switzerland applied for a group of IP addresses, the log files and analysis tools can identify the provider and tell you its location. When a user arrives with an IP 65.221.69.8, for example, we can find out that this address is assigned to a Swiss ISP, and we therefore assume that the user is in Switzerland.

  Unfortunately, even this can be deceiving. The problem is that some ISPs or commercial online services cover more than one region or country. For example, all of America Online customers look like they live in AOL's home town in Virginia, because all of the IPs designated by that company originate in Virginia.

- Are there any bad links on the Web site? The log files and analysis tools will report any errors found. For example, the log files record all the requests that a user makes. If that request returns an error like "page not found," it could reveal a bad link on the site.

- What browsers and computer platforms are users using? The log files can detect what browsers your visitors are using and what computer platforms their computers run. An analysis tool will report that X percent of users are using Windows 95 and MS Explorer 4.0, Y percent are using Windows 98 and Netscape 6.0, and so on.

- How did users find your Web site? The log files also record where a user linked from, so your analysis tool can report on referrals from search engines and Internet directories such as Yahoo.com and Excite.com.

- What do customers do at your site? The files will tell you what pages are most popular, most frequently visited, and so on. More sophisticated tools will show clicking patterns throughout a site, including what areas or pages they visit, how long they stay there, how often they jump from one page to another, and whether they make a purchase.

Very often Web sites will use "cookies" to track users' behavior. Cookies are actually little programs that are sent to a user's computer when he or she visits a Web site. Each time the user returns to the Web site, the site communicates with the cookie it planted on the previous visit. A great deal of data can be retrieved through cookies, including how often users have visited your site and what other sites they have visited. Inevitably, the use of cookies has raised significant consumer privacy concerns. Each browser is therefore equipped with an "accept cookie" option, so that consumers can refuse cookies if they wish.

Of course, the best analysis will come from user registrations and the information that users voluntarily supply. Whenever possible, your efforts should focus on getting users to identify themselves willingly. From their information, you learn far more about the users you can target; you can find out what they want or need and what you can do to better serve these needs.

Eenie Strategy

Conduct Surveys and Get Feedback from Your Users

A company called Zoomerang (www.zoomerang. com) offers the ability to conduct professional surveys, get prompt responses to questions, and analyze the results in real time. The tool is very easy to use; just choose from more than 100 modifiable report templates to get the data you need. It is easy for visitors as well. Users can access the survey from any Web browser, and answer at will as easily as using e-mail. Their information is confidential and secure; your e-mail addresses and surveys are kept private. The Zoomerang survey tool also provides dynamic real-time analysis of results, so that you can make decisions immediately. This is one cheap, easy way to take the guesswork out of managing your online business.

Cost: Free.

Meenie Strategy

Monitor Your Hosting Service for Assurance of Performance

Netwhistle.com's (www.netwhistle.com) BusinessWhistle solution offers a customizable service that can provide a full assessment of your Web site's performance and availability. This solution offers 24/7 site monitoring via HTTP, PING, SMTP, POP3, and HTTPS in intervals of 5 minutes to 30 minutes. These tools test the site to make sure it is functioning properly. If there is no response from the site, an indication that the site is not functioning, you can be notified by e-mail or pager.

The BusinessWhistle service features:

- External testing, for a true end-user perspective
- Weekly report of previous week's performance of all targets
- RTSP (Real-Time Streaming Protocol) monitoring
- Text search and verification
- Notification of slow download time

Cost: Ranges from $9.50 to $154.90 per month.

Miney Strategy

Benchmark Your Success Against Industry Standards

Reports by eMarketer (www.emarketer.com) can help you benchmark your performance against others in your industry. eMarketer is the world's leading provider of Internet statistics. It combines original analysis with aggregated results from leading sources worldwide. EMarketer's Web site has been visited by millions of online professionals from more than 140 countries; its newsletters are sent to 350,000 e-mail addresses every week. The company's articles, market projections, and analytical commentaries are featured by hundreds of news organizations and business publications every week.

Cost: Reports average $795 each.

Moe Strategy

Create a Media Presence for Your Web Site

Eric Ward, a Public Relations maven, can create a personalized linking and awareness building campaign for content-based Web launches. The success of these campaigns is a direct result of his personalized approach. His company's intricate public relations tactics involve a combination of carefully researched and selected site announcements, submissions, link requests, and site introductions. After reviewing the specific content of your site and researching your industry, Ward locates and submits press releases to outlets that are a perfect match for your business, based on your Web site's subject, content, and features. Ward, a one-person shop, offers two services located at www.netpost.com and www.urlwire.com. These activities are aimed at major Internet media contacts, editors, writers, reporters, site reviewers, portal site selectors, news outlets, news headline services, etc., that are appropriate for your particular site.

Cost: Both www.netpost.com and www.ulrwire.com are affordable for any business, but Ward is "obsessively cautious about which clients [he] takes" and scrutinizes submissions so that only major Web launches, events, and happenings are sent to his list of high-priority media contacts.

Part IV

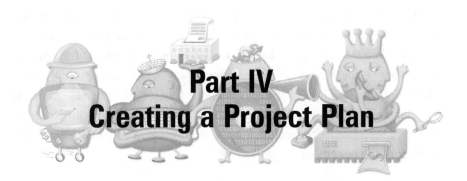

Part IV
Creating a Project Plan

Now that you have fine tuned the focus of your e-business and have developed a budget for Web site development, it is time to lay out a detailed plan of the site itself. Building even a simple Web site can be a complex undertaking, and there is no substitute for preproduction planning.

It is important to stay in touch with the Web while you are planning the project. Spend time surfing and looking at other Web sites. Be sure to subscribe to the "best sites of the week" mailing lists like the one on Yahoo!. Notice the many variations in home-page style; some site designs are conspicuously "artsy," others are straightforward directories, while still others have a "newsy" layout. Notice sites that have instant graphical impact and those that have implemented a simple and elegant home-page design. Notice the links contained on the home page: Are they intuitive enough that you know immediately just what the site offers? Be aware of the smallest details, such as font size and color combinations. All these factors contribute to the total impact of the Web site, and to the site's efficiency in achieving its goals.

The entire Web site must be designed with the expected visitors' needs and expectations in mind. The home page is the front door to the company it represents. It is imperative that the imagery of the site reflect the "voice" of the company.

The appropriate voice is defined by the objective of the site. Is the site intended to sell games and toys? If so, its voice or tone could be humorous, fun, and very colorful. Likewise, if the site is selling high-end oriental rugs, it must express that high-end quality; it must be elegant and artistically enticing. An accounting firm may want a more subdued home page that exhibits their commitment to professionalism—no joking around about money and taxes. A cutting-edge technology business needs a state-of-the-art look to be believable. Selecting the appropriate voice for your business is one of the most important steps in site development.

All these factors go into the project plan, the blueprint for the site. Once the plan is complete, any Web site developer should be able to follow this blueprint to produce a Web site to its specifications. Creating a plan that meets this goal is the subject of the next three chapters.

Chapter 17

Money Matters

Even when you have figured out exactly what your Web site is supposed to accomplish, a critical question remains to be answered: What is all this going to cost?

In this section we will focus on the cost of getting your Web site up and running. It would be nice also to project the revenue your site will generate, but that is a more difficult proposition. If this is a new venture, it may not be possible at all.

You probably know how much your company is willing to spend on the Web site. Eenie companies will go for the do-it-yourself approach, investing time wherever possible, rather than their limited funds. Meenie and Miney companies will have a set budget, probably modest when measured against what they hope to accomplish, and will measure risk/reward, while carefully considering their objectives. And Moe companies are looking at long-term scenarios with hefty budgets.

Web-site plans and budgets come in all shapes and sizes. The details of yours will depend on a variety of factors. These include:

- The size of the prospective Web site
- The design of the Web site
- The amount of graphics and multimedia planned for the site
- The level, sophistication, and quality of the programming on the site
- The types of databases, if any, to interface with

- The types of applications and partner applications that will be integrated into the site
- The amount of testing needed to validate the site
- The amount and type of marketing necessary to lure traffic to the site
- The amount of maintenance needed to keep the site fresh and dynamic
- Hosting and bandwidth requirements
- Project management and other personnel needs
- Who is doing the development? The best Web design consultants will cost a lot more than assigning the job to the hacker wannabe in your mail room, but the results are likely to be a good deal more certain.

By now, most business professionals have come to recognize that the Internet is a medium they must embrace in order to stay ahead of the competition. Many have brainstormed and discovered ways to use the Internet to increase their revenues and expand their business dramatically. Thus, reviewing, analyzing, and modifying business objectives to include an e-business strategy is becoming standard practice for businesses of all sizes.

For an ambitious e-business site, it can all become expensive, and sometimes too expensive to pay for out of existing funds. Banks and other lending and investment institutions are becoming accustomed to seeing requests for funding e-business ventures. Whether you will need their help is a question that should be addressed at the start of your project and answered firmly early in the process. If so, having a solid plan in place with realistic budgeting and expense plans becomes doubly important. A solid, professional budget is essential to getting extra funding from a bank or venture-capital firm.

In order to develop a budget for an e-business Web site, it makes sense to group costs by activity. The main activities are typically:

- Home page design
- Layout and navigation
- HTML coding
- Content creation
- Application development
- Testing
- Launching

- Marketing
- Hosting
- Ongoing maintenance

In any Web-site development budget, certain factors almost always stand out. These costly items include home-page design, layout and navigation, application development, marketing, and ongoing maintenance.

The design elements are essential to the message of the Web site. How sophisticated must it be? Do you need a top-level design firm, or will you be happy with design work from your own marketing department? These considerations obviously will affect your budget.

Depending on how large the site is, layout and navigation issues also may affect your budget. Simply getting around among dozens of Web pages can require a substantial investment in programming.

The applications your site will use will absolutely affect the budget. Look at the charting utilities on brokerage-house Web sites, home-financing software built into the sites of real estate companies, and other Web-based programs. Adding even one such function to your site can dramatically expand your costs.

You must include a budget for marketing in your overall plan. Remember, believing the old adage of "if you build it they will come" is the biggest mistake you can make.

Lastly, the site has to stay fresh, and customers have to be served from it. Someone will have to be assigned to develop new material for the site, cull obsolete pages, resolve any problems with your Internet service provider, and so on. So, the amount of ongoing maintenance dedicated to the site will greatly affect budget.

In the charts that follow, the Prophets have put together a sample budget for their respective constituencies. It should be helpful to use these charts as a guideline for producing a budget for your Web-site development endeavor.

Web Development Budgets

Eenie Development Budget

Design is typically not a critical component of your plan. You just want to get the word out there and stand tall as an Internet business with a presence on the Web. You will use tools that look the most professional and symbolize your company best. Or you will design the site yourself.

Web Site Development Budget
Simple Web site with 5 content pages

	Development time (hours)	Estimated fees/hr	Total	% of project	% of grouped activities
Developing specifications	2	20	$40.00	5%	5%
Home-page design	2	20	$40.00	5%	
Layout and navigation	0	0	$0.00	0%	
HTML coding (Sub pages)	1	20	$20.00	3%	
Application development	0	0	$0.00	0%	
Testing	1	20	$20.00	3%	
Launching	0	0	$0.00	0%	
Annual maintenance (2 hrs/mo)	24	20	$480.00	62%	72%
Annual hosting ($15/mo)			$180.00	23%	23%
Marketing			Discretionary		
TOTAL			$780.00	100%	100%

Table 17.1. Eenie's sample Web development budget

Meenie Development Budget

Your budget can support hiring a freelance designer to apply your company's look to the site. Perhaps you already have printed materials with graphics and graphic representations of your products on them. If so, you can incorporate them into your Web site. Given your budget, you will want to stay away from the bells and whistles that a more elaborate site might adopt.

Web Site Development Budget
Web site with 10 content pages and a custom shopping cart application

	Development time (hours)	Estimated fees/hr	Total	% of project	% of grouped activities
Developing specifications	10	20	$200.00	2%	2%
Home-page design	15	100	$1,500.00	15%	
Layout and navigation	10	100	$1,000.00	10%	
HTML coding	20	75	$1,500.00	15%	
Application development	20	125	$2,500.00	26%	
Testing	3	75	$225.00	2%	
Launching	2	75	$150.00	2%	
Annual maintenance (2 hrs/mo)	24	15	$360.00	4%	74%
Annual hosting ($30/mo)			$360.00	4%	4%
Marketing			$2,000.00	20%	20%
TOTAL			$9,795.00	100%	100%

Table 17.2. Meenie's sample Web development budget

Miney Development Budget

You can hire a respectable designer or Web shop to create your site. It might not be cutting edge in its look, it may not be visually stunning, but it will be very professional.

Web Site Development Budget
Web site with 30 content pages and application

	Development time (hours)	Estimated fees/hr	Total	% of project	% of grouped activities
Developing specifications	20	20	$400.00	1%	1%
Home-page design	30	100	$3,000.00	7%	
Layout and navigation	20	100	$2,000.00	5%	
HTML coding	60	75	$4,500.00	10%	
Application development			$15,000.00	35%	
Testing	7	75	$525.00	1%	
Launching	5	75	$375.00	1%	
Annual maintenance (8 hrs/week)	416	20	$8,320.00	19%	78%
Annual hosting ($30/mo)			$360.00	1%	1%
Marketing			$8,500.00	20%	20%
TOTAL			$42,980.00	100%	100%

Table 17.3. Miney's sample Web development budget

Moe Development Budget

Hire a world-class design shop to custom design the site, adding bells and whistles and robust back-end applications. This site will be able to handle a great deal of traffic, so that millions of users can access your site regularly to browse and transact with you.

Web Site Development Budget
Web site with 150 content pages and application

	Development time (hours)	Estimated fees/hr	Total	% of project	% of grouped activities
Developing specifications	250	35	$8,750.00	2%	2%
Home-page design	200	100	$20,000.00	4%	
Layout and navigation	100	100	$10,000.00	2%	
HTML coding	300	75	$22,500.00	4%	
Application development	1500	125	$187,500.00	37%	
Testing	50	75	$3,750.00	1%	
Launching	20	75	$1,500.00	0%	
Annual maintenance (40 hrs/week)	2080	35	$72,800.00	14%	62%
Annual hosting ($600/mo)			$7,200.00	1%	1%
Marketing			$175,000.00	34%	34%
TOTAL			**$509,000.00**	**100%**	**100%**

Table 17.4. Moe's sample Web development budget

Minimizing Costs for Web Development

There are several basic principles for keeping site-development costs under control. Omit even one, and your chances of budget trouble skyrocket.

Thorough planning is a must. Through careful planning, you will have nearly laid out the site before the first line of HTML code is written. You will want to give the written plan to Web-development consultants or firms to bid on the job. Once you have reviewed the designers' other work, you have an idea of the type of graphics and styles that they can provide. The developer can follow your instructions by putting the graphics and content into the style of your choice. Your planning efforts will pay off.

For smaller sites, get bids by page rather than by the hour. Many developers are willing to bill in this fashion. This is the only way to be certain that your Web project will not run far over budget at this critical early stage.

Prepare content in advance. You have built your plan and defined the content that will be placed on the site. Gather all the content in digital form, and get ready to hand it to the developer you choose for the site construction.

Text is cheap. Remember that text is cheaper to produce than graphics, audio, video, animation, or any other effect that you might want to use. Text can be copied and placed on a Web page fairly easily. Special formatting may take additional time, however.

Avoid the bells and whistles. You have seen Web sites with flashing icons and rotating buttons, and they can be impressive—to people whose love of technology causes them to lose track of the site's real purpose, which is to satisfy customers. The truth is that visitors don't particularly care for so much of this "eye candy." The less of this programming you use, the more money you will save on your site design, and the more effective your site is likely to be.

Be realistic. Do not include features you cannot maintain on the Web site. Do not make promises you cannot keep. Do not promise daily news alerts if you cannot dedicate the time to producing them.

Manage the project. No matter whom you hire for the job, the work must be overseen. This is your Web site, not anyone else's. No one will benefit from a good, efficient job of site development, or suffer from a poor one, but your company. If you hire someone outside to develop the Web site, someone in house still must manage the project. Likewise, if you hire someone in house, another in-house person must have the responsibility of overseeing the project.

Eenie Strategy

Access Low-Interest Funding Through the Small Business Administration

The Small Business Administration (www.sba.gov) offers a number of loan programs that may be perfectly suited to your business. Once a small-business borrower meets the lender's requirements for credit, the lender may request a guarantee from the SBA.

One of their programs, called SBA*LowDoc*, has the following requirements:

- The purpose of the loan must be for starting or growing a business.

- The existing business (including affiliates) employs no more than 100 people and has average annual sales for the preceding three years not exceeding $5 million.

- The business and its owners have good credit.

- The business owners are of good character.

Cost: Interest rates can be negotiated between the borrower and lender, may be fixed or variable, are tied to the prime rate (as published in *The Wall Street Journal*), and may not exceed certain SBA maximums.

Meenie Strategy

Purchase Software to Assist with Planning and Budgeting for Your Web Project

Go to www.Bplans.com and find thousands of pages of free sample plans, interactive planning and budgeting tools, and expert advice. Use the StartingCosts Tool for a quick and easy (and free) budgeting tool.

The site is sponsored by Palo Alto Software, Inc. (www.paloalto. com), a company that also produces packaged planning and budgeting software called Web Strategy Pro. The software assists in defining your Web strategy, establishing a budget for it, and planning the direction of your online business, whether it's content, commerce, or community driven.

Costs: $89.95 with a 60-day guarantee.

Miney Strategy

If Your Business Is Owned by Women, Find Venture Capitalists Who Care

An annual event called Springboard 2001/ 2002 (www.springboard2000.org) is a national initiative to accelerate women's access to the equity markets as entrepreneurs and investors. The National Women's Business Council, in collaboration with leading entrepreneurial and business organizations and key technology partners and sponsors, has launched a series of venture capital forums showcasing women entrepreneurs in technology. These forums are designed to increase investments in women-led firms and to facilitate the flow of new deals to investors. To qualify and present, you must be:

- A woman-led business seeking seed, early, and later-round investments.

- A high-growth company, primarily in the technology, e-commerce, telecommunications, and life-sciences sectors.

- A key executive with a significant equity stake in the company.

A team of leading venture capitalists and service providers screen companies' business plans and applications. Applicants are selected based on an aggressive, growth-oriented business plan, a talented management team, large target market, and a clear competitive advantage over potential rivals.

Costs: Free, though not all applications are accepted.

Moe Strategy

Seek Venture Financing for Your Dot-Com Plan

Clearstone Venture Partners (www. clearstone.com) is an independent venture capital firm with offices in Pasadena and Palo Alto, California. Clearstone has invested in dozens of successful early stage technology companies. Clearstone focuses on working closely with high-potential technology companies to help them become leaders in their industries. They invest in early stage technology companies that have the potential to dominate large markets. They focus on technology companies that combine creative and sustainable business models with exceptional management talent. Their investment parameters are flexible, but generally adhere to the following guidelines:

- Industry focus—software and communications businesses
- Stage of investment—preferred first institutional investor
- Geographic preference—nationally focused
- Investment size—seeking investment opportunities that allow for initial investments of between $1 million and $15 million and enable them to invest $10 million to $30 million over the life cycle of a company's private capital needs

Costs: Submitting a business plan is free. Accepting money will cost part of your company. But you knew that.

Chapter 18

Home Page and Web Content

Your home page usually contains very little real data, yet it may well be the most important page on your Web site. It provides the visitor's first impression of your site and your company. This, more than any other single factor, may decide whether a potential customer digs further into your products or services, or moves on to your competition.

Your home page has two main purposes: to provide branding for the company and to assure quick, easy access to your site's content areas. It almost always should include a concise description of your company's products and services and the objectives of your Web site. It must include links to all the key areas of the site.

Organizing those areas is one of the most important aspects of laying out your site. A general rule of thumb is to focus on no more than six to eight major topics or categories for a small to moderate-size Web site and up to 12 or 14 for a very large Web site. Every bit of information that you gather must fit into one of these categories. Each fact, everything you want your visitors to see, will be reached through a chain of links from your home page to the main category, and onward from there to the actual page of data. Those chains of links will form the skeleton of your Web site.

Review the site's objectives carefully. If the primary goal is to sell products, you need a link right from the home page to a products catalog. On some small shopping sites, the entire home page consists of the product listing and a series of product images. Other information is much less relevant; links to it are usually presented in a very small font in some relatively insignificant section of the page.

For example, someone who intends to buy merchandise directly from the Web site probably will not be very interested in the company's key executives. All that consumer wants is, say, to find toys for a summer outing. Your visitors are looking for red, 27-inch diameter beach balls for less than $12 each, and they want to locate them as quickly as possible. Needless company details should not get in the way.

Your site's audience also will help to shape the layout. If several different types of users are expected to visit—business users and consumers, for example—the home page should have separate, distinguishable topic areas for each group. When business users click on something that looks like a link to a business section, they should enter an area particular to their interests; consumers should be able to use a different, easily recognized link to reach features that are of special interest to them.

Let us walk through the early stages of an actual example: We will plan a Web site for the accounting firm of McKinley and McKinley, CPAs. The site is intended as a marketing vehicle for the firm. Secondarily, but just as important, there is a customer service goal: the development of an online, interactive tax planning section for McKinley's clients.

First we need to identify the "voice" of the site, which must be expressed in the home-page design: For this accounting firm, the home page should have a very professional, conservative look and feel. Maroon and blue are the firm's colors; designing the site using these colors would be consistent with McKinley's traditional marketing materials and would be an aid to branding. The firm has a professionally designed logo that will appear on the home page. The firm is proud of its size—small enough to provide personalized service, but large enough to have several areas of expertise. The management would like to place a group photo of the 25 partners, accountants, and staff on the home page, next to their slogan: "Small enough for a personal touch, large enough to have diverse experience."

On the top right corner, there will be a "client login" box, which existing clients will click to enter their personal, interactive area of the site.

Finally, the home page needs links to the main categories of information within the site. Topic areas will include history of the firm, areas of expertise, income tax news, meet the partners, client services, and "contact us." The content for these sections must be collected from existing marketing materials or further developed for the Web.

Developing Content

What should a Web site say? With time so tight these days, how much do prospective customers really want to read? In my experience, trying to get this balance right has been the most confusing and time consuming part of planning a Web site for business professionals.

First, it is no easy chore to compile all the relevant copy for a Web site. In many cases, a company already has a great deal written about it. Most firms have been the subject of articles in local newspapers, and in regional and trade magazines. Company executives will have written their own articles and speeches. And you will have the usual array of marketing materials, brochures, and catalogs to deal with. Simply taking that information and pasting it to a Web site is probably not the best solution.

Secondly, the Web is a very different medium. Television, magazine ads, and even printed catalogs are focused upon capturing the customer's attention in very short time spans, 30 seconds or less. Traditional advertising is so limiting that the messages conveyed are often mere imagery, rather than useful information. The Internet provides room to expand. Web pages have no fixed length, no limit to what they can contain, and one subject can be linked to another, in whatever order the visitor's interests direct. Every area of the company's business—its products and services, industry data, hiring needs, and much more—can be explained at length on the Web site, limited only by download times and the visitor's willingness to follow the links. This represents a radical change in the way that companies communicate with their customers and the public.

On the Internet, businesses must adopt a strategy of actively getting its message across to potential customers in a format that offers value. While the idea of providing value is not new to business, it requires different strategies and supporting tactics to be successful within the Internet community.

In the case of McKinley and McKinley, we have a relatively limited selection of printed materials to choose from. As a purely service organization, the company has relied largely on personal contacts and word-of-mouth "advertising" by existing clients to bring in new business. However, they do have several brochures promoting their skill in general accounting and tax preparation for business and private clients. In addition, General Partner John McKinley has presented several speeches about tax policy, financial planning, and entrepreneurship, and those texts are available. Beyond this, filling a substantial Web site with interesting, useful material may take some digging.

In general, the most important truth about content is true of the Internet itself. There are no rules in this new territory. There is simply no science to define what type of information a business should provide on its Web site, or how much of that information to provide. Review the following guidelines and consider the type of information most relevant to your e-business project. Chapter 19 will consider how much information to provide and how to lay out that information for maximum effect and value.

Information Is Value!

The Internet is a value-added world, and it is an information-based world. Information is value. People will keep coming back to a Web site if it offers something of value. Useful information is the most critical element of an online marketing campaign. For example, customers like to know what a company has done for them lately, so stay on top of what's new and different about what your company does or offers. Offer information about related products, rather than just strictly proprietary products. Do product comparisons, and offer industry news. Offer information that everyone in your industry knows, but isn't saying! Be the leader in this new game, and garner support from your customers and prospects alike.

Change or update this valuable information often enough to keep people coming back. Even if your products have not changed in years, find something new to say about them. This helps keep your Web pages fresh, so your visitors have a reason to come back. A successful business model can be established simply by delivering useful information to interested users/potential customers in a timely and responsive manner. Tactically speaking, this provides an opportunity to develop a relationship with the customer before a specific need arises. The business is then foremost in the customer's mind when a purchase must be made.

Product and Service Information

They say a picture is worth a thousand words. On the World Wide Web, you can have all the pictures you want, preferably accompanied by well-written text descriptions. Technical drawings, specification sheets, and other product-related data should be available to all customers and prospective customers who visit the Web site. Almost any graphic image, photograph, or video can appear on your site, so long as it captures the nature of your company's product and services.

Catalogs are an obvious place to use graphics, and online catalogs have substantial advantages over their real-world equivalent. In the tangible world, publishing a catalog requires printing thousands of brochures or magazines, often in full color. This is an expensive undertaking. In contrast, putting a catalog on a Web site is nearly free, save for the personnel cost of making up the pages. A printed catalog fixes your company's prices until the next edition appears, even if your costs have soared in the meantime; Web pages can be altered at will. And printed catalogs are seen only by the recipients, while online catalogs are accessible to everyone with an Internet account. Further, an interactive, dynamically produced catalog encourages customers to buy, because it is so easy to find interesting products and place an order without ever picking up the phone or visiting your store.

There are some basic items that should be included in any interactive catalog:

- Product images—In many industries, product pictures are critically important to the success of the sale. Animations depicting products in action are valuable selling tools. Videos and demonstrations also can be informative and very alluring. While a wholesaler of, say, industrial ball bearings might find product images less useful than some other companies, attractive pictures of the merchandise are almost mandatory for consumer-oriented retailers.

- Detailed product descriptions—Unlike an expensive printed catalog, the cost of additional pages on a Web site is minimal. Go for the details! If a prospective customer shows interest in a product, don't deny them every piece of information that can possibly be provided. Start out with the key features and perhaps a bulleted list of the benefits of the product. Then let detail-oriented consumers click through to the specifics of features and functions. Comparison shoppers are likely to resent being deprived of the chance to make a really informed decision, but appreciate a marketer who tells them everything they feel they need to know.

- Pricing—One of my pet peeves is finding a product that interests me, and then having to dig for the price. Make the product prices easy to find. Then update them at will, and capture profits that would have been missed in the days of paper catalogs.

- Order Forms—This is one of the biggest benefits of marketing on the Internet: having tireless virtual order takers at work on your Web site 24/7. Make sure the order forms are easy to find and easy to use! A visitor who finds a clumsy Web site knows that a more convenient one is just a mouse-click away.

For McKinley and McKinley, and many other service organizations, catalog-style information is a limited possibility. We will be limited to a few general Web pages describing the firm's expertise in specific areas of accounting. These are, of course, absolutely necessary to make it clear to visitors just what the firm does. However, we will need to supplement these pages with other material chosen to emphasize the company's professionalism and in-depth knowledge of its field.

News and Events

Make sure the target audience knows about upcoming activities and new offerings: Put that information on the Web site. By updating the site with news and events, you can keep users checking back for items of interest. Each new visit is another opportunity to win new customers and reinforce your relationship with old ones.

Our accountants will occasionally be able to tell of hiring a new, highly skilled employee, promoting within the firm, speeches given by executives, and perhaps the acquisition of a prestigious new client. However, most of the news at the McKinley and McKinley Web site will deal with developments in accounting practices, state and federal tax law, and related material. This will reinforce the firm's image of expertise and professionalism.

Newsletters

People regularly access newsletters with industry insight, hints, or tips. A company newsletter may work fine here, depending on the content. An original newsletter can generate considerable interest. Store current and past issues of newsletters on the Web site, so people visiting can review material from previous issues. If there is substantial demand for the newsletters, consider making this area of the site into a profit center and charge for the subscription. If you choose to send newsletters by e-mail, add links in the newsletter to lead the users back to your Web site. The more they return to your Web site, the more you influence them with your branding message.

McKinley and McKinley has not published a newsletter before this. However, the need to update its Web site with interesting, useful information will provide it with material for a print edition as well as its online publishing. The partners are now wondering whether it might be worth their effort to produce a real-world newsletter for Net-deficient clients.

Press Releases

Posting press releases is a great way to inform prospects, customers, and the media about your business. Keep the users aware of what is happening within your company.

McKinley and McKinley never saw this as a high priority for their rather traditional kind of practice. However, as long as this material is being gathered for the Web site, it seems only reasonable to spin it off for traditional media as well. Once more, it seems that the Internet is feeding its influence back into the brick-and-mortar world.

Customer Service Information

Customer support is a critical part of marketing products and services. Providing useful service information can help reduce incoming phone calls and redundant questions, and customers will appreciate the convenience of finding what they need without having to call or write. Information regarding stocking, delivery, and shipping as well as installation, configuration, and technical issues can easily be communicated to a given customer, anywhere in the world. A company may economically offer 24-hour, worldwide support and service to its customer base without concern for physical location of either its customers or support personnel.

In the case of McKinley and McKinley, much of their customer service work consists of answering routine questions about expense records needed for state and local taxes. This will be condensed into FAQ pages on the Web site. The firm is also thinking about putting an appointment calendar on the Web site, so clients who need to meet with an accountant can make the arrangements online without taking time from a secretary or receptionist. In addition, each accountant is considering a direct chat tool so their clients can chat with them when they need critical information.

Reviews

Maintaining an online listing of favorable reviews or articles about a company is a nice added touch. McKinley and McKinley has several to post on its Web site.

Contracts and Testimonials

Web pages are a good vehicle for telling others about recent contracts won by the company. Also consider posting testimonials. Again, McKinley and McKinley will be uploading a number of testimonials from satisfied clients.

Documentation

Detailed documentation about a company's offerings can be published on their Web pages. Long copy is very effective on the Internet. People want to be able to dive into specific information about a company and its products or services. In addition, many companies utilize Adobe Acrobat, an application that converts documents into a format that can be read through Adobe's browser plug-in Acrobat Reader, which is available for most popular computers and operating systems. Companies often convert large and lengthy manuals and product specifications into PDF format, so that Web users can download the file for their personal use.

Of course, for a personal-service firm, such as the one in our example, this may not really be an option. However, McKinley and McKinley does have numerous bookkeeping guidelines it makes available to their clients.

Surveys

Survey results posted on the World Wide Web will help draw attention and increase traffic on a Web site. Be creative. McKinley and McKinley may be so confident of their services that they are willing to collect and post client survey/feedback responses through their Web site.

Multimedia

Sound files and Quick-Time Video files can be added to enhance your Web presentation. However, multimedia should be used sparingly. Animated "splash" pages intended to provide a compelling introduction to the site rarely provide useful information, and for users with only modem access they can seem to take forever to download.

No, our accountants will not be using flashy multimedia presentations to make their case. However, General Partner John McKinley soon will be delivering a speech about financial planning to the local Rotary Club. It will be videotaped, and if all goes well we may post excerpts to the Web site.

Digital Delivery

For products that can be digitized, the Internet gives the added benefit of instant delivery of either samples or the product itself. Data products, such as music or business reports, can be shipped immediately.

McKinley and McKinley already delivers individual clients' tax returns to Internal Revenue via the Internet. This function will not be integrated into the Web site. However, the company may experiment with a secure page where clients who use the 1040EZ can input their tax information from home. They also are weighing the possibility of using the Web site to deliver prepared tax returns to their clients, who will then print, sign, and mail them.

Free Advice

Keep the advice relevant to your industry. For example, if you sell garden seed, you should offer tips that help people to improve their gardening. McKinley and McKinley will be putting up a Web page that offers tips for good record keeping, deductions that often are overlooked, and similar hints for keeping your financial life in order.

Something Unique

Try to offer information that is unavailable on your competitor's Web site. This will differentiate your Web site from theirs. A unique graphic alone probably will not do the trick, but a significant piece of information will. This is one more way to reinforce your image as experts in your field.

Interesting or Unusual Facts

Keeping a Web page updated with strange facts related to your industry will help to generate interest among visitors.

Our accountants hope to use this tactic to bring some welcome cheer into their often humorless industry. One of their Web pages will deal with ridiculous cases from tax court, such as the convicted burglar who attempted to deduct the cost of his tools, and other tales from the little-recognized lighter side of accounting. It is not yet clear how successful they will be in this.

Index

Creating an index of sites related to your industry can be a great addition to your Web site. People regularly refer back to indexes whenever they need to locate new information. This is an ideal chance to add value to your Web site.

Content Choices

By now, it should be clear that there are many different kinds of material that can help to attract customers to your Web site and enhance your company's image in the process. As the accountants at McKinley and McKinley decided, not all such material is suitable for all companies, even when it is clearly relevant to their practice. However, with some creative thought, you will probably find that there is much more useful information available than you realize. The key to success is in how you use it.

Eenie Strategy

Automatically and Systematically Fix Errors on Your Site

Use Net Mechanic's (www.netmechanic.com) HTML Toolbox, and immediately identify site problems and repair

HTML code with just one click. HTML Toolbox spots common HTML code errors, fixes most errors it finds on your request, and generates a repaired file for you to upload. The program offers automatic testing of your site weekly, biweekly, monthly, or on demand. It also checks for browser compatibility issues, provides a load time analysis, and performs a spell check.

Cost: Free trial. HTML Toolbox can be purchased for $40 per URL for a site of up to 100 pages, or $200 per URL for up to 400 pages.

Meenie Strategy

Make Sure All Your Web-Site Activities Are Legal and Binding

Go to www.Lawforinternet.com to find a whole host of useful, current, and accurate legal information for Internet professionals, Webmasters, Web publishers, and entrepreneurs. Their LawMaster tutorials provide "how to" information, legal forms, and checklists covering a wide array of Web activities. Lawforinternet.com also provides answers to legal questions, the latest Internet legal news, charts, sample documents (including Web contractor agreements), resource tools, and more.

The company specifically offers advice on Internet business formation, creating a Web site, building the Web site, acquiring content, building traffic, and protecting the Web site.

Their legal information is prepared and edited by qualified attorneys and is updated on a regular basis to help ensure its accuracy and reliability.

Cost: Free.

Miney Strategy

If You Are a Publisher, Extend the Value of Your Content and Brand

Using Bell and Howell's ProQuest Archiver (www.pqarchiver.com), you can market your publication online. ProQuest will create an archive of your publications: past and current issues, complete with full text and graphics. Visitors to your Web site can then click through to the ProQuest archive to search your material, downloading items of interest for a modest fee.

The ProQuest online information service is known and respected by publishers as the market-leading online research tool used in colleges, universities, libraries, and schools worldwide. What sets ProQuest apart is its patented search technology combined with its editorial team, which categorizes and summarizes each article, giving users highly relevant results.

ProQuest seamlessly integrates your content into its archive, maintaining your Web interface, so customers searching ProQuest see only your Web site. ProQuest is also e-commerce enabled so your readers will be able to purchase articles online with little effort on your part.

Cost: Visit the ProQuest Web site to see if your publication is already archived. (You may not realize that your publication is archived.) If so, there is no set-up or monthly fee. If your publication is not included, you will incur a monthly fee as well as set-up fee. The percentage of customers who pay a fee is very small.

Moe Strategy

Get the Most of Your Web Development Team

A company called MartinTate (www.projectresults.com) offers project management workshops to all levels in the organization. Their workshops are intended to help project leaders and project team members improve their project management and team skills.

Their CORE Project Management curriculum is effective in all organizations, in all types of industries, and it can be used by any type of project—technical or nontechnical; small, medium, or large.

The MartinTate CORE Method is described in the following features:

- Collaborative: fosters team participation and buy-in

- Open Architecture: allows you to use your own technical (Web development) process. It's generic and can be used on any project in your organization

- Results Oriented: produces deliverables on time and within budget, focuses on the customer, minimizes costs, creates clear accountability, and prevents problems from occurring

- Easy-to-Use: gets you up and producing results quickly

The method can be tailored to the needs of the individual project so that project teams do those steps that fit the needs of their projects and no more.

MartinTate also offers workshops that help the team work together to accomplish the goals of the company. Their facilitation workshop helps you improve your skills at avoiding unnecessary team problems, working with difficult teams or team members, and effective team interventions. Their team skills workshop improves your communication, team decision making, team idea generation, and conflict resolution skills. It also helps you to understand and work with diverse thinking and learning styles.

Cost: Public workshops are priced at $795 to $995. In-house workshops cost from $450 to $825 per person.

Chapter 19

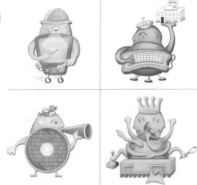

Web-Site Design

At this point in developing a Web-based business, you should have identified the main topic areas and at least some of the content that must be included in your Web site. Now we come to matters of design. This includes the structure of the site, as well as the appearance, much as a building's architecture includes both engineering and aesthetics. How should all that information be organized? How can it be presented most effectively? One factor that successful Web sites all seem to have in common is that these issues have been thought out very carefully.

Your company's brand identity may live or die as a result of the decisions you make at this step. Creating an online brand requires more than some useful information, a fancy design, and a pretty logo. Everything that shapes the user's experience helps to decide the success of your brand. Design, in the traditional graphical sense, cannot be merely attractive; it must support the corporate identity you have chosen—sober professionalism, cutting-edge technoglitz, or something in between. Design in the structural sense may be even more important, for an intuitive organization and navigation scheme is an essential part of the user's experience. If the site is not convenient to negotiate, visitors will not come back, and your brand will never get established.

Site Organization and Navigation

The site's organization—how its information is distributed among Web pages, and how users get from one topic to another—is the most basic part of designing a Web site. A graphics designer cannot make the pages pretty and coherent, or even know how many links to place on each one, until this basic skeleton is established. So let us start by thinking about matters of organization and navigation. We will turn to aesthetic design later in the chapter.

Consider this. A recent survey notes that over 44 percent of Web users say they are frustrated with Web navigation. For someone browsing Web pages, time counts. Users want to get into your site, find whatever information or products they need, and then get out. If your Web site is difficult to navigate, if it is not intuitive, they will quickly mouse-click their way to your competitor's site.

To structure a Web site effectively, try to understand what a typical user will be looking for, and place the information in a logical hierarchy. Many of these decisions may have been made already, when you chose the major topics to be included in your Web content. However, there still are details to be arranged. On a small Web site, it may be possible to branch from the home page directly to each subject page. On a larger site, the structure inevitably becomes more complicated. Does it make sense to arrange things in a strict tree structure, with major topics branching to lesser topics and subtopics, each one accessible only from the next higher level of that branch? Or should users be able to work their way out of the branch and then jump directly to some other subject branch, without returning to the home page? There may well be pages that should always be accessible—the shopping cart of a merchandise site, for example, or simply a link to a "contact us" page. Once this structure has been worked out in detail, the rest of the design process can begin in earnest.

When users click their way from the home page to one of the main topic areas, they should find navigational "hints" that both reinforce the brand and remind them of their location within the site. The company name or logo should appear on every page, and a section title should be clearly visible. Sometimes it helps to "color-code" the sections. Graphic design thus can reinforce structural design.

Within each section, there should be a "sub-navigation" menu that allows the users to "drill down" to the specific subjects presented in that section. Here's an example.

Take a look at www.e-tplastics.com, the Web site of a plastics fabrication company. The home page is simple, graphically pleasing, and right to the point with a brief welcome message and description of the company. The user easily locates navigational elements in a left side bar menu:

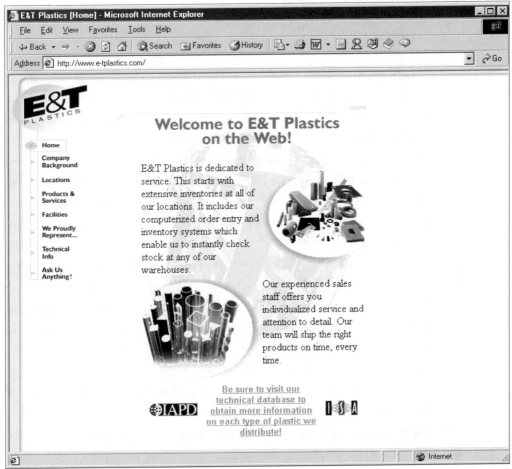

Figure 19.1. The home page of www.e-tplastics.com demonstrates the simple, clear, yet appealing kind of design suitable for a basic commercial site.

- Company Background
- Locations
- Products & Services
- Facilities
- We Proudly Represent…
- Technical Info
- Ask Us Anything!

The user intuitively navigates through these options:

- Company Background: Users click here to get a brief overview of the company history, to find out how long the company has been in business, and to get a feel for the company's reliability and going concern.

- Locations: Users may want to know if there is a location near them. Since E&T Plastics has several locations in the United States, it used a map of the United States with "roll-overs." (When you roll your mouse over the map, location addresses pop up on the screen.)

- Products & Services: Users will go immediately to this link to find out what products and services are offered by E&T Plastics. This is the "meat" of the Web site. This section is further divided into specific product categories such as Engineered Plastics, See-Through Plastics, Sign Products, and Fabrication. Users can intuitively dig deeper into each of these categories and see a complete list of products and services, each with generous descriptions and visuals.

- Facilities: Customers of E&T Plastics may want custom developed plastics products. For this reason, e-tplastics.com has a list of facilities on the site so that the prospect can see whether E&T Plastics has the proper equipment to produce their product.

- We Proudly Represent…: This page is a nice graphical presentation of all of the partner plastic manufacturers.

- Technical Info: This page is a helpful resource for prospects looking for the right type of plastic for their project. This online tool allows the prospect to research the mechanical, thermal, and electrical properties of a plastic by brand name or common name.

- Ask Us Anything!: This page is a welcome attempt to garner prospect interaction from Web site visitors.

Presentation

The home page is usually, though not always, the most graphic area of the Web site.

Regardless of the balance of graphic presentations throughout the Web site, the design of the home page should set the theme for the entire site. Graphic elements from the home page are usually repeated throughout the site. This consistency—having the company logo, color scheme, and overall layout appear on every page of the site—reinforces your corporate identity with every click. This consistency assures effective branding.

Over the past few years, many graphic designers have shifted from print publications to developing Web sites for the online medium. In the process, they have applied proven print design techniques, creating sites that look very similar to print media documents. This is great for maintaining a brand image across different media. However, recent research indicates that it may not be the best way to serve an online audience.

The Poynter Institute has released numerous eye tracking studies of how people see and use Web sites (www.poynter.org). Their studies typically review news sites, but the findings can be relevant for all sites.

In order to determine which elements of a Web site catch a viewer's attention, the studies used cameras to watch eye movement to see exactly where each reader looked on a computer screen. Eye tracking studies have been used for many years to measure the effectiveness of a wide variety of media, such as print, television, slide presentations, and other types of visual communications. The researchers measured the order in which viewers examined each element, the attention span devoted to each element, and how text and graphic links were used to navigate through the site.

You may find it surprising that readers were attracted to text more than to graphics and photos. Of users' first three eye-fixations on a page, only 22 percent were on graphics; 78 percent were on text. In general, users were first drawn to headlines, article summaries, and captions. They often did not look at the images at all until the second or third visit to a page.

Many Web site designers are enthralled with their own graphical layout. Many designers use graphics and photographs that they believe will be well received by the target audience. They choose graphics that will help users feel comfortable with the site, as well as images that help establish the corporate identity, provide brand recognition, and be used as navigation links. Many Web designers also try to balance the hefty use of graphics on a Web page with rapid download time. Yet this study demonstrates that this emphasis on graphics may be misplaced. It can be—and usually is—more effective to use text elements well.

The researchers drew a few more conclusions that can be applied to Web site design. For instance, readers have no problem scrolling. They scroll down pages and spend time viewing text elements "below the fold," as the newspaper term goes, as much as they view text higher on the page.

However, users were more than three times as likely to limit their reading to a brief summary than to read a full article. Even when reading a "full" article, users only read about 75 percent of the text. In other words, the most common behavior is to hunt for key information and ruthlessly ignore the details. So make articles shallow at first, but make in-depth information available if the user chooses to click through to the details.

Yet once their prey has been caught, users will sometimes dive into a subject more deeply. Thus, Web content needs to support both aspects of information access: foraging and consumption. Text needs to be easily scanned, but it also must provide the answers users seek.

Another interesting finding is that Internet users are getting more and more sophisticated. Not only do users bounce around Web sites very quickly, they often read more than one Web site at the same time! Users in the Poynter study frequently alternated between multiple sites. They would read something in one window, then switch to another window to visit another site, and then return to the first window and read some more on the original site. This process often continued for substantial periods, as Internet users bounced back and forth between sites.

Suddenly, it becomes easy to imagine comparison shoppers bouncing between Amazon.com and the Barnes and Noble Web site, comparing book reviews and looking for the best price in the volumes they want. They are likely to behave the same way when visiting your Web site.

The lesson for Web designers is that users are not focused on any single site, but on the information they need. Even while users are "visiting" your site, they are also checking out the competition. You cannot stop them. So, site design must accommodate people who leave and return frequently. Through intuitive design and navigation features, your Web site should help users reorient themselves. It should contain plain and simple headlines that immediately tell users what each page is about. Graphics, and even branding, are secondary.

Eenie Strategy

Participate in Web-Development Newsgroups, Subscribe to Newsletters, and View Resource-Rich Web Sites

Keep up with technology issues by visiting one of the oldest online resources, *Dr. Dobb's Journal* (www.ddj.com). You will find a wealth of information about computer, Internet, and general technology issues, as well as graphic design tips and tools. Other sites that you should frequent (and bookmark in your Web browser) include:

- www.htmlreference.com
- www.zdnet.com/developer
- www.webtools.com
- www.webtechniques.com
- www.arttoday.com
- www.animationfactory.net
- www.boogiejack.com
- www.creativepro.com

Most of the above sites are chock full of resources to help you build, manage, and promote your Web site. Be sure to subscribe to the newsletters, as they also offer valuable insights that may not appear in the Web pages.

Cost: Free.

Meenie Strategy

Create a Knowledge Base on Your Site for Easy Search and Retrieval of Information

Aestiva Knowledge Base (www.aestiva.com) is a Web site add-on that enables users to search through information databases. The product includes options for visitors to perform simple and complex searches, and a Web-based administration module for tailoring the look-and-feel of the search tool and maintaining your knowledge database.

Aestiva Knowledge Base can be installed on your server or in your account at a standard hosting provider. The advantages of utilizing a knowledge base on your Web site include:

- Improving your site's navigability—This is a sophisticated add-on designed to provide visitors to your site access to an information database of your choice.

- Enable quick searches through your databases—Aestiva Knowledge Base is powerful. It will search through 1,000 entries or hundreds of thousands of entries expeditiously.

- No development necessary—Aestiva Knowledge Base is an out-of-the-box solution. There are no development costs and no installation costs.

Cost: $650. Thirty days of voice and online support are free with purchase.

Miney Strategy

Create a Structured Information Business Portal, so Your Employees and Prospects Can Intuitively Navigate Through Your Information

If content is poorly organized, it is impossible to navigate, and all the effort you have put into content development and site design is useless. Unless your critical information can be unified and ordered, it will lose its value, become obsolete, and be a cause of frustration for your Web visitors.

A business portal solution offered by Verity Portal One (www. verity.com) can help in managing your growing volume of content. Included within Verity Portal One is the Knowledge Organizer, which automatically organizes information in a structured manner, usually by a familiar subject or theme. This makes it easier for users to find information.

Verity Knowledge Organizer uses business rules, contextual information, or an existing dictionary of classification terms—also known as metatags—to organize your data. These include all the standard concepts that conventionally organize business information, such as products, services, customers, competitors, projects, or policies.

Cost: Pricing begins at $20,000 for a development server.

Moe Strategy

Create a Sophisticated Development Environment

Using a development and tracking tool from a company called Compuware (www. compuware.com), you can free developers, testers, QA managers, and project managers to focus on problem resolution and improving quality.

Compuware's product, called TrackRecord, provides a tracking system that helps automate the identification and resolution of software defects. TrackRecord also tracks releases, projects, milestones, features, tasks, testing assets, and any other information related to application development projects.

By automating time-consuming tasks, such as documenting and reporting defects, communicating status and priorities, and locating bottlenecks, Compuware TrackRecord is an enterprise-wide tool for change-request management and defect and project tracking. It is designed to help development teams accelerate and improve their software development projects. TrackRecord can capture and share any information relating to a project including team members' schedules and defects and feature requests.

TrackRecord is a flexible, open architecture system designed around the requirements of software development, testing, and management.

Cost: Prices start at $1,200 per user, but are discounted to $850 per user for 50 or more users.

Chapter 20

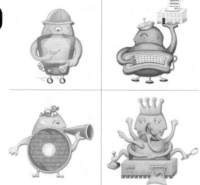

Application Development and Hosting

Thus far, nearly everything we have considered can be done in-house. Analyzing your existing business or coming up with an entrepreneurial idea, identifying the objectives of your Web site, gathering or creating content, and then figuring out how to organize it within the site. All this either is fundamentally the site-owner's job—that is, something that must be dealt with by the core development team—or is within the scope of most individuals and organizations. Even graphic design can often be handled adequately by entrepreneurs or managers with a bit of taste and imagination and the ability to learn from examples found on the Intenet.

Even if you do avoid hiring graphic designers, however, almost everyone building a serious Web site eventually needs outside help. This time usually arrives at one of two points—when you require a unique or complex piece of software to handle a special task on the site, or when you have finished the design and "construction" and it is time to take your new site onto the Internet. Writing anything but the simplest software is a task for specialists; even if you can get the job done yourself, a professional is likely to accomplish it faster and more reliably. And Web hosting—providing the hardware and software that actually puts your site out onto the Internet—is usually a waste of internal resources when there are thousands of companies to do it for you.

Finding the right helpers and making efficient use of them involves some issues that we have not faced before. It is now time to consider them.

Application Development

What I love most about technology is that you can create applications—basically, software programs—to do almost anything. You need only figure out a series of logical steps to accomplish your goal. However, that is seldom as easy as it sounds. This is a challenge you will face whenever you need to write—or have someone else write—special software or adapt an existing program to meet your needs.

So before considering how to find the right source for software, let us look at an example of the concerns you will have to address first. Say that you are creating a Web site for a business membership organization, and you need a facility where members can register on your site and be listed in your online membership directory. Let's follow a logical plan for application development:

First decide the key features of the membership directory:

- Identify the purpose of the membership directory: What value does it offer? Will it be restricted to members, or can anyone who visits your site use it to find a member?

- How will it be used? Will people be searching for members by name, or do you need to identify members by other criteria, such as category of business or location?

- What information is needed? Do you want to list the e-mail addresses for each member on the site? Do you want to list their Web address? How about the member's type of business? Location? Or special services that they offer?

Next, figure out what information is required to implement the features you have decided on. What information do you want to collect from the member? For our current purposes, let's start with the following: Business Name, Address, Phone, Fax, E-mail, Web site, Type of business, Product or service. Each of these will have to be included as an input field in your online registration form and recorded in the membership database.

Then, figure out how best to display the membership data in your online directory: sort by member name, location, or type of business. Users who come to the site will be able to locate the members they need according to the criteria you select in this design process.

Assume that you have made it possible to search by type of business, and one of your visitors is looking for an accounting firm. The search will bring up the names of all the accounting firms among your membership. Should they appear in alphabetical order, or would some other sorting order be more useful in this case? Should it be possible to limit the search still further—to accounting firms in Connecticut, say, or firms that specialize in tax accounting. These are just two of many such decisions to be made before the programming begins.

If only site members will be allowed to search the online directory, then there must be some way to screen out nonmembers trying to use the search facility. For example, each member is given a login and password in order to access the site.

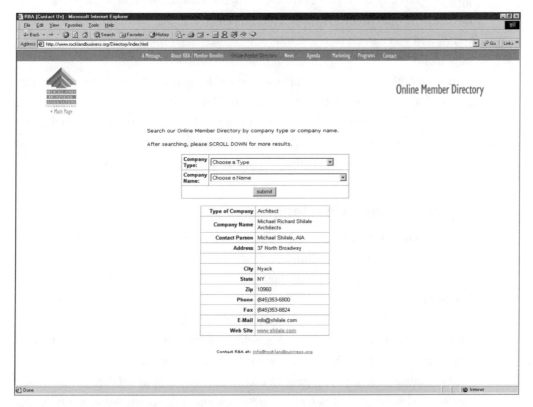

Figure 20.1. With this typical online membership directory, users can retrieve listings by type of company or name of company.

You will also need to determine where the directory will be on the Web site, on which subpage. Laying out an application like this requires quite a lot of logical thought.

Traditionally, this is the time to go looking for a programmer, either a new staff member or a consultant with the skill to turn your ideas into working software. Things are a little different in the world of the Internet, however. Many thousands of programmers around the world already have written applications to provide almost any feature you could want to include on a Web site. Chances are that you can choose from many such programs, each of which can be customized to fit your exact needs with relatively little effort. Some applications, such as database systems, even have built-in utilities to automate this process, so that you can just buy the program and tailor it yourself.

One of the reasons for writing this book was to give help in finding companies that already have this software on hand. Eenie, Meenie, Miney, and Moe have all provided information and pricing on many technologies available today, and you can go to www.internetprophets.com for an ever-growing list of new technologies.

Because of the deluge of services available, many intermediary companies called ASPs, or Application Service Providers, have emerged. The role of a typical ASP is to provide you with a range of technologies to cover one or many of your needs. Most ASPs provide software services on demand over the Internet, thus offering a substantial cost savings to their clients.

Assessing Web Developers

When considering new employees, consultants, or design firms for the creation of your Web site, it's important to evaluate their artistic talent and technical skill. This is critical, whether you are looking for graphic designers or for programmers.

If you are calling on them simply for design and layout, be sure to review other work that they have done. A single designer may have created many Web sites and claim that each has a different look. But upon careful observation, you will probably be able to recognize a consistent style among all the sites he or she has created for others. It is rare to find a designer who can achieve a totally different look for each piece of artwork. If you look close enough you will see similar color pallets are used for each. Navigational layout and graphical design will also follow a similar style on the different sites. This is not necessarily bad. You may really like the style. But careful review of the work should prepare you for what you are getting into—regardless of the promises for "uniqueness" that the designer may make.

Be careful of one "gotcha" as well. Design shops with artists and designers on staff may have a variety of styles to show you. If you select one of these styles for your Web site, be sure that designer still works for the firm when you are ready to begin!

Similarly, programmers put their own spin on the applications they produce. By reviewing the work of prospective programmers, you will also get a feel for their style. Take a look at the logical layout of the applications they have created for other Web sites. Are they intuitive to use? Does the layout look friendly and approachable? There is nothing worse than an intimidating registration form or order form on a Web site.

Most importantly, ask for credentials of the key people involved in the project, and for references from other companies they have worked with. The Internet is a brand new medium, only six years old, and many newbie computer users may be quick on the keyboard but have no clue about business. The individuals you want working on your Web site should have some business experience and background in other fields. Anyone working on a Web strategy with you should be able to draw on resources in his or her past as well as introducing new technologies for your business on the Web.

Also remember that although a designer may claim to have artistic talent and design experience, the Internet is a totally new medium. Many traditional design concepts must be unlearned or reformatted for the Web.

Finally, make sure you can speak to the person or firm you are considering to team up with for this Web project. When I say speak, I mean speak clearly. There is no need for anyone to try to impress you with techno-babble. Of course, they can try to educate you a little, because you will inevitably be confronted with technical issues that are unique to this field, but make sure you can build a friendly and professional working relationship with the people who will carry your project to fruition.

There are many pieces to the Web-site puzzle. You may need to work with multiple vendors on your project. The vendors may include an ISP who hosts your site, a Web development firm that designs and codes your site, an Application Service Provider that integrates Web applications into your site, and your project manager and in-house content manager. Be prepared to manage all the pieces of this puzzle.

Hosting Requirements

Every Web site that is visible on the Internet is hosted on a Web server. A Web server is merely a computer that is connected to the Internet 24 hours a day, 7 days a week. Your server can be hosted within your company, or offsite, typically with an Internet Service Provider (ISP) or Internet Presence Provider (IPP).

If your site is hosted with an ISP or IPP, it may "live" on a Web server that is shared with many other Web sites. This is not a problem. A Web server can handle many Web sites at one time, and no one knows the difference. We call this "virtual hosting." To the outside world it looks as if your Web site is on its own computer, when in reality it resides on a shared server.

The advantage of virtual hosting is that you get the benefit of a robust computing environment with adequate bandwidth without incurring the costs of buying, renting, or leasing your own server. You also gain the advantage of a professional staff that monitors and maintains the server 24/7. You will have your own domain name and your own database or transaction system. However, the server software usually will be chosen, provided, and maintained by the ISP. If you require special software, it may not be possible for the ISP to install it on its server for you. In this case, you may want to go to a dedicated or a co-location environment or host and manage the server yourself.

You can choose an ISP that is located anywhere in the world. Basically, for a virtual or dedicated setup, geographic location is irrelevant. Once the server or site is configured on the network, it can be accessed from across the globe with a simple Internet connection.

Different ISPs offer varying levels of connectivity. Make sure that the ISP has enough bandwidth to handle your expected demand. Bandwidth is the amount of data that can be transmitted through the lines. Ask the ISP about the types of lines they have and their capacity. Ask what percentage of bandwidth capacity is used at peak times; this should be less than 50 percent at all times. You also want to make sure they are up and running 24/7/365. To verify this, ask them about their percentage of server uptime—and make sure it is 99.5 percent or better! We all know that computers are vulnerable to tampering and can malfunction even without outside interference, so be sure to ask the ISP what security and backup procedures they have in place.

Most ISPs will bill based on use. That is, you will get a monthly rate for a certain amount of usage. This is typically only a concern when the site receives millions of hits daily or has video and heavy audio. Whether you are contemplating your own server or using the services of an ISP, bandwidth is a critically important issue.

Eenie Strategy

Scan the Web for Cool Tools to Incorporate into Your Site

Visit sites like The JavaScript Source (www.java script.internet.com), an excellent JavaScript resource with tons of "cut and paste" JavaScript examples for your Web pages. Also visit these helpful sites:

- www.flashkit.com
- www.internet.com
- www.itprodownloads.com
- www.streamingmediaworld.com
- www.scriptsearch.com
- www.webcoder.com
- www.webmonkey.com

Most of these sites have newsletters and discussion groups. Don't be shy. Join them. Hear the issues that other Web developers face. You will find many inexperienced developers chatting with seasoned professionals. The beauty of the Internet is this open, free, and supportive environment.

Costs: Free.

Meenie Strategy

Set Up an E-Commerce System Using a Packaged Storefront Application

Miva Merchant (www.mivamerchant.com) is a dynamic browser-based storefront development and management system that allows merchants to create one or multiple online stores.

Miva Merchant has a complete set of "wizards" to simplify the process of building your store; tell it what features you want in your store, and it will automatically configure the software to meet your needs. The browser-based administration interface provides access to an array of sophisticated tools to maintain your catalog and inventory, manage customer and affiliate accounts, create comprehensive promotional campaigns, handle order fulfillment responsibilities, and generate detailed sales and Web-site traffic reports.

Costs: Initial Domain Licenses (includes first store) are $595 per domain.

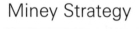

Miney Strategy

Conduct Real-Time Performance Measurement on Your Web Site

Using webHancer e-Business View, you can have real-time insight into your site's performance and an examination of users' quality of experience at your site.

e-Business View quantifies and clarifies behavioral issues like the following:

- Why do users abandon pages?
- What page-load times turn people off?

- Which pages load slowly and why?

- Which pages get and keep user interest?

- What is the efficiency and effectiveness of a commercial site when compared with that of the competition?

- Which parts of the site generate cash flow?

- Which infrastructure problems are the source of delay? Ad banner servers? ISP? Web server? Content server?

webHancer data helps to prove payback for expenditures like site infrastructure, co-location services, content distribution services, increased bandwidth, or caching services.

Cost: Pricing begins at $12,000 per month; volume discounts are available.

Moe Strategy

Recognize the Tools Your Internal Developers Are Using

If you have in-house developers working on your project, you should get to know some of the most common development tools for integrating database applications on a Web site and for creating graphically rich user experiences.

A product called ColdFusion by Allaire (www.coldfusion.com) is widely known and used for database integration. Allaire ColdFusion is a complete development and deployment platform. Your developers can create quick and easy databases to interface with the Web or very sophisticated service oriented databases to assist customers on your Web site.

In January 2001, Allaire announced its intention to merge with one of the most well known interactive graphic and multimedia masters, Macromedia. This merger brings together two software development leaders and creates the most comprehensive resource for dynamic

Web design and development. Macromedia's Flash, a vector-based animation program, is used to design and deliver low-bandwidth animations and presentations. It offers scripting capabilities and server-side connectivity for creating engaging applications, Web interfaces, and training courses. For examples of Flash presentations, visit www.flash.com.

Costs: Cold Fusion license approximately $4,995. Macromedia Flash license approximately $500. Total cost, of course, includes the price of hiring or dedicating personnel to master this software and apply it to your needs.

Part V

Part V
Marketing Your Web Site

In any business venture, advertising and promotion are necessary to let prospective customers know that the business exists and that it has something to offer them that is worthy of their attention—and their hard-earned cash. How you intend to use these techniques, and use them effectively, is a fundamental part of every business plan. This is as true in the ethereal world of e-business as it is in the traditional offline economy.

There are a whole host of advertising venues in the physical world. Most of these traditional media outlets and advertising techniques are found, slightly transformed, in cyberspace as well. Some smaller businesses are successful with simple word of mouth advertising. On the Internet, this is referred to as "word of mouse." Direct mail's online counterpart is direct e-mail. Banner advertising on Web sites is equivalent to an advertisement in a typical printed publication. In the New Economy, it makes sense to advertise in both traditional and online venues, if possible. Your traditional ads should complement your electronic ads, and vice versa.

This does not mean that you have to launch a high-powered and expensive ad campaign to be successful on the Internet. While advertising is important, one of the lessons we have learned during the fall of so many dot-coms is that you will go bust trying to capture the Web's entire audience. Pets.com, for example, spent four times its sales on advertising, a policy that likely helped seal its fate.

Which marketing, advertising, and promotion techniques to choose and how you develop the right strategies for online and offline campaigns will depend on the size of your budget. It is true that the bigger the budget, the more exposure

207

can be bought. However, using a budget wisely is just as important. One of the great advantages of the Web, especially for businesses that must start with limited funds, is that it is inexpensive—often free—to let people know where to find a new and useful site.

Here are some common-sense tips for you to consider as you put together your marketing program.

Set clear goals and objectives. Marketing is far too expensive a proposition to go at it without a clear plan. Make sure you know specifically what you want to accomplish before getting started. Do you want to lure qualified traffic to your Web site? Increase sales by 5 percent? Sign up X new customers? Or will it be enough just to generate awareness among potential customers? You can think big, but with a small budget you have to be realistic. Setting goals from the outset will help you determine what and how much you need to do. Setting realistic, quantitative objectives will help you benchmark your success.

Learn about your target audience and what media channels are typically successful in reaching them. Before jumping into any program, you must understand your audience. Find out what magazines they read, trade shows they attend, sports they like, and so on. This will help you in targeting your activities to them. You can either use an established marketing firm to do the research or dedicate some staff time for research. E-mail surveys, phone surveys, and Internet research offer tons of information to help you plan a successful marketing campaign!

Create materials with long life and multiple utility. If you are creating a marketing piece for your company, design it so the copy and graphics work for a number of different situations. For example, brochure copy and photos can be used on the Web site, which can be converted to a flyer. These can be converted to a trade show ad, and so on. Leveraging the money it costs to create the original can go a long way toward keeping your budget in balance. At the same time, the consistency of message and look will help in building your brand.

Use viral marketing techniques. Make your efforts and message contagious! Create something that your customer can pass on, that builds your brand and sends a consistent marketing message to new prospects. As an example, AOL offers a $50 refer-a-friend incentive for its instant messenger service. NextMonet (www.nextmonet.com) an online art gallery, gave its customers blank postcards of artworks that were featured on the site. Iconocast (www.iconocast.com) an Internet industry newsletter, offered incentives to its customers for referring potential attendees to its annual conference. Viral marketing can reach prospects on an exponential basis.

PR is wonderful. PR is very effective and less expensive than a broad-based advertising campaign. It can have phenomenal results. The credibility that you get from good press coverage is impossible to match. Successful PR efforts create buzz and excitement. You can do it yourself, hire an agency, or hire a competent consultant on a contract or hourly basis.

In Chapters 21–24, we will examine these and other techniques for marketing and promotion, and the Internet Prophets will offer a variety of resources that can help grow your e-venture to meet or exceed your goals.

Chapter 21

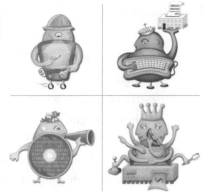

Search Engines

The key to any site's success is qualified Web traffic. Once you have the Web site up and running, you have to get people to visit it. It is growing harder every day.

By the first quarter of 2001, there were an estimated 8 billion Web pages available on the Internet, more Web pages than there are human beings on Earth, and the number was growing rapidly. With all those pages to choose from, how can anyone possibly find what they want? And how can any business keep its message from being lost in the vastness of cyberspace? After all, some 29 million domain names have been registered to date, and more than three-fourths of them are registered as .coms.

The vast majority of visits to a Web site—between 93 percent and 97 percent, according to most studies—originate with a link from another Web page. It only makes sense; people who find one page to be of interest are likely to follow up on its links to other, similar sites. Making that possible was the whole point of developing hypertext in the first place. So the most efficient way to bring customers to your Web site may be to trade links with the operators of related, preferably noncompetitive, sites.

Users find sites in other ways as well. They click through banner ads; read about them in books (such as this one); learn of them from e-mail and from friends; read about them in magazines and newspapers; hear or see advertising in print, on radio and TV, and at trade shows; see them mentioned on Usenet newsgroups. The list is nearly endless, and any of these methods could be a source of customers for your site.

However, one way in which visitors arrive at a site is particularly important for the development of new business. When people have no idea how to find what they want, they are likely to use a search engine. Learning how search engines work may be one of the most productive things you do to promote your online business.

When I first discovered the Internet, I used search engines to search for all the information I could find regarding local events, activities, and goings-on in my little community. The fact is, I found none. So I set up my own local interest Web pages and submitted them to the search engines. Lo and behold, Rockland County, New York, suddenly had a place on the cybermap! My Web pages stayed high in the rankings for a good year and a half, but by 1996 the Internet had expanded so dramatically that such limited-interest pages were bound to fall behind.

With such an influx of Web sites—and the many hundreds of millions more that have arrived since then!—the search engines were inundated with listings. Today, it is not uncommon to get 60,000 or 600,000 results to a simple search. The results listed up front—those with the best ranking—are going to get the visits. Getting your Web site there is not as easy as it was when the territory was virgin.

If you can get high ranking in search engines—that is, be one of the first results listed after the user enters a request or keyword—your Web site will be visited regularly, and your opportunities for success can be great. The traffic you get from search engines and directories is highly qualified. People find you through a search engine when they are actually searching for your product—they are pre-qualified as specifically seeking the product or service that you offer. There are people looking for your products and services 24/7 from around the world. If you are not at the top of the list, they will go to your competitor.

Until recently, all search engines accepted listings without charging a fee. Whether your site was actually posted to the search engine was another matter. Yahoo! was notorious for *not* accepting listings. Recently, it has begun charging to add Web sites to its commercial category listings. The cost is a one-time, non-refundable $199 for a single listing. Yahoo! claims that this fee guarantees that its editors will review your Web site and consider it for inclusion within seven business days. In most other search engines, however, listings remain free. Ranking is another story.

So clients very often ask me the obvious question: "How do I get into these Internet search engines and make sure that my Web site appears at the top of a results list?" Unfortunately, that is not so easy.

Over the last several years, as the number of Web sites has increased dramatically, and high search-engine rankings have become harder and harder to achieve, search-engine submission services have sprung up. These companies claim to have developed technology that can increase the ranking of Web sites by search engines. They accomplish this by studying the algorithms of the search engines (at least the 10 major search engines) and developing techniques that they say can manipulate those algorithms to result in successful submissions. These services typically charge for the service. Their fees could range from a $99 annual fee to up to $1,500 setup and per "hit" transaction fee.

Most of these submission services appear confident about achieving their claimed results. Usually the per-hit transaction service is offered as a guarantee. You do not have to pay anything unless your site gets the ranking.

A few examples of search engine submission services are:

- www.did-it.com
- www.tssubmit.com
- www.1stplaceranking.com
- www.siteannounce.com
- www.worldsubmit.com
- www.searchenginemonkeys.com

You can also buy placement on some search engines. As an example, www. goto.com claims to have revolutionized the way consumers find Web sites and advertisers reach consumers. It is the first search engine where advertisers pay only when someone clicks on a Web link. Advertisers determine where they appear in the search results listings by bidding on search terms in an open auction. This method enables advertisers to target customers at lower cost and with more precision and accountability.

Consumers win because:

- They locate only the most relevant commercial Web sites on their unique topic of interest.
- Results are based on an open system by which advertisers vie for consumer attention.
- There are no hidden tricks with phantom keyword placement and other methods that companies can use to force their Web site to the top of a results page.
- All search-term bids must adhere to GoTo's strict policy of Web-site relevance to its corresponding keyword.

Advertisers win because:

- A bidding system allows them to determine placement in the search results.
- They can target a measurable share of topic-specific consumer attention.
- They only pay for actual visits to their site.
- Flexible pricing suits the business models of large and small advertisers.

The beauty of GoTo is that smaller, more targeted advertisers now have an affordable way to gain prominence on a search engine in exactly those searches that are most valuable to them. Where a large company might buy the top placement for the search term "auto," a smaller business specializing in antique car parts would be able to purchase prominence in a more specialized category where it might otherwise have never been listed at all.

Eenie Strategy

Implement Search Engine Optimization Techniques in Your Web Site

The best way for Eenie companies to get ranking in search engines is to roll up their sleeves and get to work. It can be time-consuming to optimize your site and submit it to search engines, but it can be highly rewarding. One site dedicated to education about search engine technology, technique, optimization, and placement is none other than www.searchengines.com.

Sections on the site include: a listing of search engines by geographical area, topic, or general directories; a section about how to optimize your site; another that deals with how to submit your site; and a membership-based "Inside Scoop," which includes inside information on major search engines and optimization techniques.

You will also find product reviews and advice for monitoring your site's activity.

Cost: Free.

Meenie Strategy

Purchase a Search Engine Optimization and Submission Program

WebPosition Gold (www.webposition.com) is a handy tool that optimizes your Web site and submits it to all the major search engines. WebPosition Gold analyzes your existing Web pages and gives plain-English advice on how to improve them. It also includes a simple, built-in HTML editor that makes it fast and easy to change your Web pages and generates HTML pages designed to rank near the top of the search results.

Once your Web pages are optimized, WebPosition assists in uploading your new and changed pages to your Web server and automatically submits them to the major search engines.

WebPosition also:

- Reports your positions on each search engine for each keyword you are targeting.

- Tracks the number of visitors to your site, where they came from, and what keywords they used to find you.

There are two editions of WebPosition Gold, one intended to meet the needs of the average user and one intended for the professional Web-marketing consultant.

Cost: Standard Edition (supports 5 different Web sites), $149; Professional Edition (supports an unlimited number of Web sites), $349.

Miney Strategy

List Your Site on Sprinks

Sprinks is a self-service advertising tool for professional sites that want to reach high-quality, targeted audiences. On Sprinks, which is similar to goto.com, you bid for keyword placement. The more sites bidding on the keyword you want, the higher the per-click cost will be.

But Sprinks is not a stand-alone search engine. It is partnered with more than 700 topic-specific sites through About.com. About.com serves more than 500,000 searches daily on its site and will allow advertisers to name their price and control their results.

The interface for submitting your search terms is easy, especially if you focus on only a limited number of keywords. Sprinks allows only 25 characters for each keyword. For your site title it allows 50 characters, 200 for site description, and 255 characters for your URL.

After submitting your keywords, site description, URL, and site title, you are asked to bid on each keyword individually. Sprinks shows you the ranking of each of your search terms as you bid on them, which can come in handy when bidding to a specific rank.

If one of your keywords is ranked in the top 10, you will appear on the first page of search results for that keyword. The next 40 results appear on the next page. If you are not ranking in the top 50, your site will not be listed.

Sprinks offers reports that show your bids, rank, number of clicks, total cost of clicks, and the highest bid for each keyword. It is updated daily and shows only the latest bid on your keywords.

Cost: You bid on cost per click.

Moe Strategy

Participate in a Rewards Web Site

iWon, an innovative search engine, had a terrific idea upon launch—design a major Internet portal along the lines of Yahoo!, Excite, and the like, but give the users who visit it a reward of some sort, just for coming to the site. iWon rewards users with guaranteed cash giveaways—something in the neighborhood of $10,000 a day, and $1 million per month! From the user's perspective it's an iWin—why not win something while searching the Web?

iWon is one of the most popular destinations on the Web. Advertising here gives you a chance to get your company in front of millions of users.

iWon has built a highly sticky and loyal audience—a benefit for marketers interested in brand building and those seeking highly involved consumers with positive brand associations. Among all portals, iWon ranks first in time spent, days visited per month, and unique page views per month, as well as consumer site and feature satisfaction.

As the fifth most trafficked site on the Web, iWon offers a wide variety of advertising opportunities, including direct marketing with iWon e-mail and postal address rental, content newsletters, iLead, and survey opportunities. iWon has a full media package posted to its Web site at www.iwon.com.

Cost: CPM rates range from $15 to $100.

Chapter 22

Affiliate Marketing

Affiliate marketing may be one of the best innovations in the electronic realm. The combined power of this new medium with astronomical numbers of Internet users creates an incredibly rich marketing resource for businesses of all sizes.

Affiliate marketing programs are partnerships between online merchants who want to extend their reach beyond their own Web sites, and affiliates— other sites on the Web that agree to host merchant links in exchange for a piece of the revenue. From the merchant's perspective, this is free advertising, with the potential to drive traffic and generate sales. From the affiliate's perspective, it is a viable source of additional revenue in exchange for a small piece of advertising on its Web site.

Amazon.com offered the first affiliate program on the Internet and called it the "Associates" program. The Associates program offered commissions to referring Web sites when Amazon.com sells merchandise to referred visitors. It was and still is incredibly simple to get started. You just place a link on your site, either a graphic or simple text. The link contains special code that tells the system at Amazon.com which visitors came from your site. If a visitor who came from your site buys a product, you get a piece of the action.

Amazon.com's program is extremely successful, especially now that Amazon.com has expanded its line of products well beyond just books. Being an

Amazon.com associate allows the affiliate site to customize offerings from Amazon's huge inventory of books, CDs, videos, software, toys, and other products. The neat thing about the Amazon program is that it allows you to link not just to the home page, but to pages that sell individual products. Thus, if you review a book on your site, you can have a link that lets visitors jump to Amazon and order the book. When visitors click through the link to Amazon's site and make a purchase, you get a commission for referring the buyer. Associates earn up to 15 percent revenue on all items sold to the customers they refer. Amazon now has more than 500,000 affiliate partners promoting its products all across the Web.

You can seek affiliates for your business or be an affiliate for others. Seeking affiliates for your business through affiliate marketing programs has great potential for increased sales. Using the power of the Internet, affiliate marketing strategies afford a business the opportunity to reach an exponential number of prospects in a cost-effective and efficient manner. Today's technology enables companies to build and manage thousands of marketing partnerships with the snap of a virtual finger. These partnerships can be managed with a minimum of internal resources and tightly controlled costs.

Advanced affiliate marketing management software allows direct marketers to track the relationships with their customers and measure the success of their marketing efforts in real time. Reports can be run on the conversion to sale of each link on the affiliate sites, based on information that is updated regularly. Marketers can tell immediately which offers are most effective. This knowledge ensures that only the most effective offers stay alive.

Best of all, this is a pay-per-performance business model; affiliates are paid only when products are sold or other criteria are met. In all cases, marketing is free until that performance objective is met. Sophisticated affiliate marketing management software enables companies to customize compensation to affiliates based on impressions, click-through rates, completed forms, percentage of sales, flat fees, monthly minimums, or any combination of these elements that makes sense for the marketer's specific business goals. And you can get creative. For example, you might raise the commission as sales volume grows, to give your affiliates an even greater incentive. The objective is to lower customer acquisition costs significantly. And it works.

Growing your affiliate base is obviously one critical part of affiliate marketing. Managing an affiliate program can become time-consuming and expensive if you let it. Consider joining an existing affiliate network, which can supply you immediately with willing affiliates. Networks with proven success records attract the most qualified, knowledgeable, and serious affiliates, the ones who are the most effective resellers of your products.

There are several affiliate directories on the Internet. Take a look at some of these:

- www.refer-it.com
- www.affiliatematch.com
- www.associate-it.com
- www.associateprograms.com
- www.cashpile.com

You can submit your affiliate program to any of these directories, or you can have a submission service like Affiliate-Announce.com do it for you. The convenience is worth the low price of $79 for the submission service.

A last note on affiliates. Once you have your affiliates, treat them well. They are your business partners. Communicate with them as often as feasible. Send them newsletters and e-mail announcements to keep them updated. Regular contact keeps affiliates informed about what is new with your program, so they are encouraged to update content and links regularly and take advantage of limited-offer promotions. Establishing regular contact builds the relationship between you and your affiliates, making affiliate marketing true partnership marketing. And do not forget to reward your partners for great referrals. Many direct marketers give their top affiliates a bigger chunk of the pie. They also offer them other perks and packages to keep them loyal and active.

Eenie Strategy

Earn Additional Revenue Through Affiliate Marketing

You are a do-it-yourselfer. You can create and manage your own affiliate marketing program, generating more income for your business without paying fees to online service providers. There are so many free or low-priced scripts and applications that you can use to launch and manage your program. Check out the listing of affiliate scripts at the CGI Resource Index (cgi.resourceindex.com). Several dozen scripts are listed, ranging from freeware and shareware to scripts costing a few hundred dollars.

For more information and to conduct research on affiliate marketing, go to www.Affiliatehandbook.com

Be sure to check out all the listings of affiliate marketing conferences. There may be one in your area. Your time will be well spent on education in this unique and powerful marketing technique.

Cost: Free.

Meenie Strategy

Start a Simple Banner Referral Affiliate Program

An application called My Affiliate (www.myaffiliateprogram.com) is a great tool for starting a simple banner-referral affiliate program. The application automates the entire banner-referral process. Affiliates can sign up for your program, copy HTML for a referral banner, and easily post it to their site. The program will thank them for signing up, show them how to place the banner on their site, and tell them where to go to view their statistics.

The My Affiliate software also tracks affiliate-referred visitors from click-through to sale. You will be able to analyze who is sending you traffic and who is sending you sales. The program also produces reports, so you can thank your affiliates with well-deserved commissions.

If you manage your accounting using Quickbooks, My Affiliate Program even has an export function, so that you can move your sales information into your Quickbooks program. Costs: software access fee, $795; monthly maintenance fee, $50.

Miney Strategy

Outsource Your Affiliate Program Management

Only around 10 percent of all affiliate mer-chants really make a significant profit from their programs, according to industry estimates. Yet the remainder, who only get a dribble of traf-fic, still increase their exposure and revenue. These merchants often recognize that their affiliate program is the most cost-effective of all their marketing initiatives, but lack the time to commit to it, so that their productivity wanes. The solution is to hire a professional.

Your company can work with a marketing specialist who spends time each and every day managing and growing your affiliate pro-gram. Among the services AffiliatePeople.com provides are affiliate strategy development, communicating with current and potential affil-iates, advertising and creative options, targeted affiliate recruitment, technical integration, and affiliate-content provision.

Costs: Starts at $2,995 per month for basic outsourced program management.

Moe Strategy

Use a Combination of Web-Marketing Tactics to Drive Results

A company called E-Base Interactive (www. ebaseinteractive.com) offers a comprehensive array of marketing campaigns designed to fit the specific needs of your business. Its affiliate program includes affiliate rela-tionship management, recruitment, affiliate application review, support, and communications. E-Base can also develop strategic alliances, analyze affiliate site traffic, and create necessary reports.

In addition to affiliate programs, E-Base Interactive offers banner advertising, targeted e-mail, search engine submission, and e-zine publication and distribution.

Another unique offering by E-Base is a press release service. Its sources provide local, regional, national, country-specific, or global press release coverage. It also offers press releases targeted to special topics, categories, or industries. The releases reach a wide assortment of media outlets: radio, TV, cable providers, magazines and trade journals, Web sites, newspapers, and more.

Cost: Fees for an affiliate program range from $2,000 monthly for 32 hours of management to $5,400 monthly with a one-year contract for full-time 40-hours-per-week program management.

Chapter 23

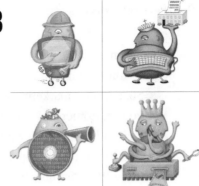

E-Mail Marketing

E-mail is an effective mechanism for driving traffic to a Web site and one of the most effective online marketing tools available for generating repeat traffic. Think about your own online habits. If you are like me, checking your e-mail is the first thing you do every morning and the last thing you do each night. During the day, you are reviewing, sorting, categorizing, and replying to e-mail on a very frequent basis.

Naturally, I get e-mail from friends, family, business colleagues and customers—it's all very relevant and important. I also get a wealth of information about my industry and sort it neatly into categories, so that I can refer to each item when I need to.

But I also get tons of so-called junk mail. But that "junk" does not bother me. It is easy to sort through, and I know that there is often a diamond in my daily rough. What do I look for? Well, I like to travel, so I have signed up with a variety of travel lists that specialize in cheap tickets and last-minute specials. I like theater and art, so I'm on lists that announce what is going on in my area. I keep up on grass-roots social concerns through e-mail. I trade on eBay and look for my auction updates. And, of course, Amazon.com sends me information about new books that I might like. All of these interests either specifically provide commercial e-mail or tell advertisers that I might be interested in their products and thereby bring more advertising to my in-box. There is not much of it that I really think of as junk.

So, consider marketing by e-mail. As a marketer, you want to get right in front of your customers, to visit them where they live. Most people spend more time in their in-box than anywhere else on the Internet!

Because e-mail campaigns are so lucrative and cost effective, it makes sense to use every communication channel possible to gather e-mail addresses from your customers and prospects. Develop your own in-house e-mail marketing database. In-house lists are the best, because you can be certain that no one "touches" your customer except you. Having a centralized database will maximize security, integrity, and efficiency.

Privacy has been a big concern on the Internet, so be sure to follow the rules as best you can. Rule number one: Get the customer's consent. Be sure to ask your prospects and customers whether you can use their e-mail address to send them information about your products or services; it's called opting-in. Even if you purchase e-mail lists from commercial sources—and there are many of them—you should make sure the lists you receive are also opt-in lists.

Sending e-mail without the consent of the recipient is called spamming. There are many regulations that govern spamming, so be certain you comply with state and federal law. Spamming is a serious offense, and you can risk losing business by sending out unsolicited e-mails. Irate recipients may even reply simply to cost you money by creating unproductive demand on your systems. Occasionally, spontaneous waves of "counter-spam" have clogged Net servers so badly that ISPs have closed the original spammer's account.

Due to the proliferation of e-mail in the last few years, a national e-mail council has been established to set guidelines protecting consumers and businesses alike. The guidelines consist of six separate resolutions designed to safeguard receivers from getting consistently unwanted, erroneously labeled, or intentionally deceptive e-mail. Each of the resolutions complements the next, and they all should be taken into consideration as a collective entity. In full they are:

- Marketers must not falsify the sender's domain name or use a nonresponsive IP address without implied permission from the recipient or transferred permission from the marketer.

- Marketers must not falsify the subject line to deviate and mislead readers from the content of the e-mail message.

- All e-mail marketing messages must either include an option for the recipient to unsubscribe from receiving future messages from that sender, list owner, or list manager, or valid and responsive contact information of the sender, list manager, or list owner.

- Marketers must inform the respondent upon online collection of the e-mail address for what marketing purpose the respondent's e-mail address will be used. (Inform either online or via e-mail.)

- Marketers must not harvest e-mail addresses with the intent to send bulk unsolicited commercial e-mail without consumers' knowledge or consent. ("Harvesting" is defined as compiling or stealing e-mail addresses through anonymous collection procedures such as via a Web spider, through chat rooms, or other publicly displayed areas listing personal or business e-mail addresses.)

- Marketers must not send bulk unsolicited commercial e-mail to an e-mail address without a prior business or personal relationship. (Business or personal relationship is defined as any previous correspondence, transaction activity, customer service activity, personalized marketing message, third-party permission use, or proven offline contact.)

The Association for Interactive Media Council for Responsible E-Mail also made the following recommendations:

- Do not falsify e-mail addresses.

- Do not falsify subject lines.

- Give recipients the chance to stop future messages.

- When collecting e-mail addresses, disclose how those addresses are to be used.

So, how do you entice prospects and customers to provide you with their e-mail address so they can be part of your opt-in program? Think of how you can implement some of the following strategies for your business:

- Offer promotions to your physical world customers: Offer a discount, say 10 percent off every customer's next purchase if they allow you to send them e-subscriptions. This is a great, low-cost method to migrate offline users online. Give away a free shirt, a free lunch, or something to get more addresses. Have a spot where customers can leave their business card or e-mail address next to the cash register. Your physical world customers are a proven market, so use this valuable tool to get their permission to join your e-marketing program.

- Incorporate a similar promotional offer in every customer's billing statement: "Save $20 on your next bill if you provide us with your e-mail address."

- Many Web sites offer sweepstakes or giveaways that entice customers to leave their e-mail when surfing through the site. Offer a vacation package, money, or a free sample of your product. Also, offer to send free e-newsletters or e-zines. Of course you need their e-mail address for that! Be sure to ask what interests them, so you can tailor your offerings accordingly.

- For business-to-business sites, consider working with trade directories to collect e-mail addresses. One Web site, www.B2Bworks.com, delivers qualified audiences of trade-publication Web-site users, who have an immediate need for news and information about their business. B2BWorks is organized to provide targeted access to the largest, most powerful business-to-business buying audience.

Here are some other resources for B2B lists:

- www.cahnerslists.com, "the world's largest publisher of business magazines"

- www.postmasterdirect.com, which claims to be the leader in opt-in e-mail lists, including B2B

- www.thomasregister.com, operated by the publishers of the largest real-world directory of manufacturers, which offers lists of manufacturers

- www.topica.com, a good aggregator of lists that could give you some ideas on targets or segments that you might be interested in pursuing

When you have your list and are ready to start an e-mail campaign, there are still more issues to consider. First, determine the style and format you will use when sending your e-mail message. Will your message be sent in plain-text, HTML, or rich-media format? Will you be sending a newsletter-type promotion? Next, determine the frequency of the mailings and the level of personalization. Will you send something every week, once a month, or only when you have a special offer? Will you address customers by name? Will you send personalized content to your prospects?

How will you assess the results of your campaign? You can track a variety of behaviors, such as how many recipients opened the message, which specific links were clicked, how many e-mails were forwarded, how many recipients made a purchase, and more. You need to decide in advance what information is important to your goals.

Here are a few more basic tips for e-mail marketing success:

- Keep subject lines (the most important line of the e-mail) to 35 characters.

- Include more than one link per e-mail, just in case the primary offer and link do not arouse the customer's interest.

- Monitor unsubscribe (opt-out) rates to make sure your e-mail is remaining relevant.

Eenie Strategy

Send Personalized Messages to E-Mail Lists Containing as Many as 500 Recipients

Create sharp and snappy e-mail messages with Broadc@st HTML, from MailWorkZ (www.mailworkz.com). This tool allows you to create dynamic looking e-mail messages that include graphics, multiple fonts, and plenty of color.

Broadc@st HTML allows you to create a professional looking brochure, personalize it with data from your mailing list, and send it to everyone on your bulk mail list. Managing your e-mail lists is critical, so with this application, you also can easily add, edit, or delete addresses. The e-mails can be sent to groups of addresses at predetermined times throughout the day, week, or month.

Broadc@st HTML is easy to use and provides comprehensive reports, so that you can effectively manage your campaign.

Cost: $249.

Meenie Strategy

Use a Multifunctional, Robust Online E-Mail Service

An online service called EmailFactory (www. emailfactory.com) offers a dynamic, versatile, and very affordable e-mail marketing service. Using a simple point-and-click system, EmailFactory's easy-to-use tools allow complete control over your marketing campaign.

EmailFactory offers list creation and management tools that allow you to create and manage your e-mail list. You can easily add or edit addresses and get list statistics. EmailFactory offers a powerful and responsive tracking system.

Using EmailFactory's robust e-mail management system, you can also establish, run, and manage viral marketing campaigns. Email-Factory also boasts about its contest features, allowing you to establish and track contests as part of your e-mail marketing campaign.

Cost: Starts at $100 per setup and $25 per month for up to 20,000 addresses.

Miney Strategy

Use Viral Marketing Strategies

Using a service from Clickability (www. clickability.com) is the quickest way to establish a viral distribution channel for your content and brand. By adding Clickability's EMAIL THIS button to your Web pages, visitors to your Web site can send e-mail links to your content to their friends, who forward those links to other friends. With a compelling site and a little luck, you may have just spread a site-clicking virus as everyone clicks their way back to your site. Viral marketing tools are used to drive traffic, increase revenue, allow for content popularity tracking, and build readership.

EMAIL THIS is brand transparent; it uses your logos and colors to reinforce your brand. Your brand is carried throughout the application, even when e-mailed links are forwarded all over the Web.

Clickability tracks and compiles reports on the aggregate viewing habits of your readers and delivers this information to you. The benefit of using Clickability is that it hosts and maintains the application, saving you development and maintenance costs. Clickability offers support to get you up and running. Establishing an account is easy. Just insert a few lines of JavaScript into your Web pages, and you are ready to go.

Cost: Varies, depending mostly on traffic, but can range from $500 to $2,000 per month.

Moe Strategy

Increase Your Brand Through Desktop Branding

Nothing gets closer to your prospects than a branding image that wiggles, dances, or sings to them whenever they are sitting at their computer. A company called AdTools (www.adtoolsinc.com) creates animated characters that users can download to their desktop. Once there, these characters have a mind of their own! They can talk, sing, burp, hop, skip, and jump—anything you want them to do. These animated characters are a tremendous reinforcement for your brand. Users interact with them, because they are unique and entertaining.

These animated applications can also be sent via e-mail to friends and associates, adding that viral component to your marketing plan. AdTools creates animation and multimedia desktop software products, as well as products for online community technology, palmtop, and wireless applications.

AdTools's products are extremely small in file size, usually less than 500k, so they are quick to download. The user does not need a plug-in or player. AdTool products allow for two-way communication and can feature full multimedia.

Cost: $15,000 to $25,000.

Chapter 24

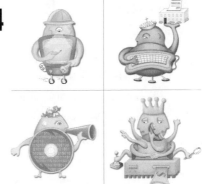

Banner Advertising

Banners are little digital billboards that advertisers place on other companies' Web sites. They may be small "thumbnails" (60 × 125 pixels) or long and thin (468 × 60 pixels) in shape. They may be static messages, though many are animated. When visitors click on a banner, they hyperlink to the advertiser's Web site.

Just as with traditional billboards, where banner ads are placed makes all the difference. A billboard on a site with few visitors will not generate as many customers as a billboard by the Lincoln Tunnel into New York City, where millions of commuters travel each day. A cyber-billboard on a tiny, private Web site will not generate as many views as a banner on Yahoo!.

Most companies that buy banner advertising space on very heavily trafficked sites such as Yahoo! and MSNBC have lavish advertising budgets and have committed huge investments toward their Internet-based enterprises. The cost of running a banner ad on these popular sites is probably around $40 to $60 per thousand "impressions"—the number of times the page is seen by Web surfers. As you might imagine, on these sites the term "heavily trafficked" is an understatement. Advertisers on these sites can run through not thousands, but millions of impressions in just a few hours. At those rates, you had better have a hefty budget.

Now, you may have heard that banner advertisements on the Internet do not work. In fact, there have been many reports and articles written attempting to disprove the theory, practicality, and return on investment of banner advertisements on Web sites. However, the early fear that Web surfers ignore "annoying" banner ads and that banner ads are therefore fruitless has largely passed.

Over the last few years, methods for recording and reporting accountability for banner advertisements have been greatly improved. The true effectiveness of banner advertising can now be measured, using sophisticated software that records the number of times a banner ad is viewed, as well as the number of times users click through to the advertisers' Web sites. New technology even allows companies to track results all the way from the initial click-through to the sale. This improved accountability allows researchers to gather information about the choices that shoppers make at many points along the path to the final sale. Thus, advertisers now can constantly improve upon their strategies.

The result is that we now know Internet advertising works. In fact, it works so well that Internet ads have become more valuable than any other form of advertising a company can engage in. In any other medium, there is a lag between the time the prospects see the ad and the time they respond to it. The Internet is "real time," so customers can act instantly, companies can hone their advertising immediately.

Predictably, banner advertisements have become big business. According to a report by the Internet Advertising Bureau (IAB), Internet advertising reached over $4.62 billion in 1999, representing an increase of 141 percent over the $1.92 billion spent on online advertising in 1998. More than half of the money spent in 1999 was for banner ads.

The goal of any advertising campaign is to promote sales by getting the right message to the right audience at the right time. Once you have identified your target audience and have defined a method of reaching them, you need to develop specific, measurable objectives to guide your campaign. The purpose of your campaign will probably fall under one of these categories:

- Branding or Awareness
- Traffic-Building
- Direct Sales

Branding

The objective of a branding campaign is not to go for the immediate sale, but to impress your company's brand identity upon potential customers. The hope is that by putting a message about your company in front of enough people, enough times, they will be able to identify your logo, sing your song, whatever. The point is that they will think about you first when they do decide to buy.

Traffic Building

The objective of a traffic-building campaign is to get as many Web surfers as possible to click on your ad and visit your site—to generate traffic. The advertisement is really just the teaser offer that brings the prospective customer through the door; you can worry about selling to them once they arrive. Your advertisement should have an immediate call to action, it must be provocative, and it must be creative.

Direct Sales

The objective of a direct-sales campaign is to get site visitors to take action, usually by buying something. While the objective of a traffic-building campaign is to get customers to come to your site, the success of a direct-sales campaign is measured in actual purchases made. Here you are trying to do two things at once, not only to attract good prospects but to motivate them to buy.

Jargon and Statistics

If you are setting out to buy banner ad space, getting familiar with banner ad lingo is the first order of priority. Banner advertising is most often sold in units called CPM, or costs per mil (Latin for thousand). This is the amount you will spend for 1,000 "impressions" of your banner ad. An impression occurs when your banner ad is displayed on a Web page requested by a Web surfer. For example, if your ad had 50,000 impressions on a site that charged $10 CPM, you would pay $500. CPM rates vary widely from site to site. A publication like *The New York Times* can demand a CPM of $65 to $80, while a general-interest publication with few readers might only be able to sell banners for $1 CPM.

Some sites will agree to "hard-code" your banner ad onto a page. A hard-coded banner ad is permanent on that page of the site on which it is hard coded. In that case, 1,000 views of that page will count as 1,000 impressions of your ad. However, most sites use an "ad server" or a third-party ad server service. With an ad server, your ad can appear anywhere on a site at any time. The ad server can be configured to rotate ads at random on particular Web pages, or it can serve an ad based on the user's request for information. Did you ever notice that when you use a search engine to search for something on the Internet banner advertisements specifically relating to your search happen to appear? For example, you might use a search engine like Lycos (www.lycos.com) to locate information about how to control roaches or household bugs. Ad servers recognize and analyze your specific request for information and could serve up ads (which appear at the top of your results page) for exterminator services or bug spray products.

The "click-though rate" (CTR) is another important concept to understand. A click-through occurs when a Web surfer actually clicks on a banner ad and visits the advertiser's Web site.

Page views, hits, and unique visitors are more key ideas relating to Web sites and banner ads. Specifically, these concepts relate to a Web site's "traffic." Traffic is the quantitative analysis of a site's exposure. This is analyzed by counting either the number of page views, hits, or unique users recorded by a Web site or a specific Web page.

Page views are the number of times a particular page—and any advertisements on it—appeared in a visitor's browser. Hits are the number of requests to a server that take place when a Web page is downloaded. Depending on the number of elements on a Web page—graphics, banners, text, and so on—one page request could result in as many as 15 or 20 hits.

Unique users are the numbers of different people who visit a site within a specific time period.

There are three main ways of pricing online advertising—impressions, cost per click, and pay per performance, which is based on customer action.

Impressions (CPM)

Most purchasers buy ads on the Web in multiple thousands of impressions. Purchasing banner advertising with this pricing model is similar to purchasing traditional print advertising. Therefore, this pricing model carries the same disadvantages as print. When you place an ad in a magazine that has say, 50,000 subscribers, you only know that 50,000 sets of "eyeballs" are given an opportunity to see your ad, not whether they actually looked at it. The same is true with purchasing banners on a "number of impressions" basis. Of course, this model also carries the same advantages of print advertising—the ability to brand your business's name by placing it in front of thousands of eyeballs, even if only for subconscious effects.

Below are some industry guidelines of CPM fees you can expect to pay for banner advertising at various types of sites:

- Search engines—$20 to $50
- Search engine keyword advertising—$40 to $70
- Targeted content sites—$10 to $80
- Ad networks—$10 to $70
- Sponsored content—$45 to $85
- Auction sites—$1 to $25

Cost Per Click (CPC)

A huge advantage of advertising in an information- and data-rich environment like the Web is the technological ability to track the number of people who are actually clicking on your banner ad and linking to your Web site. The CPC pricing model is designed to pay the advertiser only when a prospect clicks on their ad. In theory, cost per click pricing is a great idea, and a number of companies now offer it. But it is controversial, and advertising sites have been slow to adopt it on a large scale. Publishers do not want to be penalized if your ad does not attract any clicks. It could be the ad's fault—maybe it is not provocative or imaginative enough. The banner ad still takes up ad space, and your company still gets the potential eyeballs each time an ad is served up, whether or not it is clicked on.

Average CPCs usually run between $.25 and $.50. However, I have seen them as high as $.90 and as low as $.10, depending on the site's make-up.

Customer Action

While the click-through model is based on how successful your ad is at getting customers to your site, the customer-action model is based on actual sales or another direct customer action that results from an ad lead. The best example of this model may be Amazon.com's Associates program. In essence, Amazon is the advertiser, and when a customer who is referred from an associate's site purchases a product, that Web site is paid a referral fee for the ad. In this case, the banner ad is simply the special Amazon URL, which is built into the link from the referring site.

As you consider banner advertising, browse rate cards, and talk with ad-sales reps, remember that there is always room for negotiation. There is more inventory than demand on the Web, so negotiation in the industry is standard. In addition, you can often budget your costs by choosing to run an ad for a certain length of time until the agreed upon number of impressions is reached. Also, read on to see how banner advertising is frequently auctioned off on the Internet.

When beginning any advertising campaign, a company should have reasonable expectations of the outcome, given a certain set of established criteria. In other words, advertising is not purchased as a leap of faith. It is helpful to know your costs for acquiring customers and industry performance averages, so you can best anticipate your results. Of course, ad campaigns must be carefully monitored and adjusted, based on actual results achieved.

Knowing how and where to buy banner ads is a key factor in an online advertising campaign. There are many options. Perhaps your traditional marketing agency has become literate in banner advertising. Maybe you would prefer to make your own deals by visiting related sites and directly purchasing advertising space. You can also work with a third-party ad server, ad service provider, or banner management service. You can join an ad network, an ad auction, a banner exchange, or an affiliate network. Or you can do it all yourself and own and operate your own ad server.

Making Your Own Deals

For small businesses with a limited ad budget, the most critical factor in an ad campaign is a focused approach to getting the most exposure for the least money. Making your own deal may be the most cost-effective method for you to seek banner exposure. You have to invest only time to contact related sites—not competitors, but sites with products and content that complement yours. Go through the search engines, and enter keywords or terms associated with the products you are selling. Then contact the sites that come up highest in the results. Take advantage of their traffic. Contact them, find out what they charge for banner ads, and select the best sites to advertise with.

Working with Ad Servers

Banner ad management systems range from simple shareware scripts to six-figure systems that require a team of people to operate and manage. These technologies are designed to configure and place advertisements on Web sites and track all advertising results. Until recently, most Web sites were using their own proprietary ad-serving technology and software. While the ad-serving technologies did what they were supposed to do—that is, serve ads—proprietary campaigns lacked consistency in reporting activity. The industry could not agree on standard counting and measurement guidelines for online activities. In addition, it had to contend with myriad reporting formats for assessing advertising effectiveness. The need to develop consistent standards for recording data soon became painfully clear.

Enter third-party ad servers, ad networks, and every possible combination of third-party services. Trying to get a grip on all these players is quite an undertaking. The Internet advertising industry has become one of the most confusing enterprises in the new electronic realm.

Third-party companies got into the game in a variety of ways. Some simply ran ad servers for clients seeking to run advertising campaigns on the Internet. What the third-party ad server promised its clients was centralized campaign management, the development and dissemination of the banner ads, and for the first time a fair and accurate comparison of campaign activity. Even if the data were somewhat inaccurate, the counting methodology was the same in every instance. Finally, advertisers and publishers had one place that could show them how the campaign performed. For a directory of Internet ad servers go to www.digitrends.net/adserver.

Other third-party organizations created ad networks that do all the work of selling and running ads and collecting money from clients. Their main promise is that an advertiser can place a message within scores of categories, on a wide variety of sites, in one fell swoop. This is convenient, and relatively less expensive. This broad outreach to an identified, targeted audience is a fabulous low-cost strategy for a beginner's online campaign.

Yet other service organizations have created advertising auction houses. They are predicting that Internet advertising will be bought, sold, and traded like commodities. The truth is that even with all the advertising programs in place, as much as 80 percent of online space frequently goes unsold each month, even on prime Internet real estate. These new markets push this unsold inventory through auction clearinghouses and open exchanges.

Finally, there are banner and link exchanges. A banner ad exchange is a low- to no-cost way to advertise. Members of a banner ad exchange agree to host banner ads on their Web sites in exchange for placing their ads on the sites of other members. In many banner ad exchanges, there are thousands of participant Web advertisers and Web sites to advertise on. Usually, there is a two-for-one split, so that if you provide 1,000 banner ad impressions, your banner will be displayed 500 times on other member sites, but this ratio can vary. Banner exchanges boast great success for their network of companies.

There are hundreds of banner exchanges. Microsoft's Bcentral (www.bcentral. com), formally LinkExchange, has been around for a long time and has a good reputation. Yet many of the lesser-known exchanges also can provide good results for their members.

These free banner exchanges are unlike any other advertising medium in the world. You only need to have a Web site of your own, and a banner to display on other sites. Other than that, these banner exchanges are entirely automated. You just register with the network. The network provides you with a line of HTML code to be inserted into the page on your Web site where the hosted advertisements are to appear. (The exchange will provide easy instructions.) This line of code acts as a retrieval mechanism, sending out a call to the banner network's computer to display a banner. The computer sends different banner ads each time the page is loaded.

Banner exchanges use ad servers behind the scenes to keep track of how many times your site has displayed a banner from their network and how many times your banner has been displayed on other members' sites. Banner exchange programs also place paid advertising on their member sites, so they also keep track of an overall program credit ratio, the "multiplier" that defines how much free and paid advertising a banner network will accommodate. If your exchange's credit ratio is two-to-one—that is, your banner will be displayed somewhere else once for every two ads you host—half of the ads that appear on your Web page will be paid advertising. Those paying advertisers subsidize the cost of placing your ads on member Web sites. Naturally, it is in your best interest to obtain the best credit ratio possible.

Many banner exchange programs allow limited targeting of your advertising. Targeting simply means choosing a category of Web site to display your banner ad on. Obviously you want your ad to appear on sites that are complementary to yours. If you sell toys on your new Web site, you may want your ad to appear on various children's entertainment sites.

How well is the ad working? Your banner exchange network will provide statistics through your member account on their Web site. First, the exchange will show how many credits you have earned by displaying someone else's banner on your site. It will also show you impressions, the number of times your banner has been shown on someone else's site. And it will report on "click-throughs," the number of times an Internet user has actually clicked on your banner and been transferred to your site.

Remember that although your primary goal is to generate traffic to your site, it is much more important to make sure the user identifies in some way with your company. Once users come to your site, you must somehow get them involved in your business. Objectives run the gamut from product purchasing to registering with you for future prospecting. All of the banner advertising in the world is useless unless you have a clear sense of purpose and can articulate that your site has value to those who "click through" your banner.

Designing Banner Ads

When the time comes to create a banner ad, you will find that each banner network has its own set of rules for what is acceptable in banners—whether or not the banner can be animated, which graphic format is acceptable, and so on. The exchange may also limit the number of kilobytes of storage space your banner can occupy.

It makes sense for new advertisers to take advantage of the free services available through companies like BCentral (www.bcentral.com), who are extremely helpful to new members and provide extensive information on their sites about Internet banner advertising.

Banner ads are much like traditional advertisements. Successful banners are clever and catchy. Make your banners bright, succinct, and inviting. On the Web, it costs no more to produce color than black and white, and advertisements can be animated to attract more user attention. Some research indicates that more users respond to animated banners than to static ones. Many marketers recommend boosting click-through rates by including a call to action within banner copy, such as a simple phrase "Click Here." Others have found that headlines printed in larger fonts pull in more visitors than smaller headlines.

Several new forms of banner ads also have appeared recently. As faster Web connections with greater bandwidth become more widely available, many companies are experimenting with streaming commercials and expandable banner ads that allow customers to obtain further information without leaving the original site.

Also, some marketers promote unconventional advertisements to overcome customer resistance. They create banner ads that look like part of the Web site, so when people click on them, they have no idea that they are clicking on an ad. Banner ads may look like radio buttons, check boxes, hypertext links, drop-down menus, "Click Here" buttons, and other innocuous parts of Web sites. There is room to wonder whether these techniques result in sales to customers who otherwise would not have visited the advertiser's site or merely irritate users, who may feel they have been tricked into clicking on the ad. So far as I know, there is no firm evidence either way; would-be advertisers will have to experiment for themselves.

Either way you go—with an unconventional ad or a more traditional, sparkling, star-spangled banner ad—consider where the click will land the prospect. Have the banner link to your home page for "general" ads. That is, if your objective is to promote your company or brand, then your Web site's home page is probably a sufficient place for the visitor to land. From the home page they should get the best overall idea of what your company offers.

But, not all banner ads should point to your Web site's home page. When developing your advertising plan, include a banner linking strategy based on the specific action you want potential users to take. For example, a banner that encourages users to subscribe to an online newsletter should point to a page that contains a brief description of the newsletter and the complete data-entry form, not to a home page that links to the registration form five levels deep. Likewise, if the goal of your Web site is to sell products or services, link your banners directly to product or service information. Be sure that the page includes specs for your product or service, and consider including a "buy me now" button for items that can be ordered directly from your site.

Tracking Effectiveness

Once your ad is up on a site, how do you know whether it is working? It is not enough to note that sales are up. Say you bring 1,000 new visitors and 10 people buy, and that is your normal rate. What if, through adjusting the banner ad or the design of your site, you could double the number of sales? Without good tracking, you do not know what is converting prospects into customers. You may be wasting thousands of ad dollars without realizing it.

In addition to measuring CTR and customer action, you need to also measure banner effectiveness. Let's say that you created two banners and have them each rotating on multiple sites. Banner 1 receives the better click-through ratio at 14.5 percent. Banner 2 received a much less impressive click through ratio of 1.5 percent. However, Banner 2 had a much more appropriate message and brought in people more likely to become customers. Banner 2 received a conversion ratio of 6 percent, where as Banner 1 received a conversion ratio of 0.15 percent. This ultimately meant that Banner 2 made twice as many sales as Banner 1.

When you look deep enough, you have a better opportunity to test the effects of creative ads, price, location on a publisher's site, and much more. You will also notice that some sites where you advertise cater to people who are more apt to purchase, while others draw people more apt to browse.

Publisher Strategies
(Selling Advertisements on Your Web Site)

If you are the advertiser, you want to place your banner advertisements on other Web sites. If you are the publisher, you recognize an opportunity to create a revenue stream by hosting other companies' banner ads on your site. Like www.internetprophets.com, you may be both an advertiser and a publisher. You want to increase traffic to your Web site, so you advertise on related opportune sites, and you want to benefit from a new revenue source through hosting ads on your own site.

Publishers have responsibilities to both advertisers and those who visit the site—with the heavier emphasis on the advertisers who feed them. The publisher's goal is to target readers who have some sort of value to the advertisers.

Consider traditional magazine programs, for example. Take technology magazines. The readers of tech magazines are almost by definition users of technology as well, and probably fairly sophisticated ones. This audience is the perfect audience for technology advertisers. However, Ferrari and makers of other high-end sport cars and luxury items also advertise in tech magazines. Why? Well, demographics show that the tech market consists of young readers who have great wealth. Anyway, prospective advertisers examine the magazine's full media package, which tells both how many readers the magazine has and who those readers are—everything the magazine knows about them from their income level to the last purchase they made.

In principle, it is no different on the Web. In fact, Web publishers have much greater opportunities to collect valuable information about their visitors. Yet many Web-based publishers seem to get sidetracked. Because of the Web's incredible reach, the concept of traffic is often misapplied to the Internet publisher's business model. Traffic by itself is meaningless. What counts is a clearly defined audience. Identifying each visitor and recording his or her buying preferences will enable you to attract those advertisers dying to target your specific audience and ready to pay for the privilege. And because they can target their advertisements so effectively, they will achieve the success they need to keep advertising with you.

Also, Web publishers often are overly concerned about the performance of the Web site. True, the Web site has to deliver what visitors want, but from a business standpoint this is secondary to recruiting qualified prospects for its advertisers.

Think of it this way: If your main source of revenue is derived from selling advertising on your site, then your advertisers, not your visitors, are your real customers. Your Web visitors are actually the product that you are selling to the advertisers. In order to generate the best price for that product, you need a product that is in high demand. An effective publishing Web site will be constantly improving its customer bases. This is no simple task. You must consider all aspects of the site—site content and functionality—expressly from the perspective of its role in attracting a desirable audience.

Think about proving the value of your Web site's audience to your advertisers in exactly the same way you would need to prove the value of any other product. The idea is simple: Gather information, create knowledge, leverage the knowledge, make money. A successful publisher will meticulously identify his audience (product) and convert the demographic profiles into advertising revenue (sales).

Based on the type of site you run and the offerings that you extend, you should know approximately who the Web site's potential visitors will be, even before the site goes online. If you know who the visitors will be, then you have an idea of which advertisers will be interested in relating to those visitors. To increase the value of your product, you can try to lure visitors with specific content that relate to your advertisers' offerings and watch them react. Now you have very specific profiles and behaviors that increase the market value of each visitor.

Properly analyzing reactions to targeted content gives you the power to regulate the make-up of your audience, and consequently the value of your advertising space. You will be able to charge higher rates per impression, since each impression is more targeted, and you will have more ad inventory to sell.

There is good benefit here for the visitors as well. The more you know about your visitors, and the more you fine-tune your message to them, the more you personalize their experience. They get content that they have shown interest in, and they see advertisements for products and services that they are likely seeking. The result of happy visitors is that they will return again and again. Your click-through rates will improve, and your campaign will be a success.

Many publishing model Web endeavors offer a variety of opportunities to their advertisers. These packages of online ad vehicles are typically referred to as sponsorship opportunities. Sponsorships offer your advertisers extra value. With a sponsorship package, there are more places to advertise and a greater variety of vehicles to use. The advertiser could have a banner ad, a mention in an e-zine, or even sponsor an online conference. Combining all these activities is destined to give better results.

Publisher sponsorships make good sense for a lot of reasons. First, if you are selling many spots in one package, you will probably need fewer advertisers to make a given income. In a sponsorship model, you want to target advertisers looking for the bigger piece of the pie, rather than seeking advertisers banner by banner. Fewer advertisers require less work to obtain, reducing solicitation costs. Next, since the advertisers you want are looking for the big slice of your advertising real estate, you can charge more, thus increasing your revenues. With a sponsorship package, you are selling a group of tools that have an obviously higher value than each part of the whole. You have greater room for negotiation.

As the industry matures, the pricing for banner ads, direct e-mail and newsletter advertisements will become more and more defined. But with a sponsorship model, you will always be able to make up your own unique package and have more flexibility in defining your own pricing.

Take a look at other Web sites that have sponsors. You are likely to find that sponsors take part in multiple content, advertisement, and listing features on a Web site. One excellent example is www.fool.com. Register to receive newsletters. You will receive very interesting, timely, and worthwhile material about five times per day. And you will find that each newsletter has a different sponsor. The newsletter offers content blurbs which, when clicked, return you to the Motley Fool site, where you will be exposed to many more advertisers.

Eenie Strategy

Join a Banner Exchange Program

One of the best known banner exchange programs is called Link Exchange—a product of Microsoft's bCentral at www.bcentral.com. Link Exchange claims to be the Web's largest ad network, with more than 400,000 sites. It also claims to reach more than 65 percent of Web users. For every two ads you show on your site, you earn one credit to have your banner shown on another member's site. The amount of free advertising you receive is directly proportional to the amount you give others.

Joining a banner exchange is a way to pull traffic to your site and acquire new customers. Using Link Exchange, you can choose what type of site to advertise on to reach your prospective audience. When you join the network, you categorize your site in at least one of 2,000-plus categories. This allows you to target your banner ad to your specific audience.

Link Exchange offers free statistical reporting, so you can track visitors to your site and measure advertising effectiveness.

Cost: Free.

Meenie Strategy

Hire a Product Management Company to Guide and Direct Your Web-Advertising Campaigns

Porthos Consulting (www.porthosconsulting. com) is a consulting firm that will act as a product manager for all of your online projects. Porthos bases its work on the principal that understanding and evaluating your business needs and the environment you compete in are key to developing a strategy that will set your business apart and ultimately drive bottom-line growth.

Porthos will evaluate your current processes and recommend ideas to increase efficiency, customer satisfaction, and long-term profitability, fitting suggestions to your business and budget. Porthos works to assist you in establishing strategic partnerships, penetrating target clients more effectively, and driving channel and distribution relationships.

Porthos provides direction in the following areas:

- Recommend hosting environments for the online operation

- Implement and manage double opt-in e-mail newsletters and lists

- Review and recommend tracking and database software for Web operations

- Research and recommend or build referral or affiliate programs

- Business plan analysis and development on all online components

- ROI calculation and management
- Traffic-building activities

Cost: Porthos charges a variable, usually modest, up-front fee and an ongoing percentage of sales.

Miney Strategy

Sell Advertising Space on Your Web Site

If you would like to sell advertising on your content-oriented Web site, you may want to contact DoubleClick (www.doubleclick.com), one of the first and largest online advertisement agencies.

The DoubleClick Network represents hundreds of publishers from around the world and offers them incremental revenue streams from online banner advertising. Sites within their network leverage DoubleClick's worldwide sales force, global reach, and multiple sales channels to sell a designated amount of inventory on run-of-category and run-of-network buys.

DoubleClick Network site benefits include:

- Non-exclusive sales representation
- Incremental revenue from advertisers purchasing your inventory
- A sales force covering national, local, e-commerce, and international markets to complement your current sales efforts
- DoubleClick DART ad serving and reporting technology
- Exposure to an established base of more than 4,300 advertisers
- Higher CPMs generated from unique targeting innovations for re-marketing to existing and prospective customers

Cost: Variable, but substantial. DoubleClick accepts only larger companies as clients, and prices accordingly.

Moe Strategy

Incorporate a Multichannel Advertising Strategy for Your Advertisers

Engage the services of Engage (www. engage.com), which offers a suite of multi-channel advertising programs. Engage's Multichannel AdManagement Suite helps publishers better serve their advertisers by automating the trafficking, proofing, and delivery of ads for print, Web, e-mail, and other advertising media. Its powerful digital asset-management system allows publishers to merge online and offline advertising operations so that they can sell, traffic, and manage integrated multichannel campaigns.

With the Engage Multichannel AdManagement Suite, you can attract more advertisers with flexible and innovative online inventory packages and cross-sell online and offline customers, directly increasing your revenue.

Cost: Again, variable, but over-budget, even for a Miney company.

Part VI
Appendices

Appendix A
A Method to the Madness

Did you know there is really a method to the madness of the U.S. highway systems? (And why are we suddenly talking about highways in a book about e-business?) Well, the U.S. government had a very effective strategy in mind when the highway system was laid out. If you take a look at the map of the area around any major U.S. city, you will see that the major highways encircle the city. The reason? Washington did not want any of these major cities cut off in time of war. If any one road were destroyed, there would be alternative routes into and out of every large city in the country.

Several decades later, the U.S. Department of Defense (DOD) had a brilliant idea. Why not build a computer infrastructure similar to the highway infrastructure? One that could transfer data from any major computing center in the country to any other center, through many different routes? One that could not be disrupted if a war blocked one, or even many, of the paths?

DOD found its infrastructure in the U.S. telephone system, which had already spread its cables throughout the country: If we could reliably send a voice from the Atlantic to the Pacific, why not send digital data from one point to another using the same circuits? When a telephone line or switching station went down, the phone system was already designed to route calls around the trouble. Find a way to send data over the same system—the data that was becoming increasingly important to modern warfare—and there would be no stopping it.

In 1968 the Department of Defense Advanced Research Projects Agency (ARPA) successfully transmitted data between four mainframe computers located at the Stanford Research Institute, the University of California at Los

Angeles, the University of California at Santa Barbara, and the University of Utah. ARPA called the network connecting these four sites the "ARPANet."

Once the Internet protocol for data transfer was developed, around 1973, not only was the intelligence system protected, but unbelievable new opportunities arose. The Internet, more or less as we now know it is the direct result of that early work. E-mail, newsgroup messages, and the vast collection of sites on the World Wide Web all eventually grew out of this primitive beginning.

Now, of course, 20 or 30 years ago, few of us had any idea that this "underground" system existed. And even if we had known about it, we would not have figured out what good it would do us. In the late '80s, we learned that Oliver North had used something called e-mail for his various escapades, but we still did not understand what e-mail really was.

Throughout the '70s and '80s, the Internet was used mostly by government, large universities, research institutions, and big corporations. At first, access was restricted to government agencies and approved contractors. Later, the Internet was officially open to the public, but it was effectively limited to the computer elite: First, you had to have access to a computer, then you had to be really knowledgeable in order to use the primitive Internet software then available. Nonetheless, the data and educational resources freely offered by these early users created a worldwide library of unprecedented proportion.

The first personal computers appeared in the 1970s, but PCs did not become widely available until IBM entered the game in 1981, and their descendants really did not go mainstream until the early '90s. It took 15 years for the PC to reach 25 percent of U.S. households. However, as personal computers gradually proliferated in the '90s, the Internet's popularity soared. Now more than 65 percent of Americans have access to the Internet. PCs are a must for every school, library, and business. Many families have more than one computer in their home.

Put simply, the Internet is a network of computers—well over 100 million of them at this point—that are located around the world, all of them connected through the telephone system, as well as some dedicated cables and fiber-optic lines. Once you connect to one of the Internet computers, you are literally connected to the entire network. Your computer becomes part of the Internet, and you can browse through all the files on each computer across the world. You can also add files of your own.

The Internet is not privately owned, and there is no central control. As a result, the Internet is either wildly free and exciting, truly capitalistic and democratic, or dangerously anarchical. This all depends on your point of view.

Types of Internet Access

With the Internet protocol (IP)—the technology that could connect two computers together—many business opportunities arose. Private commercial services like America Online, Prodigy, and Compuserve grew up quickly. These services did not connect users to the Internet; rather, they merely used the technology to allow subscribers to connect to their proprietary computers and view data that these private services offered. In other words, in the '80s, if you had a computer, you could sign on to Prodigy and access a host of information provided by Prodigy partners such as Newsweek and Grolier's, but you could not get to the information on the growing network of computers called the Internet.

At the same time, bulletin board systems (BBSs) appeared. These were usually hobby setups that allowed users to call up a central computer, explore the files on it, and often exchange messages with other users. They used the new communications technology (though not necessarily IP), but did not actually connect to the Internet. It was easier for users to join these private BBSs, but even these systems were rather arcane, and membership stayed within a relatively sophisticated minority of computer users.

To use the Internet directly, you would have had to locate an Internet service provider (ISP) in your area. An ISP provides a host computer that is part of the Internet and allows users to access the Net through it. In the '80s and early '90s, they were relatively rare and did not always give full access to the Internet. That changed with the launch of the World Wide Web. The Web is just one facet of the Internet, but it is the part that made the Internet easy enough for the nontechnical masses to use. In doing so, it paved the way for the growth of the massive, largely commercial world that is today's Internet.

Appendix B
Launch of the World Wide Web

The World Wide Web was the brainchild of a computer scientist named Tim Berners-Lee. While working at CERN, the European high-energy physics laboratory in Geneva, he had an idea that information on the Internet should be accessible through a simple interface from any kind of computer, anywhere in the world. Further, it should be connected as "hypertext," so that readers could click on part of the text and follow the link to related documents, images, multimedia objects, and other computer files. Berners-Lee was not the first to have this idea—an American computer scientist named Ted Nelson conceived hypertext as early as 1965 and spent most of 30 years trying to create a practical hypertext network—but Berners-Lee was the first to make it work.

While working at CERN in the early 1990s, he developed all basic technologies of the World Wide Web. He devised the domain-name convention, which translates numerical IP addresses into the familiar www format that even nongeeks can cope with. He created HTML, or HyperText Mark-up Language, which made it possible to link one document to another and to display them more or less predictably on a variety of different computer screens. He also devised the first Web browser, a graphical user interface for the Internet. It was called *WorldWideWeb*, the first use of that term.

A simple interface was the key. In 1993, the Internet got a phenomenal boost with the release of Mosaic, a simple, freely available Web browser that could be made to run on virtually any personal computer. The Internet hid its cryptic computer mumbo-jumbo behind a slick new point-and-click interface.

Netscape and other companies polished *Mosaic* further and brought commercial versions to market.

However, just being simple to use was only a part of the story of the new Internet. With graphical browsers suddenly common, the Internet gained an attractive new look. It now sported full-color pictures, music, even video. Instead of grim screens of monochrome text that only a hacker could love, users found vivid pages full of attractive, functional media. This was the World Wide Web—or simply "the Web," as it is now being called—a place where consumers could be entertained and feel at home.

And it is the Web that has attracted savvy marketing executives throughout business and industry. They have recognized a unique opportunity to create new and better ways of promoting their products and services to millions of potential buyers who have made the Web a part of their daily lives.

As the Web exploded, the commercial online services had no option but to expand their closed computer worlds. Around 1995, America Online, Prodigy, and Compuserve offered their users gateway access to the Internet. Today the service of these independent providers is very similar to what it used to be; it is still, for the most part, a proprietary environment, with gateway access to the Internet added as something of an afterthought. Because they rely on this gateway access, these services tend to be slower than Internet access one can get from a direct Internet Service Provider.

Internet Addresses

So, how do we really get around the Internet and the World Wide Web? Technically, here is how it works:

Every host computer on the Internet has an address made up of four numbers. Each number is one byte long, so it must be between 0 and 255. The address is usually shown with periods between the numbers. Thus an address might be something like 209.225.277.51 or 195.46.8.120. Numbers are hard to remember, though, so we now associate names with the numbers. So when someone looks for a Web site whose IP address is, say, 122.65.777.9, she types in www.mycomputer.com, a computer somewhere on the Internet looks up the numerical address associated with that name, and she is sent to the appropriate Web site.

This mechanism, called the Domain Name System, or DNS, is used on every Internet computer. Thus, today you almost never need to know the IP address of the computer you are trying to reach. Odd as it seems, this unobtrusive piece of technology sparked a commercial frenzy in the '90s.

Domain Names

As the Web became commercialized, companies raced to stake their claim. Claiming domain names was a lot like claiming land and territories during the expansion of the American West. Anyone who owned the name could build a business on it—and some of the names were valuable indeed. Since there was no restriction on the registration of domain names, some very astute individuals and companies gobbled up hundreds or thousands of them and put them up for sale to the highest bidder. Today, it is said that 90 percent of the English dictionary has been used in registering Internet domain names. Even more amazingly, more than 60,000 domain names are registered every day—and that's just for the .com, .net, and .org sites.

Maybe you've read or heard about these fantastic domain name auctions. The domain name beer.com was sold for several million dollars to a major brewer. Drugs.com sold for over $800,000. The words beer and drugs are as generic as they come. But think of how valuable they become to their respective product manufacturers. Domain names are extremely powerful for any business. Domain names are so scarce that people are paying huge sums of cash, and a new cottage industry, name appraisal, has been spawned to dupe nascent entrepreneurs. One might think there are no more of these domains left—but I believe we have seen only the tip of the iceberg.

All this raises a question for Internet startups: "How does one find a suitable name?"

Let's start by reviewing the reasons for registering a domain name. In the previous section we saw that a domain name is actually a "user-friendly" equivalent of an arcane numbering system. Obviously, a domain name like pizzaexpress.com is easier to remember than a string of numbers like 199. 324.87.2.

The most obvious reason to register a domain name is to give your company a home on the Web. Why is it important to do this immediately? Because domain names are unique—that is, there can only be one smithandjones.com registered in the entire the world. If your firm's name is Smith and Jones, and you have not registered that domain name yet, you should probably hurry. A PR firm in Great Britain already uses smithandjones.co.uk, and a law firm in Canada already holds smithandjones.net. The .com variation cannot remain open for long.

By the way, your firm does not have to be named Smith and Jones in order for you to register smithandjones.com. As with beer.com, the person that registered it knew this was a valuable domain name that could be sold at a substantial price. He bought the domain name just to sell it. This happens all the time.

The next reason to have a domain name is to have an e-mail address or URL that is similar to your company name or that has some affiliation with what your company does. A domain name allows you to receive e-mail at a customized e-mail address. If your organization's name is Smith and Jones, PC, you could register the domain name smithandjones.com and your e-mail address could be yourname@smithandjones.com. Your customers would also be able to access your organization's Web site by visiting www.smithandjones.com with their Web browser.

Finally, and in some ways most important, a domain name represents a branding opportunity. A company name or a domain name can inspire, excite, motivate, and entice. At the same time, it can repel, bore, confuse, and polarize. Coming up with a domain name that is not only memorable, but original and compelling, for your company can be one of the most difficult and critical early challenges for getting your business on the Internet.

The reason I say domain names are still at the tip of the iceberg is that you can be very versatile and flexible when choosing a domain name. Let's say smithandjones.com has been taken—registered to another firm—by the time you get there. You will have to think of a different domain name that describes your firm. Be flexible. Dream up alternatives to your perfect domain name if you've found it has been taken. Say you were a law firm in Kansas. How about bestlawyersinkansas.com? Now that's a memorable domain name that really lends itself to marketing. All your advertisements in the papers, on television, and radio will refer to you as being the best lawyers in Kansas. You will tell the public to reach you on the World Wide Web at www.bestlawyersinkansas.com. That kind of domain name can be extremely powerful. In fact, a domain name can be one of your most valuable assets.

There are some general rules about domain names that you should know before trying to create one of your own: The only valid characters for a domain name are letters, numbers, and a hyphen "-". Other special characters like a question mark "?" or an exclamation mark "!" are *not* permitted. And absolutely no spaces are allowed in a domain name. Top level domain names can be up to twenty-six characters long, including the dots "." and the three characters used to identify the type of domain. The following are top level domain (TLD) suffixes:

.COM—The most popular domain suffix refers to a COMmercial entity. All businesses should have a .COM suffix to their corporate name if possible. Outside the United States, .COM is replaced by .CO, followed by a two-letter code for the country. For example, a commercial domain name in Great Britain would end, ".co.uk."

.NET—This suffix was traditionally used for the computer nodes that were a part of the Internet NETwork. However, there is no restriction for registering a .NET domain. Many companies who find "theircompanyname.com" taken now register as "theircompanyname.net." Many companies register both versions to provide the broadest protection of the domain name.

.ORG—This suffix was traditionally used to register domain names for ORGanizations, usually nonprofits. Again, anyone can register a .org domain. However, this suffix still strongly suggests that the Web site is operated by a nonprofit group, so companies seldom register .org domain names.

.EDU—Predictably, these domain names are assigned only to EDUcational institutions.

.GOV—Again, this one is obvious. Only GOVernment institutions can register a .GOV domain name.

The rules for naming Internet domains have been changed recently to allow for longer names, with several new domain suffixes, and more suffixes are under consideration. However, domain names that use these novelties are not yet common, and most Internet users still think only of sites that end with .COM, .ORG, .NET, and .GOV. For the time being, it is probably just as well to keep names as short as possible and stick to the traditional suffixes.

What else? A domain name should be easy to type, the simpler the better. It should be easy to spell, pronounce, and hear. When at all possible, avoid acronyms and numbers in a domain name.

The name should also be memorable. It can be your business name, the name of your product, or a word that describes your product or service. Make it something that people will not have to write down—something that they will remember. Consider a descriptive or provocative name. You can choose to be literal, metaphorical, esoteric, or something else. Do you want your name to describe what you do (housecleaners.com), be a metaphor (Amazon.com), be more esoteric (Yahoo.com), or would you like to spice things up with a foreign tongue, like vivalarevolucion.org?

Decide who you are and what type of personality you want your company to reflect. Are you bold, innovative, and aggressive, or friendly, playful, and outgoing? Are you a technology company, or are you service driven? Do you want to come across as big, traditional, and all-encompassing or comfortable and intimate? All of these traits can be reflected in a name, and the best names should match the traits you want people to associate with you.

Be sure to think about the future. When selecting a name, be careful not to paint yourself into a corner. A highly specific name might not give you "permission" with your customers to branch out to new, yet related areas of business. A name like greatplantfood.com is not likely to attract customers to your new line of garden tools.

Avoid trademarked names. The company who trademarked that name in the real world probably will try to defend its ownership on the Internet as well. It might well succeed, and even if it fails, the court case will be long and expensive.

Choose a name that will last a long time. In the last few years the trendy "E"s (for e-commerce), "I"s (for information revolution), and DOTs (for dot-com) have been used in thousands of variations. Five years from now, names with these appendages could sound like dinosaurs. Do not be trendy. Name your company so that it will sound relevant in the future.

Consider registering more than one domain name. Assuming that they are still available, you can have www.smithandjones.com *and* www.bestlawyersinkansas. com. You can have both domains "point" to the same Web site and to the same e-mail address. Why have both? Because a prospect or customer who knows your firm name may try to find your Web site by using that name. Likewise, someone who listens to the radio may not remember your firm's name, but go instead to the more memorable, marketed address www.bestlawyersinkansas.com.

Now, there is still a bit more to understand about domain names, and it may be important. Like so many other facets of this new world, domain name registrations are still evolving.

When the Internet was born, Washington assigned a government organization to act as the Internet registration authority. Called InterNic, it was responsible for assigning all the domains that ended in EDU, GOV, COM, NET, and ORG. In 1997, the Clinton Administration published an executive order calling for privatization of the Internet Domain Name System (DNS). It published a "White Paper" entitled "Management of Internet Names and Addresses." The White Paper asked that a private, nonprofit corporation be formed to assume responsibility for the overseeing of domain names: "The new corporation should operate as a private entity for the benefit of the Internet community as a whole. The development of sound, fair, and widely accepted policies for the management of DNS will depend on input from the broad and growing community of Internet users. Management structures should reflect the functional and geographic diversity of the Internet and its users. Mechanisms should be established to ensure international participation in decision making."

In response, the Internet Corporation for Assigned Names and Numbers (ICANN) was established. ICANN's role is to qualify and approve of private companies that want to operate a domain name registration service. (So far half a dozen such private registrars have set up shop.) Pay attention to ICANN in the news, because ICANN is responsible for setting policy when it comes to domain registrations. It will shape the future of the Internet in fundamental ways in the years to come.

ICANN has begun the process of considering whether, how, and when to add new generic top-level domains (GTLDs) to the domain name system. In recent years, a number of plans have been proposed to create new GTLDs, such as .firm, .store, .law, and .arts., and some companies have even taken orders for them. If these top level domain names are adopted, Mary Jones and Robert Smith would have a shot at registering their domain name as jonesandsmith.firm, if jonesandsmith.com has been taken.

There are many arguments for and against new GTLDs. Those in favor of new GTLDs argue that there are no technical obstacles to establishing new generic top level domains, and that doing so will help relieve perceived scarcities in existing domain names. This, they say, would be consistent with a general push towards consumer choice and diversity of options. Those opposed fear that new domains will bring greater opportunities for consumer confusion and the risk of increased trademark infringement. Those concerned about intellectual property are highly concerned about protecting trademarked names, and some trademark holders lucky enough to own ".com" domains fear that new GTLDs will pose additional risk of trademark infringement.

If ICANN approves these GTLDs, it will proceed with caution, because there is no recent experience in introducing new domain extensions. They recommend that a limited number of new top level domains be introduced initially and that additional top level domains be added only after careful evaluation of the initial introduction. Implementation should promote competition in the business of registering domain names.

Eenie and Meenie Domains

If you have a real business, register a real domain name. Do not accept a name that is simply grafted on to the name of a portal site. If your URL begins with geocities.com/ or homesiteaol/ members or tzlink.com~tripod.com/, you will be lost in the morass of similar names.

In order to register a domain name, you can go to any of the authorized ICANN registrars listed below. These are companies accredited, and currently operating, as registrars:

- NameSecure.com (United States)

- Networksolutions.com (United States)

- register.com (United States)

Each of these services has instructions on how to register a new domain name. They are very intuitive. Typically, they have an input box on their home page that simply says, "Name to be registered." You enter your name there, and select your suffix. If the name desired has already been registered, the service will return a listing including information about the organization that holds the name, the name servers, and the contacts responsible for administering it. If it is not in use, the answer will be: AVAILABLE.

Miney Domains

Buy or build? Sometimes, you just have to have a name that someone is selling. In that case, what is it worth to you? The eCompanies folk paid $7.5 million for the name business. com. Perfect.com paid somewhat less for its name—$100,000—but that is still a lot of money for a small start-up company to invest in a domain name. Some names can be acquired for $5,000 or less. My feeling is that unless you must have the name up for sale, do not spend more than it would cost for a consultant to help you develop a new one.

Moe Domains

Hiring an agency or consultant to help with developing a name for your company and Web site can be a good idea. It can take enormous amounts of time and energy to name a company. Having a strong process and experienced leadership will make that time more fruitful. When looking at firms, make sure they walk you through their process. Also, look at past projects, and contact references. Fees for help with domain names can range anywhere from $15,000 to $100,000, or even more. Make sure you get the service, attention, and experience for which you are paying.

Appendix C
Using Search Engines

We looked at the role of search engines in promoting a Web site in Chapter 21. This appendix is about the other half of the process, using search engines to find a site. This is the route that many potential customers will take to locate your site.

There are literally thousands of search engines on the Internet today. The familiar names—Yahoo!, Excite, Infoseek, Netscape search, Netfind, Google, askjeeves, and so on—barely scratch the surface. Some are general-purpose utilities, like the ones above, while others are specialized to find pages only in the sciences, for example, or pages originating in certain countries. Some have even finer specialties. One, cyclesearch.net, finds only pages that deal with motorcycles. There also are meta-engines, which automatically call up other search engines, have them make the search, and combine the results into one comprehensive report. Search engine technologies are still being developed, and thousands of companies are vying to lead the race for the perfect engine. One day soon, it may be necessary to create a specialized search engine, just to find the right search engine for your purpose.

See the end of this chapter for a list of the most popular search engines.

Building a Catalog

Most people tend to use the term "search engine" generically: If you go to a Web site, enter some search terms, and it comes back with a list of resources to look at, it must be a search engine. In fact, there are two different kinds of search engines to consider, true search engines and Web directories. They are not the same. The difference lies in how the listings are compiled.

True search engines build their listings automatically. They send out "robots" or "spiders" that automatically visit a Web page, read it, and then follow links to other pages listed within the site, and scan them as well. (This is what it means when someone refers to a site being "spidered" or "crawled.") The search engine's spiders may return to a site as often as every week to look for changes.

Everything the spiders find goes into an index. When a user calls up the search engine and enters keywords, the engine searches through the index that its spiders have built. This catalog contains hypertext references to the actual pages on the World Wide Web.

Web directories depend on human beings for their listings. Web site owners submit a short description to the search engine, or editors write descriptions or reviews of sites they have seen. When a user asks one of these facilities to make a search, the engine finds matches only in the descriptions submitted.

There also are hybrid search engines. These facilities search the Web and also maintain an associated directory.

Search engines and Web directories each have some advantages and disadvantages: Search engines have their spiders out on the Internet at all times, constantly searching for new or altered Web sites, so they tend to find great numbers of pages. However, it may take the system time to enter a Web page into the index after it has been "spidered," and until it is added to the index, it is not available to anyone using the search engine.

In addition, spiders do not have much in the way of judgment. If a site mentions John Donne, that page will wind up being indexed under the poet's name, even if it appears only in passing, say as a tortured metaphor in a technical review of a new computer processor.

In a Web directory, a human being has contributed to the indexing process, so one can at least hope that a site indexed under John Donne's name will have at least something to do with him. However, the results depend in large part on the accuracy of the site owner's description or the skill of the reviewer.

And, because they require manual labor, Web directories tend to index far fewer pages than true search engines. Sites that a spider would have found may be overlooked, simply because no reviewer has gotten to them yet.

Which type of index will serve the user better depends largely on the search being carried out. For subjects where a good, comprehensive special-interest directory is available, they often yield the best ratio of good, on-topic "hits" to dross, and they are likely to pick up sites that either would be missed by less selective engines or would be lost in a mass of tangential or off-topic material. (Any e-business that fits into one of these fields definitely should ask to be listed in relevant directories!) For other topics, it can depend on exactly how the engine pulls up "hits" from its index.

Finding the Pages

Search for almost any topic using your favorite search engine, and the results can be amazing.

Almost instantly, the search engine will sort through the millions of pages it has categorized and present you with ones that it thinks best match your topic. The matches are typically ranked, so that the most relevant ones come first. And this complicated process is *fast*. Search engines often brag about how quickly they operate, listing the search time along with the results. Google, for example, scans some 1.3 billion Web pages and seldom reports search times much longer than 0.2 seconds.

Of course, search engines do not always get it right. Their reports usually contain irrelevant pages—often many of them—and it takes more digging to find what you are really looking for. To make it more confusing, the same search on different search engines often produces different results. Each search engine uses different algorithms to produce the "best" results possible, according to whatever criteria made sense to its creators.

There are some basic "relevance" rules that most search engines follow. The main rules involve the location and frequency of keywords on a Web page. Pages with keywords appearing in the title are assumed to be more relevant to the topic than others. Most search engines also check to see whether the keywords appear near the top of a Web page, in the headline or the first few paragraphs of text. They have been programmed to "assume" that any page relevant to the topic will mention those words right from the beginning.

Frequency is the other major factor in how search engines determine relevance. A search engine will count how often keywords appear in relation to other words in a Web page. Those with a higher frequency are often deemed more relevant than other Web pages.

Of course, in the case of Web directories, relevance ratings also depend substantially on the judgment of the reviewers who entered them into the index, or the keywords suggested by the site owner who contributed the links.

Now, why do you get different—often very divergent—results from different search engines? To begin with, some search engines index more Web pages than others. Some search engines also index Web pages more often than others. The result is that no search engine has the exact same collection of Web pages to search.

Some search engines also may rate some Web pages higher than others might. For example, some use link popularity in ranking pages. It can tell which of the pages in its index have a lot of links from other sites pointing at them. These pages are given a slight boost during ranking, since a page with many links to it is probably of broader interest than others.

Some hybrid search engines with associated directories may boost the relevancy rank of sites their editors have reviewed. The logic is that if the site was good enough to earn a review, chances are it is more relevant than an unreviewed site.

Many Web designers mistakenly assume that metatags are the "secret" to propelling their Web pages to the top of the rankings. Metatags are keywords and descriptions hidden within the code of a Web site and not visible to Web viewers. Some search engines do give a slight boost to pages with keywords in their metatags. But there are plenty of examples where pages without metatags still get ranked highly.

Search engines may also penalize pages or exclude them from the index, if they detect search-engine spamming. An example is when a word is repeated hundreds of times on a page or in a metatag, to increase the frequency and propel the page higher in the listings. Search engines watch for common spamming methods in a variety of ways.

There is a method called "deep crawl." Search engines doing deep crawls will list many pages from a Web site, even if the pages are not explicitly submitted to them. Some search engines will search for variations of a word, based on its stem. For example, entering "golf" might also find "golfs" and maybe "golfing" depending on the search engine. This can be more or less helpful, depending on the user's particular needs.

Honing Your Search Skills

Why do search engines feed you so much irrelevant information? It may not be their fault; the truth is that most search engines today work pretty well. You just have to learn some search techniques to get better results. Most Internet users do not really know how to use a search engine. They just guess at a few keywords that might work and hope for the best.

The Internet is an information resource, so approach it systematically, as you would carry out any research. First, you should know what type of information you are seeking. Are you looking for statistics, in-depth books, magazine articles, expert comments, product reviews, or what?

There are some obvious rules to follow in making a search. They will serve you well, no matter which search engine or Web directory you use.

- Identify keywords that describe or pinpoint what you are looking for. Perhaps a phrase better describes your quest. Play with the keywords a bit; use synonyms and alternative spellings.

- Search by category, topic, company, product, person's name, etc. Some search engines will also let you limit the query to specific resources, such as images or multimedia files, or sites with a particular kind of domain—a .EDU or .GOV. These can be particularly useful if you know, for example, that the economic data you need is collected by a government agency.

- During your review of the search engine results, look at some of the most relevant results, analyze the terms used within them, and see whether there are other terms that you can use to narrow or widen your search.

- Always use more than one search engine. Although there is considerable overlap among the Web sites indexed by different search engines, pages overlooked by one often will be picked up by another. Using several search engines—or a good meta-engine—gives the best chance of picking up as many relevant sites as possible.

- Since each search engine is unique, be sure to read the instructions and tips and techniques for using the search tools you use.

Sometimes, you want to make sure that a search engine finds pages that have all the words you enter, not just some of them. In many search engines, the "+" symbol lets you do this. For example, imagine that you want to find pages that have references to both "fish" and "stew" on the same page. You could search this way:

+fish +stew

Only pages that contain both words would appear in your results. Try adding another term:

+fish +stew +Moltomario

That would find pages that have all three of the words on them; with a little luck, it will turn out to be a recipe for fish stew by the great chef, Moltomario.

Sometimes, you want a search engine to find pages that have one word on them but not another. The "-" symbol lets you do this. For example, imagine you want information about President Clinton, but do not want to be overwhelmed by pages relating to Monica Lewinsky. You could search this way:

Clinton -Lewinsky

That tells the search engine to find pages that mention "Clinton" and then to remove any of them that also mention "Lewinsky." Similarly, you could eliminate further with a search like this:

Clinton -Lewinsky -Starr

In general, the - symbol is helpful for focusing results when you get too many that are unrelated to your topic. Simply begin subtracting terms you know are not of interest, and you should get better results.

Another type of search you might need to do is a phrase search. Say you are looking for a dog-friendly hotel. You could enter the keywords

dog friendly hotel

This search could bring back pages that have all those words on them, but there's no guarantee that the words will be near each other. For example, it would pick up someone's account of a recent vacation on their family Web site: "Then we visited the Johnsons in Ann Arbor (you remember that big, friendly old dog of theirs, don't you Maude?) and didn't get back to the hotel until after midnight!" That is not quite what you needed.

Doing a phrase search avoids this problem. This tells a search engine to give you only those pages where the terms appear in exactly the order you specify. You do this by putting quotation marks around the phrase, like this:

"dog friendly hotel"

Unfortunately, phrase searches seldom appear to be entirely reliable. On many search engines, they yield a better proportion of the desired pages, but still call up pages that contain only one or two of the search terms. One popular search engine that claimed to be capable of phrase searching used to call up more spurious "hits" when the search terms were surrounded by quotation marks than when they were simply linked by plus marks—a result that in theory should not be possible.

Other Search Mechanisms

There are a number of different mechanisms to search for information on the Internet. The most common search mechanism is called Boolean Logic. Boolean Logic uses three primary search operators—AND, OR, and NOT—to combine search terms in useful ways.

- Using AND narrows the search. A search using the terms *space* AND *shuttle* will return only documents that contain both words. The plus mark discussed above is just a shortcut for the AND operator.

- Using OR broadens search results. A search using the terms *space* OR *shuttle* will return documents that contain either or both words. Only one of the words needs to be present to retrieve a document.

- The NOT operator—equivalent to a minus—will drop any documents that contain the excluded term. For instance, if you are looking for semiconductor chips, you might want to state your search as *chip* NOT *potato*.

Still, many World Wide Web search tools do not support true Boolean searches. Instead they are limited to some form of relevancy ranking. Relevancy ranking automatically assumes that there is an OR operator between words in the search term and relies on relevance criteria to make sure that the useful pages appear at the top of the list, with the junk farther down.

Each of the search engines on the Internet utilizes different forms of this search. Some place the highest emphasis on the first word in the search string; others allow you to specify that some words must (or must not) be present in the Web page to be considered—a sort of pseudo-Boolean search that is used to fine-tune the relevance rating. Most of the relevance-based search engines now allow at least three forms of search expressions:

- ALL, which corresponds to the Boolean operator AND

- ANY, which corresponds to the Boolean operator OR
- PHRASE, which looks for the search terms adjacent to each other

Using a subject guide on the Internet is similar to using a subject catalog in a library. Many of the search engines have classified the documents/sites covered by the guide into a number of broad, and often hierarchical, subject categories. A keyword search allows you to find more information because the computer looks at words in the title and content of a resource as well as the subject. The challenge is to refine your topic so that the search yields an adequate number of useful citations.

The best bet is to use both a keyword search engine and a subject index, and preferably more than one of each. This is the same as using more than one book, print index, or CD-ROM in the library. You maximize your opportunities to find what you want.

How to Choose the Best Search Tools

As we have just seen, there are any number of ways to search for information on the Internet. The keys to success are knowing the kind of information you want and understanding how each search tool works, so that you can decide which is most likely to give the desired results and how best to phrase your search question.

The services below are generally regarded as being among the major search engines:

- AOL Search, search.aol.com
- AltaVista, www.altavista.com
- Ask Jeeves, www.askjeeves.com
- Direct Hit, www.directhit.com
- Excite, www.excite.com
- FAST Search, www.alltheweb.com
- Go/Infoseek, www.go.com
- GoTo, www.goto.com
- Google, www.google.com
- HotBot, www.hotbot.com
- iWon, www.iwon.com

- LookSmart, www.looksmart.com
- Lycos, www.lycos.com
- MSN Search, www.search.msn.com
- Netscape Search, www.netscape.com
- Northern Light, www.northernlight.com
- Open Directory, www.dmoz.org
- RealNames, www.realnames.com
- Snap, www.snap.com
- WebCrawler, www.webcrawler.com
- Yahoo!, www.yahoo.com

While there are many other search engines on the Internet, the above are either well known or well used. For Webmasters, these services are the most important places to be listed, because they can potentially generate the most traffic. For searchers, these well-known, commercially backed search engines generally mean more dependable results. These search engines are more likely to be well-maintained and upgraded when necessary, to keep pace with the growing Web.

Not all of the services are "true" search engines that crawl the Web. For instance, Yahoo! and the Open Directory are "directories" that depend on human beings to compile their listings. However, most of these services offer both search engine and directory information, though they will predominately rely on one mechanism more than the other.

Appendix D
Internet Regulation

A s we have seen, the rise of e-commerce has stripped away many of the fundamental rules that limited business in the brick-and-mortar world. Suddenly, special-interest sellers can serve boutique markets too small to be reached effectively by any other means. Tiny businesses can look as substantial as multinational giants, and they can reach potential customers and partners half a world away. With the right idea, a tiny workforce, and a budget that would not have supported a mom-and-pop candy store 20 years ago, a smart Internet entrepreneur can become a billionaire. For business, it is an exhilarating time.

There is another side to this revolution, however. Stripping away so many of the old rules has made it much more difficult to govern the abuses that always seem to follow where legitimate business leads. In the physical world, someone who violates zoning laws and sets up a pornography shop is simply taken to court and shut down. An illegal gambling hall is easily closed as well. Someone who fails to file state sales tax is subject to fines and penalties. But on the Internet, these actions are hard to track and harder still to control.

Many governments have attempted to regulate the Web sites they consider socially unacceptable, such as gambling and pornography. Most of the time, however, it is impossible to identify the perpetrator, or even the true location of the crime. Historically, laws have been created to govern within the geographic boundaries of the state or country that passed them. The Internet has no boundaries, and so governments have no clear jurisdiction over activities there.

The Internet is a free and open system. In the increasingly capitalistic world, freedom and openness are generally considered good. The Internet is one exception. In the universal view of governments, and also of many private citizens concerned with issues of safety and ethics, there is such a thing as too much freedom and openness.

Anyone can set up shop on the Internet and sell products across the world. In effect, there are no import regulations, no export controls, no effective safety regulations for children's toys, no FDA approvals required for the sale of medicines. Sales tax, gambling, and even the regulations of the Securities and Exchange Commission can be avoided. A Pakistani manufacturer can set up an Internet site and sell rugs anywhere in the world. If the rugs do not meet American safety standards, or happen to violate Swiss import restrictions, there is not much that legal authorities can do. The U.S. Consumer Product Safety Commission has no power to tell the Indian company how to make its products and has no ability to monitor its sales. Neither can the Food and Drug Administration do much about it if American citizens go to a Web site based in Mexico to buy pharmaceuticals not approved in the United States, or even approved drugs for which they do not have a prescription.

How can the Securities and Exchange Commission crack down on stock scams whose operations originate out of a foreign country but are run on the Web? Even if the users are U.S. citizens, they cannot! How can New York sales tax authorities collect money from out-of-state buyers? They cannot! And how about bootlegged books, videos, music, and software being sold from worldwide countries? U.S. courts do not have jurisdiction to penalize Web site operators residing in other countries. No state or nation in the world has jurisdiction over activities that occur beyond its borders—though in the case of drug trafficking and the weapons trade the United States often tries.

Inevitably, governments everywhere are looking very carefully at establishing laws that will govern Internet policies and Internet commerce, none more actively than that of the United States, where the Internet originated and still is based—to the limited extent that this concept retains any meaning in the cyberworld. To date, the most promising target for government regulation of e-commerce appears to be ICANN, the Internet Corporation for Assigned Names and Numbers. Technically, ICANN just assigns the domain names and IP addresses required by every Internet user. (Recently, several other organizations have begun to share this power; however, ICANN retains the ultimate control of domain names.) Yet everyone recognizes that the management of domain names is more than a matter of IP routing and infrastructure growth. ICANN may be the choke point where the law can finally regulate Internet commerce.

Many lawmakers believe that domain name holders should be subject to rules and regulations, which would be enforced through ICANN. One proposal would require ICANN to impose contracts under which domain name registrants would be subject to restrictions or compliance requirements governing their activities. These contracts might, for example, detail rules for product sales in certain countries, so the FDA could maintain control over pharmaceuticals, or rules governing the use of intellectual property, so that publishers and music producers were protected from copyright infringement. What if someone violated their contract? Well, advocates of this idea say the law would just take the domain away from the registrant, effectively banning them from the Internet. It is a penalty as harsh as closing down the store.

The future of Internet regulation is still uncertain. It is in everyone's interest to see that whatever rules eventually are enacted provide only as much control over the Net as is truly required, without needlessly restricting legitimate e-commerce. ICANN will be increasingly important in the years ahead. It must not only be controlled, but protected from heavy-handed over-regulation. Industry and government must work together to shape reasonable rules for the Internet.

Appendix E
Technical Overview of HTML

HTML is a language designed to format documents so that they can be displayed on a computer system. The software needed on each computer to view HTML documents is called a browser. The most popular browsers are Netscape and Internet Explorer, though there are many lesser-known alternatives. Each contains an interpreter that displays HTML documents in exactly the same way, no matter what computer or operating system you use.

HTML is a modest programming language. It is not one of those languages that you need four years of college and a special degree to master. In fact, most of the individuals who "publish" a Web page about their family, hobbies, and other interests have taught themselves HTML. Many books are available from which to learn HTML, and we will be able to cover all the basics needed to create a professional-looking Web page here in this brief appendix.

HTML files are text files. If you understand the language, they can be written in any text editor or word processor so long as they are saved with a dot-HTML (.html) extension. We usually refer to an HTML file as a page, because it makes up a single Web page.

HTML is referred to as a "tagging" language. HTML pages contain codes, or instructions, known as tags, that tell a Web browser how it should be displayed. These tags are placed within angle brackets <> so that the HTML interpreter built into your Web browser will recognize them as instructions, rather than treating them as regular text. Anything within the <tags> does not appear on the screen when the file is displayed in the browser.

Just about everything that appears on a Web page is ordered by HTML tags. Tags tell a Web browser to make the text bold, italicize it, make it into a header, or treat it as a link to another document anywhere on the Internet. Using the bold <b> tag, the following sentence will appear bold in an HTML document viewed in a browser:

<b>I like apples in the fall.</b>

I like apples in the fall.

Note that the ending tag contains the slash "/" character. This slash tells the Web browser to stop whatever it is doing to the text. HTML tags must be paired this way. If you forget the slash, a WWW browser will continue to make the text boldface (or italic, or a headline, or whatever) until it comes to the end of your document. In this case, all the text that follows the statement "I like apples in the fall" will be made bold until the interpreter finds the </b> tag.

This section provides only a general overview of HTML, just to help you understand the basics of this essential skill. From this beginning, you can go on to learn many complex and subtle applications of HTML, as well as a variety of extensions to the fundamental language. You also can examine the HTML code on any Web page that interests you. Just select View/Source (or the equivalent command) from your browser's tool bar.

Despite the simplicity of HTML, many programs are available that make it even easier to create Web documents. You can use Microsoft Frontpage, Adobe Page Mill (for the Mac), Dreamweaver, and others. These software applications are like specialized word processors. From their toolbars you select the font style, size, color, and position on the page, and many other options. Some of these functions even are included in certain word processors, such as Microsoft Word, but the dedicated programs are more versatile. Some of these programs are very good, but I believe it's helpful to understand HTML, so that if you become interested in advancing your skills, you have an adequate foundation.

Let's create a simple Web page. In general, to create Web pages you will need to use at least two applications at the same time and multitask. You will need a basic text editor like Notepad to code your text and images, and a Web browser to view the results of your work. Set up a workspace by opening your text editor and Web browser, and get ready for multitasking.

Note: You do not need to be connected to the Internet to open your browser or to view Web pages. The Web page that you create now, and wish to examine, will be available on your computer's hard drive.

It may help to resize the two windows (text editor and Web browser), so that they both fit on your screen. Alternatively, you can layer your windows so you can click on either of them to bring it to the front, or simply use the task bar and minimize button to open and close a window session.

Creating an HTML Document

Go to the text editor window, and enter the following information using the designated tags:

<title>Your business name</title>

Your business name

Then type a brief overview of your business objectives (see Figure E.1).

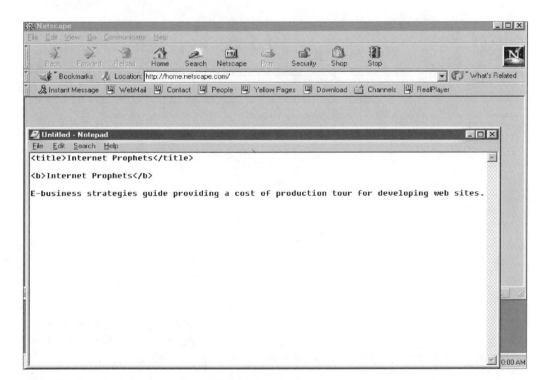

Figure E.1 Both the browser window and text editor are open.

Save the document as "myco.html". Using the ".html" file name extension tells the Web browser to read this text file as an HTML page and properly display it as such.

All HTML documents start with a title tag. This is the name the Web browser will display in the title bar at the top of the browser's screen.

To display what you have just created, go to or activate the window to the Web browser you are using for your production. Then select File, Open from the menu bar.

Use the dialog box to locate and open the file you created, "myco.html" (see Figure E.2). You should now see your business name in the title bar (uppermost top left in the browser next to the browser icon), your company's name in bold, and a description of your company's objectives. You will notice, however, that the text needs positioning to make a more attractive, readable page.

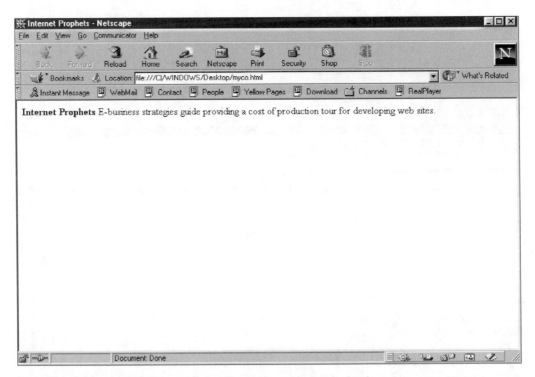

Figure E.2. From your Web browser, select file, open, and find myco.html on your computer.

Now that you have created your first HTML document, you will learn how to change your document quickly and view the updates within the Web browser. In HTML, you must include paragraph breaks when you want to separate text. So, let's go back to the text editor and place a paragraph break after the company name. The paragraph break tag is <p>.

Select: File, Save to update the changes in your HTML file.

Return to the Web browser window where the previous version of your file was displayed. Note that the text has not changed at all! To see the changes, select Reload or Refresh from the Tool Bar. This instructs the Web browser to read in the same HTML file and display it with whatever changes have been made. You should now see the text in a new position, thanks to the inclusion of the paragraph tag (see Figure E.3).

You may want to use blank lines and extra spaces within the code of your document to make your HTML files more readable in your text editor.

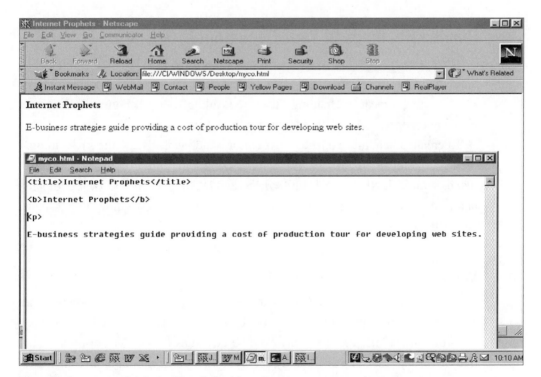

Figure E.3. Be sure to click "reload" or "refresh" to view changes to your html document.

Text Styles

HTML offers several tags for text style attributes. Just remember to be judicious and consistent in the use of styles; too many can make the text uncomfortable to read. Here are four of the basic tags for stylized text:

    <b>Make this text Bold...</b>

And it looks like this: **Make this text Bold...**

    <i>Make this text Italic...</i>

And it looks like this: *Make this text Italic...*

    <u>Make this text Underlined...</u>

And it looks like this: <u>Make this text Underlined...</u>

    <tt>Make this text typewriter...</tt>

And it looks like this: Make this text typewriter...

Here is an example of how to combine style tags:

    <b><i>Make this text Bold and Italic...</i></b>

And it looks like this: ***Make this text Bold and Italic...***

Placing Headings in Your Document

There also are heading styles. Headings are created in HTML by tagging certain chunks of text with heading tags. The format for an HTML heading tag is <hN>Text to Appear in Heading</h> (see heading styles in Figure E.4), where N is a number from 1 to 6 that identifies the heading size.

To create a heading, go to the text editor window. Let's use the <h1> to display your company name. Just replace the <b> (bold) and </b> (end bold) commands with <h1> (heading 1) and </h1> (end heading 1) around your company name. Now go to your browser, refresh the page, and see how things have changed.

Lists

Many Web pages display lists of items. These items may be unordered and preceded with a "bullet" or may be numbered sequentially. These lists are easy to format in HTML, and they may even be nested as lists of lists to produce an outline format. Lists are also handy for creating an index or table of contents to a series of documents or chapters.

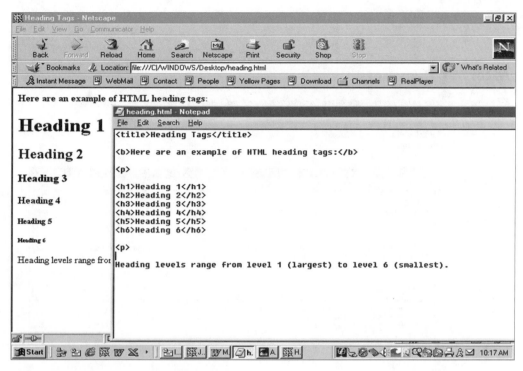

Figure E.4. Headings 1 (h1) through 6 (h6).

Unordered Lists, or ul tags, are ones that appear as a list of items with "bullets" or markers in the front. Let's open your editor, and add an unordered list to myco.html. Under or within the business objectives paragraph, we will use an unordered list to list and punctuate keywords used to emphasize your products and services. Enter the HTML code to create a list of terms. For example:

<ul>

<li>Easy reference directory of service providers sorted by product cost

<li>Newsworthy articles and industry information

<li>Event and seminar listings

<li>Personalized services

</ul>

Save the file, and reload the page in your browser.

The <ul> tag marks the beginning and </ul> marks the end of the list. The <li> indicates each list item.

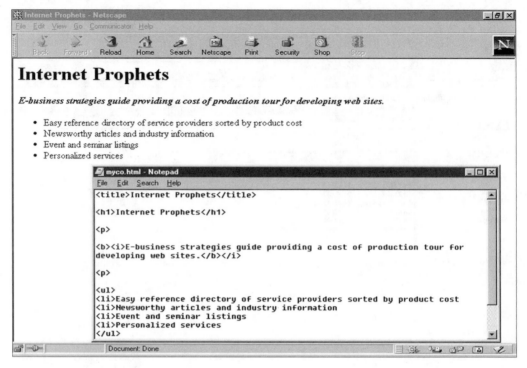

Figure E.5. Creating bulleted lists.

Ordered lists are ones where the Web browser numbers each successive list item, starting with "1." To produce an ordered list, simply change the <ul> and </ul> tags to <ol> and </ol>.

Print vs. the Web

At the beginning of this appendix, I stated that HTML pages appear the same, no matter which computer, browser, or operating system is used to display them. Unfortunately, this was an oversimplification. That is how HTML was intended to work, several years ago when the language was first being developed. Since then, some complications have crept into the relationship between HTML code and the Web pages they represent.

In the world of print, designers and typesetters have a great deal of control over page layout. But in HTML, there is no absolute positioning; an image that the designer placed on one part of the page may appear slightly out of place, or far away from its intended location.

In addition, and to make matters excruciatingly frustrating, each version of each browser can render HTML code differently. As browser versions are released, more and more code freedom and restrictions are introduced. So what you may be seeing on your IE 4.0 browser may look different on someone's IE 5.0 or Netscape 6.0 browser.

Consider some of the limitations: In HTML, you can't specify that an element on the page should appear a specific distance from the left or right margin. You can't specify that an image will nest three lines down to the right. You also can't specify how much space will appear between one line of text and another. Combine all that with the variations introduced by Web browsers, and a perfectionist Web designer can go simply nuts!

To get around these limitations Web designers use tables to lay out pages. Tables are invisible, but they form "controls" within the page. The table is made up of cells in which text, images, and other elements can appear. Tables can control the width of the document, sort of forcing margins to take positions they otherwise could not. Tables can be measured by either pixel width (width = 600) or relative width (width = 90%). This is an important distinction, because monitor sizes vary greatly among Web users. Lay out the page according to pixels, and the margins of the Web page will appear N pixels apart, regardless of how large the user's monitor is or what resolution it is configured for. Lay it out according to percentages, and the margins will appear at the same relative positions on the screen—say, 5 percent of the width in from the left edge and 5 percent in from the right.

Tables can be complicated. This is HTML code for a sample table:

```
<Table Border="2" Align="left" Cellpadding="5"Width="75%">
<Caption    Align="top"><h2>Introducing    the    Internet    Prophets:</hr>
</Caption>
<tr>
<th>Eenie</th>
<th>Meenie</th>
<th>Miney</th>
<th>Moe</th>
</tr>
</Table>
```

Complicated as this appears, it all becomes understandable with a little practice. Placing images on a Web page is not difficult. Tricky is a better word for it.

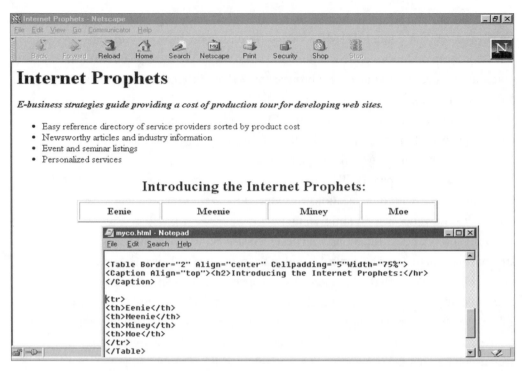

Figure E.6. Creating a table for better alignment.

The first thing to understand is that the image file must be formatted properly for the Web. A properly formatted image can be stunning, while an improperly formatted image will look sloppy, fussy, and distorted.

Briefly, there are two image types that can be viewed through Web browsers. They are .gif (graphics interchange format) and .jpg (a compressed graphics format). Many graphics programs can save image files in GIF and JPEG format. If yours does not, several shareware programs can perform the conversion.

A Web page with many large images in a sophisticated layout may look great on a high-end computer, but they will frustrate users who must wait for images to arrive over a slow modem connection. The Internet is a 72 dpi world, which means that those high-end images must be scaled down, both in file size and in pixel definition. Because large files take longer to download and because you want your Web pages to load quickly, you must be conscious of the size of the images that you put on your Web page. As a rule of thumb, keep images less than 20k in file size. The entire Web page should be less than 50k.

When possible, it helps to reuse images. Because the Web browser downloads the Web page and images into its cache, a temporary holding place in memory, a single image can appear several times in a Web document with little added delay for each extra use. The second time the image is requested, the Web browser looks in its cache and loads it very quickly.

Here are some tips for scanning photographs and images: Scan the image in at 300 dpi, and take the image into Photoshop or a similar image-editing program. Once in Photoshop, go to Image—>Image Size, reduce the file size to 72 dpi, and adjust the dimensions of the final image (e.g. 125 pixels x 56 pixels.) Then go to Image—>Adjust—>Brightness/Contrast, and increase the contrast and the brightness by a few notches. You will have to experiment with this to get the best result, because there is no formula that will work for all scans. But this is crucial to enhance the image quality in a simple, easy way and reduce the file size.

Save the image as a JPEG or a GIF, depending on the makeup of the image. Use GIFs for pictures with large flat areas of color and JPEGs for pictures that have photographic details. Again, you will have to experiment with some of the options provided by your software to achieve the best compromise between image clarity and file size.

To add images to a Web site, you use the tags <img>, which stands for inline image, and <scr>, which stands for source. Between tags, you must identify the image name and image location. For example:

     <img src = images/eenie.jpg>

This will look for the image eenie.jpg in the folder or directory called images.

Also, changing the table border to "0" will eliminate the lines around the table, making them invisible, but will leave the table still holding the images in proper place. For example:

<Table Border="0" Align="left" Cellpadding="5"Width="75%">

<Caption Align="top"><h2>Introducing the Internet Prophets:</hr></Caption>

<tr>

<td><img src=images/eenie.jpg></td>

<td><img src=images/meenie.jpg></td>

<td><img src=images/miney.jpg></td>

<td><img src=images/moe.jpg></td>

</tr>

<tr>

<th>Eenie</th>

<th>Meenie</th>

<th>Miney</th>

<th>Moe</th>

</tr>

</Table>

Now, we will add links to your Web page. Go back to your editor, and below the heading, enter the following text:

Based on the book "Internet Prophets"

published by <a href="http://www.infotoday.com">Information Today, Inc.</a>

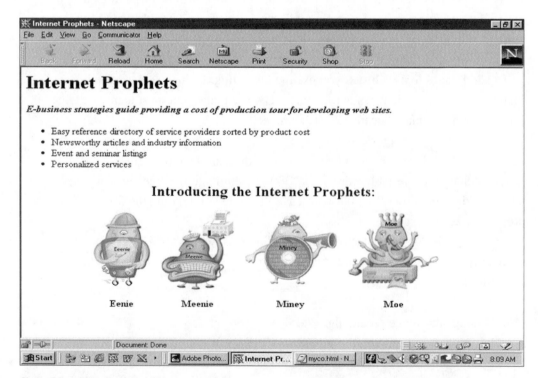

Figure E.7. Adding images within your table.

Then save and reload.

Notice that the link is highlighted and when clicked will take you to the Internet Prophets home page. <a href="full url"> is the HTML tag for linking to other documents on the Web. This tag must be closed by </a> tag. Notice also that the copy within the tags "Information Today, Inc." is highlighted.

All this is just a taste of HTML, proof that the task of making your own Web pages is well within your ability. Even with the basics we have looked at here, simple, professional-looking Web pages can be made. However, far more is possible. For further information about creating your own HTML documents, go to:

- http://www.htmlreference.com
- http://www.zdnet.com/developer

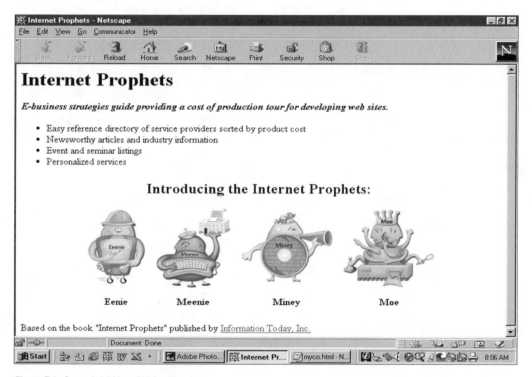

Figure E.8. Great job! Your Web page is done.

Appendix F
Index of Prophet Strategies

Eenie Strategies

- Automatically and Systematically Fix Errors on Your Site (p. 180)
- Participate in Web-Development Newsgroups, Subscribe to Newsletters, and View Resource-Rich Web Sites (p. 191)
- Scan the Web for Cool Tools to Incorporate into Your Site (p. 201)
- Implement Search Engine Optimization Techniques in Your Web Site (p. 214)
- Earn Additional Revenue Through Affiliate Marketing (p. 221)
- Send Personalized Messages to E-Mail Lists Containing as Many as 500 Recipients (p. 229)
- Join a Banner Exchange Program (p. 246)

Meenie Strategies

- Build a "Shopping Cart" Web Site (p. 32)
- Launch a Sweepstakes (p. 44)
- Conduct Live Meetings Online (p. 53)
- Implement Online Project Management Tools (p. 58)
- Host Moderated Discussions on Your Web Site (p. 66)
- Turn Your Site into a Microportal (p. 74)
- Automate the Management of Your Auction (p. 82)
- Join an E-Marketplace (p. 88)
- Increase Productivity of Your Sales Force (p. 95)
- Set Up Shop in a Regional Mall (p. 102)
- Host Online Charitable Auctions (p. 108)
- If You Are a Municipality, Make Your Code Available on Your Web Site (p. 116)
- Use the Resources of One of the Web's Most Popular "Research Marketplaces" to Create an E-Business Plan (p. 128)
- Implement Audio Training Initiatives to Help Your Employees Grasp E-Business Concepts (p. 143)

Miney Strategies

- Implement Content Management Software for Teachers to Publish Curriculums on the Internet (p. 116)
- Access Industry-Focused Research When Planning Your E-Business (p. 129)
- Conduct In-House Training to Create Employee Awareness of E-Business Requirements (p. 144)
- Benchmark Your Success Against Industry Standards (p. 153)
- If Your Business is Owned by Women, Find Venture Capitalists Who Care (p. 168)
- If You Are a Publisher, Extend the Value of Your Content and Brand (p. 182)
- Create a Structured Information Business Portal, so Your Employees and Prospects Can Intuitively Navigate Through Your Information (p. 192)
- Conduct Real-Time Performance Measurement on Your Web Site (p. 202)
- List Your Site on Sprinks (p. 216)
- Outsource Your Affiliate Program Management (p. 223)
- Use Viral Marketing Strategies (p. 230)
- Sell Advertising Space on Your Web Site (p. 248)

Moe Strategies

- Create Real-Time Customer Sales Assistance (p. 34)
- Build an E-Commerce Site, and Optimize Your Marketing Efforts While Targeting and Tracking Visitors (p. 45)
- Offer Rich-Media Content on Your Web Site (p. 54)
- Create Customized Sticky Applications on Your Web Site (p. 60)
- Give Visitors to Your Web Site the Ability to Build Their Own Interactive Web Site (p. 67)
- Create an Information Portal (p. 75)

Appendix G
Index of Service Providers

Auctions

- AuctionSearch: www.auctionsearch.com
- Beyondsolutions: www.beyondsolutions.com
- Bidland: www.bidland.com
- eBay: www.eBay.com
- Onvia: www.onvia.com
- QXL: QXL.com
- Worldbid: www.worldbid.com

Customer Service

- Ask Jeeves: www.askjeeves.com
- ICQ: www.icq.com
- LivePerson: www.liveperson.com
- Salesforce: www.salesforce.com

Digital Delivery

- Burstware: www.burstware.com
- Ipublish: www.Ipublish.com
- Iuniverse: www.iuniverse.com
- Mshow: www.mshow.com
- WebEx: www.webex.com
- Xlibris: www.xlibris.com

Dynamic Pricing Models

- AuctionBroker: www.auctionbroker.com
- Biz2biz: www.biz2biz.com
- Imandi: www.imandi.com
- SAQQARA's: www.saqqara.com

One-to-One

- BrightStreet: www.brightstreet.com
- ePrize: www.eprize.com
- Peppers and Rogers Group: www.1to1.com
- Responsys: www.responsys.com

Online Communities

- CommerceCity: www.commercecity.com
- eShare Technologies: www.eshare.com
- Liveuniverse: www.liveuniverse.com
- Talk City: www.talkcity.com

Online Shopping

- Excite: www.excitestores.com
- Frontline Communications Corp.: www.frontline.net
- Gateway: www.gateway.net
- Mindspring: www.mindspring.com
- Verio: www.verio.com
- Yahoo!Store: www.yahoo.com
- Zshops: www.amazon.com
- Stickiness
- E-Vis: www.e-vis.com
- iSyndicate: www.isyndicate.com
- Your Compass: www.yourcompass.com

Appendix H
Glossary of Internet Terms

Ad Server. A computer on the Internet that "serves" ads to one or many Web sites. The ad server uses technology to strategically place ads on various sites across the Web, based on an advertiser's set of criteria.

Ad Network. A network of partner Web sites that agree to host advertisements.

Adobe Acrobat. A program commonly used to share documents on the Internet so that they will appear exactly the same on any computer, monitor, or Web browser; also the file format used by this program.

Anonymous FTP. A File Transfer Protocol where the user does not have to be registered with the server receiving the file transfer request.

Archie. A search tool, now largely obsolete for finding files residing on Internet servers around the world. More specifically, it was a directory of FTP (file transfer protocol) sites on the ever-expanding Net.

ARPANET. Advanced Research Projects Agency Network, the name given to the first network of computers that used the IP protocol for transferring data through the existing telecommunications infrastructure—the embryonic form of the Internet.

ASP. Application Service Provider, a company that markets specialized software, such as database managers or "storefront" applications, to be incorporated into Web sites.

Bandwidth. A measure of how much data can be sent through an Internet connection, usually quoted in bits-per-second.

BBS. Bulletin Board System, a pre-Internet technology, now largely obsolete, in which people shared files and communicated with each other via a non-networked computer, usually accessed by telephone modem.

Boolean. A form of logic used in making a search request. It uses three primary search operators—AND, OR, and NOT—to combine several terms for the search. For example, a request for "Internet AND commerce" would locate only those files in which both "Internet" and "commerce" appear; a request for "Internet OR commerce" would locate files containing either "Internet" or "commerce."

Brick and mortar. A New Economy term for businesses that have physical stores and buildings.

Browser. A software application that interprets HTML to display a Web site on the computer screen.

Click-through rate (CTR). The result of the number of times a user clicks on the banner ad divided by the number of impressions a banner ad receives.

Click and mortar. A New Economy term used for businesses that have both an online presence and a physical world presence.

Co-location hosting. A service offered by ISPs to host a company's computer in their facility and maintain its connection to the Internet.

Commercial Service Providers. A provider of information services via computer routed over the telecommunications infrastructure.

Cookie. An application that downloads from a Web site to a visitor's browser and thereafter is stored on the user's computer. This application communicates with the Web server to record the visitor's path through the Web site and may also provide the Web site's owner with other information about the user.

CPC. Cost Per Click, a means of pricing for Internet banner advertisements.

Crawler. A technology used to scan Web sites for purposes of indexing data.

CRM. Customer Relationship Management.

Dedicated hosting. A service offered by ISPs to dedicate a computer in their facility that will be used for hosting and transactions on the Internet.

DNS. Domain Name System, the systematic numbering of IP addresses; also Domain Name Server, the computer that reads this address from a message and routes it to the proper destination.

DOD. Department of Defense, the U.S. government agency that developed Internet technology.

Drip irrigation. Slowly acquiring data about customers on a Web site by using a variety of surveys, registration forms, and other online forms.

e-book. A handheld device that connects to the Internet and downloads electronic books.

e-business. A firm for which the Internet forms a basic part of its business model.

e-commerce. Conducting any form of commerce electronically (on the Internet).

eCRM. Electronic Customer Relationship Management.

e-zine. An online magazine; electronic magazine.

FTP. File Transfer Protocol, a software standard used to move files from one computer to another via the Internet.

Gateway. A Web site that serves as a point of access to other sites.

Hits. The number of requests to a server that take place when a Web page is downloaded. Depending on the number of elements on a Web page—graphics, banners, text, and so on—one page request could result in as many as 15 or 20 hits.

Hosting. The storage of data on an Internet computer; usually refers to providing an online "home" for someone's Web site.

HTML. Hypertext Mark-up Language, the language used for programming documents on the World Wide Web.

Hyperlink. A special piece of text within a document that, when clicked, moves the user to another document.

Hypertext. A text file that includes one or more hyperlink-related documents on the World Wide Web.

ICANN. The Internet Corporation for Assigned Names and Numbers, an organization responsible for setting Internet policies.

Impressions. The number of times a banner ad has been viewed.

IP address. Internet Protocol address. Every system connected to the Internet has a unique IP address, which consists of four groups of numbers. The IP address is attached to messages being sent to that computer so that they can be routed to their destination.

ISP. Internet Service Provider. A service company that offers dial-up or high-speed access to the Internet.

Javascript. A specialized programming language that can interact with HTML source code, enabling Web authors to spice up their sites with dynamic—that is, active or spontaneously changing—content.

Killer Application. Slang for a very popular application, often applied to a kind of software so useful that it justifies buying the technology used to run it. For example, spreadsheets were the "killer ap" that many observers believe justified the purchase of early personal computers and brought PCs into the mainstream.

Page views. The number of times a particular page and any advertisements on that page appeared in a visitor's browser.

Plug-in. A small software program that works with a Web browser to read special file types, such as streaming audio or video.

Portal. A Web site that offers a gateway to other Web sites.

Spam. Unsolicited commercial e-mail; as a verb, to send unsolicited commercial e-mail.

Streaming. Technique for transferring audio and video files over the Internet whereby the receiver can begin playing the file before the total transfer is complete.

URL. Universal Resource Locator, the Internet address of an e-mail recipient or Web site, as: http://www.InternetProphets.com.

Vortal. The combination between an Internet portal and a "vertical," subject-specific Web directory.

WAP. Wireless Application Protocol, a worldwide standard developed to allow mobile phones to access the Internet.

Webcasting. Broadcasting on the Web, as when a radio station sends its programs out over the Net.

About the Author

In 1996, Mary Diffley created a successful Internet and computer company, United Computer Specialists, Inc. (UCS), which provided dial-up Internet access, training, consulting, and Web development services to businesses in the New York tri-state area. The company grew through creative self-promotion campaigns, public speaking engagements, published articles, and Internet consulting. The company was featured in local and national publications including the *New York Times*.

Mary has a background in accounting (CPA, New York) and business processes. She is expert in providing innovative Internet strategies and Internet integration solutions to businesses of all sizes. A publicly held company, Frontline Communications, Corp. (FNT), acquired her Internet firm in 1999.

Recognizing that many small and medium-size businesses and organizations need a much better understanding of Internet technologies and strategies to help them plan their e-business initiatives, Mary began writing *Internet Prophets* in 2000. Mary provides active support for the book at its companion Web site, www.internetprophets.com.

Mary has published dozens of articles in local publications such as the *Rockland Review* and the *Hudson Valley Business Journal*. *Internet Prophets* is her first book.

Index

More CyberAge Books
from Information Today, Inc.

Internet Business Intelligence

How to Build a Big Company System on a Small Company Budget

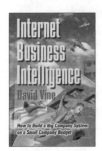

By David Vine

According to author David Vine, business success in the competitive, global marketplace of the 21st century will depend on a firm's ability to use information effectively—and the most successful firms will be those that harness the Internet to create and maintain a powerful information edge. In *Internet Business Intelligence*, Vine explains how any company—large or small—can build a complete, low-cost, Internet-based business intelligence system that really works. If you're fed up with Internet hype and wondering, "Where's the beef?" you'll appreciate this savvy, no-nonsense approach to using the Internet to solve everyday business problems and stay one step ahead of the competition.

CyberAge Books • 2000/448 pp/softbound/ISBN 0-910965-35-8 • $29.95

International Business Information on the Web

Searcher Magazine's Guide to Sites and Strategies for Global Business Research

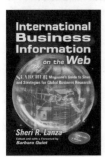

By Sheri R. Lanza • Edited by Barbara Quint

Here is the first ready-reference for effective worldwide business research, written by experienced international business researcher Sheri R. Lanza and edited by *Searcher* magazine's Barbara Quint. This book helps readers identify overseas buyers, find foreign suppliers, investigate potential partners and competitors, uncover international market research and industry analysis, and much more.

CyberAge Books • 2001/380 pp/softbound/ISBN 0-910965-46-3 • $29.95

Smart Services

Competitive Information Strategies, Solutions, and Success Stories for Service Businesses

By Deborah C. Sawyer

Here is the first book to focus specifically on the competitive information needs of service-oriented firms. Author, entrepreneur, and business consultant Deborah C. Sawyer illuminates the many forms of competition in service businesses, identifies the most effective information resources for competitive intelligence (CI), and provides a practical framework for identifying and studying competitors in order to gain a competitive advantage. *Smart Services* is a roadmap for every service company owner, manager, or executive who expects to compete effectively in the Information Age.

CyberAge Books • 2002/256 pp/softbound/ISBN 0-910965-56-0 • $29.95

Super Searchers Do Business

The Online Secrets of Top Business Researchers

By Mary Ellen Bates • Edited by Reva Basch

Super Searchers Do Business probes the minds of 11 leading researchers who use the Internet and online services to find critical business information. Through her in-depth interviews, Mary Ellen Bates gets the pros to reveal how they choose sources, evaluate search results, and tackle the most challenging business research projects. Loaded with expert tips, techniques, and strategies, this is the first title in the Super Searchers series edited by Reva Basch.

CyberAge Books • 1999/206 pp/softbound• ISBN 0-910965-33-1 • $24.95

net.people

The Personalities and Passions Behind the Web Sites

By Eric C. Steinert and Thomas E. Bleier

In *net.people*, get up close and personal with the creators of 36 of the world's most intriguing online ventures. For the first time, these entrepreneurs and visionaries share their personal stories and hard-won secrets of Webmastering. You'll learn how each of them launched a home page, increased site traffic, geared up for e-commerce, found financing, dealt with failure and success, built new relationships—and discovered that a Web site had changed their life forever.

CyberAge Books • 2000/317 pp/softbound/ISBN 0-910965-37-4 • $19.95

The Invisible Web

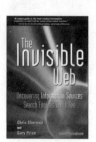

Uncovering Information Sources
Search Engines Can't See

By Chris Sherman and Gary Price
Foreword by Danny Sullivan

Most of the authoritative information accessible over the Internet is invisible to search engines like AltaVista, HotBot, and Google. This invaluable material resides on the "Invisible Web," which is largely comprised of content-rich databases from universities, libraries, associations, businesses, and government agencies around the world. Authors Sherman and Price introduce you to top sites and sources and offer tips, techniques, and analysis. Supported by a dedicated Web site.

CyberAge Books • 2001/450 pp/softbound/ISBN 0-910965-51-X • $29.95

Ask for CyberAge Books at your local bookstore
or order online at www.infotoday.com

For a complete catalog, contact:

Information Today, Inc.

143 Old Marlton Pike • Medford, NJ 08055
609/654-6266 • email: custserv@infotoday.com